Computational Methods for Communication Science

Computational Methods for Communication Science showcases the use of innovative computational methods in the study of communication.

This book discusses the validity of using big data in communication science and showcases a number of new methods and applications in the fields of text and network analysis. Computational methods have the potential to greatly enhance the scientific study of communication because they allow us to move towards collaborative large-N studies of actual behavior in its social context. This requires us to develop new skills and infrastructure and meet the challenges of open, valid, reliable, and ethical "big data" research. This volume brings together a number of leading scholars in this emerging field, contributing to the increasing development and adaptation of computational methods in communication science.

The chapters in this book were originally published as a special issue of the journal *Communication Methods and Measures*.

Wouter van Atteveldt is Associate Professor of Political Communication at VU Amsterdam, the Netherlands. His research interests include computational communication science and the role of news and journalism in the functioning of democracy. He co-founded the ICA division on Computational Methods and is Editor-in-Chief of the journal *Computational Communication Research*.

Tai-Quan Peng is Associate Professor at the Department of Communication, Michigan State University, East Lansing, USA. His research interest lies in the application of computational methods to examine structure and dynamics of human communication phenomena on social and mobile media. He was the Inaugural Chair of the Computational Methods division at the International Communication Association.

Computational Methods for Communication Science

Edited by
Wouter van Atteveldt and Tai-Quan Peng

NEW YORK AND LONDON

First published 2021
by Routledge
52 Vanderbilt Avenue, New York, NY 10017

and by Routledge
2 Park Square, Milton Park, Abingdon, Oxon, OX14 4RN

Routledge is an imprint of the Taylor & Francis Group, an informa business

Chapters 1, 2 and 5–7 © 2021 Taylor & Francis
Introduction © 2018 Wouter van Atteveldt and Tai-Quan Peng. Originally published as Open Access.
Chapter 3 © 2018 Elena Rudkowsky, Martin Haselmayer, Matthias Wastian, Marcelo Jenny, Štefan Emrich and Michael Sedlmair. Originally published as Open Access.
Chapter 4 © 2018 Damian Trilling and Jeroen G. F. Jonkman. Originally published as Open Access.

With the exception of Introduction, Chapters 3 and 4, no part of this book may be reprinted or reproduced or utilised in any form or by any electronic, mechanical, or other means, now known or hereafter invented, including photocopying and recording, or in any information storage or retrieval system, without permission in writing from the publishers. For details on the rights for Introduction, Chapters 3 and 4, please see the chapters' Open Access footnotes.

Trademark notice: Product or corporate names may be trademarks or registered trademarks, and are used only for identification and explanation without intent to infringe.

Library of Congress Cataloging-in-Publication Data
A catalog record for this title has been requested

ISBN13: 978-0-367-53616-9 (hbk)
ISBN13: 978-1-003-08260-6 (ebk)

Typeset in Minion Pro
by codeMantra

Publisher's Note
The publisher accepts responsibility for any inconsistencies that may have arisen during the conversion of this book from journal articles to book chapters, namely the inclusion of journal terminology.

Disclaimer
Every effort has been made to contact copyright holders for their permission to reprint material in this book. The publishers would be grateful to hear from any copyright holder who is not here acknowledged and will undertake to rectify any errors or omissions in future editions of this book.

Contents

	Citation Information	vi
	Notes on Contributors	viii
	Introduction: When Communication Meets Computation: Opportunities, Challenges, and Pitfalls in Computational Communication Science Wouter van Atteveldt and Tai-Quan Peng	1
1	Applying LDA Topic Modeling in Communication Research: Toward a Valid and Reliable Methodology Daniel Maier, A. Waldherr, P. Miltner, G. Wiedemann, A. Niekler, A. Keinert, B. Pfetsch, G. Heyer, U. Reber, T. Häussler, H. Schmid-Petri, and S. Adam	13
2	Extracting Latent Moral Information from Text Narratives: Relevance, Challenges, and Solutions René Weber, J. Michael Mangus, Richard Huskey, Frederic R. Hopp, Ori Amir, Reid Swanson, Andrew Gordon, Peter Khooshabeh, Lindsay Hahn, and Ron Tamborini	39
3	More than Bags of Words: Sentiment Analysis with Word Embeddings Elena Rudkowsky, Martin Haselmayer, Matthias Wastian, Marcelo Jenny, Štefan Emrich, and Michael Sedlmair	60
4	Scaling up Content Analysis Damian Trilling and Jeroen G. F. Jonkman	78
5	How Team Interlock Ecosystems Shape the Assembly of Scientific Teams: A Hypergraph Approach Alina Lungeanu, Dorothy R. Carter, Leslie A. DeChurch, and Noshir S. Contractor	95
6	Methods and Approaches to Using Web Archives in Computational Communication Research Matthew S. Weber	120
7	Disentangling User Samples: A Supervised Machine Learning Approach to Proxy-population Mismatch in Twitter Research K. Hazel Kwon, J. Hunter Priniski, and Monica Chadha	136
	Index	159

Citation Information

The chapters in this book were originally published in the *Communication Methods and Measures*, volume 12, issue 2–3 (June 2018). When citing this material, please use the original page numbering for each article, as follows:

Introduction
When Communication Meets Computation: Opportunities, Challenges, and Pitfalls in Computational Communication Science
Wouter van Atteveldt and Tai-Quan Peng
Communication Methods and Measures, volume 12, issue 2–3 (June 2018) pp. 81–92

Chapter 1
Applying LDA Topic Modeling in Communication Research: Toward a Valid and Reliable Methodology
Daniel Maier, A. Waldherr, P. Miltner, G. Wiedemann, A. Niekler, A. Keinert, B. Pfetsch, G. Heyer, U. Reber, T. Häussler, H. Schmid-Petri, and S. Adam
Communication Methods and Measures, volume 12, issue 2–3 (June 2018) pp. 93–118

Chapter 2
Extracting Latent Moral Information from Text Narratives: Relevance, Challenges, and Solutions
René Weber, J. Michael Mangus, Richard Huskey, Frederic R. Hopp, Ori Amir, Reid Swanson, Andrew Gordon, Peter Khooshabeh, Lindsay Hahn, and Ron Tamborini
Communication Methods and Measures, volume 12, issue 2–3 (June 2018) pp. 119–139

Chapter 3
More than Bags of Words: Sentiment Analysis with Word Embeddings
Elena Rudkowsky, Martin Haselmayer, Matthias Wastian, Marcelo Jenny, Štefan Emrich, and Michael Sedlmair
Communication Methods and Measures, volume 12, issue 2–3 (June 2018) pp. 140–157

Chapter 4
Scaling up Content Analysis
Damian Trilling and Jeroen G. F. Jonkman
Communication Methods and Measures, volume 12, issue 2–3 (June 2018) pp. 158–174

Chapter 5
How Team Interlock Ecosystems Shape the Assembly of Scientific Teams: A Hypergraph Approach
Alina Lungeanu, Dorothy R. Carter, Leslie A. DeChurch, and Noshir S. Contractor
Communication Methods and Measures, volume 12, issue 2–3 (June 2018) pp. 175–199

Chapter 6
Methods and Approaches to Using Web Archives in Computational Communication Research
Matthew S. Weber
Communication Methods and Measures, volume 12, issue 2–3 (June 2018) pp. 200–215

Chapter 7
Disentangling User Samples: A Supervised Machine Learning Approach to Proxy-population Mismatch in Twitter Research
K. Hazel Kwon, J. Hunter Priniski, and Monica Chadha
Communication Methods and Measures, volume 12, issue 2–3 (June 2018) pp. 216–237

For any permission-related enquiries please visit:
http://www.tandfonline.com/page/help/permissions

Contributors

S. Adam Institute of Communication and Media Studies, University of Bern, Switzerland.

Ori Amir Department of Communication, UC Santa Barbara Media Neuroscience Lab, USA. Institute for Collaborative Biotechnologies, UC Santa Barbara, USA.

Wouter van Atteveldt Department of Communication Science, VU University Amsterdam, the Netherlands.

Dorothy R. Carter Department of Psychology, University of Georgia, Athens, USA.

Monica Chadha Walter Cronkite School of Journalism and Mass Communication, Arizona State University, Phoenix, USA.

Noshir S. Contractor Department of Communication Studies, Northwestern University, Evanston, USA.

Leslie A. DeChurch Department of Communication Studies, Northwestern University, Evanston, USA.

Štefan Emrich Drahtwarenhandlung (dwh) GmbH, Vienna, Austria.

Andrew Gordon Institute for Creative Technologies, University of Southern California, Los Angeles, USA.

Lindsay Hahn Department of Communication, Michigan State University, East Lansing, USA.

Martin Haselmayer Department of Government, University of Vienna, Austria.

T. Häussler Institute of Communication and Media Studies, University of Bern, Switzerland.

G. Heyer Computer Science Institute, University of Leipzig, Germany.

Frederic R. Hopp Department of Communication, UC Santa Barbara Media Neuroscience Lab, USA.

Richard Huskey School of Communication, The Ohio State University Cognitive Communication Science Lab, Columbus, USA.

Marcelo Jenny Department of Political Science, University of Innsbruck, Austria.

Jeroen G. F. Jonkman Department of Communication Science Amsterdam School of Communication Research, University of Amsterdam, the Netherlands.

A. Keinert Institute for Media and Communication Studies, Free University Berlin, Germany.

Peter Khooshabeh Human Research and Engineering Directorate, US Army Research Laboratory, Adelphi, USA.

K. Hazel Kwon Walter Cronkite School of Journalism and Mass Communication, Arizona State University, Phoenix, USA.

Alina Lungeanu Department of Communication Studies, Northwestern University, Evanston, USA.

Daniel Maier Institute for Media and Communication Studies, Free University Berlin, Germany.

J. Michael Mangus Department of Communication, UC Santa Barbara Media Neuroscience Lab, USA. Institute for Collaborative Biotechnologies, UC Santa Barbara, USA.

P. Miltner Institute for Media and Communication Studies, Free University Berlin, Germany.

A. Niekler Computer Science Institute, University of Leipzig, Germany.

Tai-Quan Peng Department of Communication, Michigan State University, East Lansing, USA.

B. Pfetsch Institute for Media and Communication Studies, Free University Berlin, Germany.

J. Hunter Priniski Department of Mathematical and Statistical Sciences, Arizona State University, Phoenix, USA.

U. Reber Institute of Communication and Media Studies, University of Bern, Switzerland.

Elena Rudkowsky Faculty of Computer Science, University of Vienna, Austria.

H. Schmid-Petri University of Passau, Germany.

Michael Sedlmair Computer Science, Jacobs University Bremen, Germany.

Reid Swanson Institute for Creative Technologies, University of Southern California, Los Angeles, USA.

Ron Tamborini Department of Communication, Michigan State University, East Lansing, USA.

Damian Trilling Department of Communication Science Amsterdam School of Communication Research, University of Amsterdam, the Netherlands.

A. Waldherr Department of Communication, University of Münster, Germany.

Matthias Wastian Center for Computational Complex Systems, Technical University of Vienna, Austria.

Matthew S. Weber Department of Communication, Rutgers University, New Brunswick, USA.

René Weber Department of Communication, UC Santa Barbara Media Neuroscience Lab, USA. Institute for Collaborative Biotechnologies, UC Santa Barbara, USA.

G. Wiedemann Computer Science Institute, University of Leipzig, Germany.

INTRODUCTION   🔓 OPEN ACCESS

When Communication Meets Computation: Opportunities, Challenges, and Pitfalls in Computational Communication Science

Wouter van Atteveldt ⓘ and Tai-Quan Peng ⓘ

ABSTRACT
The recent increase in digitally available data, tools, and processing power is fostering the use of computational methods to the study of communication. This special issue discusses the validity of using big data in communication science and showcases a number of new methods and applications in the fields of text and network analysis. Computational methods have the potential to greatly enhance the scientific study of communication because they allow us to move towards collaborative large-N studies of actual behavior in its social context. This requires us to develop new skills and infrastructure and meet the challenges of open, valid, reliable, and ethical "big data" research. By bringing together a number of leading scholars in one issue, we contribute to the increasing development and adaptation of computational methods in communication science.

The role of computational methods in communication science

"We are on the cusp of a new era in computational social science" (Wallach, 2016). As evidenced by the many reviews, special issues, and position papers, a growing community of scholars is using computational methods for analyzing social behavior (e.g., Alvarez, 2016; Boyd & Crawford, 2012; Huberman, 2012; Lazer et al., 2009; Parks, 2014; Shah, Cappella, & Neuman, 2015; Trilling, 2017). The recent acceleration in the promise and use of computational methods for communication science is primarily fueled by the confluence of at least three developments:

1. A deluge of digitally available data, ranging from social media messages and other "digital traces" to web archives and newly digitized newspaper and other historical archives (e.g., Weber, 2018);
2. Improved tools to analyze this data, including network analysis methods (e.g., Lungeanu, Carter, DeChurch, & Contractor, 2018; Barabási, 2016) and automatic text analysis methods such as supervised text classification (Boumans & Trilling, 2016; Collingwood & Wilkerson, 2012; Odijk, Burscher, Vliegenthart, & de Rijke, 2013), topic modelling (Maier et al., 2018; Blei, Ng, & Jordan, 2003; Jacobi, Van Atteveldt, & Welbers, 2016; Roberts et al., 2014), word embeddings (e.g. Rudkovsky et al., 2018), and syntactic methods (Van Atteveldt, Sheafer, Shenhav, & Fogel-Dror, 2017); and
3. The emergence of powerful and cheap processing power, and easy to use computing infrastructure for processing these data, including scientific and commercial cloud computing, sharing platforms such as Github and Dataverse, and crowd coding platforms such as Amazon MTurk and Crowdflower.

Many of these new data sets contain communication artifacts such as tweets, posts, emails, and reviews; and many of these new methods are aimed at analyzing the structure and dynamics of human communication. As such, these developments are especially relevant for communication science and computational methods have been used to analyze a variety of communicative

---

This is an Open Access article distributed under the terms of the Creative Commons Attribution License (http://creativecommons.org/licenses/by/4.0/), which permits unrestricted use, distribution, and reproduction in any medium, provided the original work is properly cited.

phenomena (e.g., Colleoni, Rozza, & Arvidsson, 2014; Grimmer, 2016; Jungherr, 2014; Tucker et al., 2016) . Moreover, communication theories, such as agenda-setting, two-step flow of information, selective exposure, and interpersonal persuasion have been widely cited as major theoretical backbones in many computational studies (e.g., Russell Neuman, Guggenheim, Mo Jang, & Bae, 2014; Tan, Niculae, Danescu-Niculescu-Mizil, & Lee, 2016; Wu, Hofman, Mason, & Watts, 2011; Xu et al., 2013; Yang & Leskovec, 2010). As will be argued in this volume, these three developments have the potential to give an unprecedented boost to progress in communication science, provided we can overcome the technical, social, and ethical challenges presented by these developments.

Like "big data," the concept of computational methods makes intuitive sense but is hard to define. Sheer size is not a necessary criterion to define big data (Monroe, Pan, Roberts, Sen, & Sinclair, 2015), and the fact that a method is executed on a computer does not make it a "computational method"—communication scholars have used computers to help in their studies for over half a century (e.g., Nie, Bent, & Hull, 1970; Stone, Dunphy, Smith, & Ogilvie, 1966). Adapting the criteria given by Shah et al. (2015), we can give an ideal-typical definition by stating that computational communication science studies generally involve: (1) large and complex data sets; (2) consisting of digital traces and other "naturally occurring" data; (3) requiring algorithmic solutions to analyze; and (4) allowing the study of human communication by applying and testing communication theory.

Of course, computational methods do not replace the existing methodological approaches, but rather complement it. Computational methods are an expansion and enhancement of the existing methodological toolbox, while traditional methods can also contribute to the development, calibration, and validation of computational methods. Moreover, the distinction between "classical" and "computational" methods is often one of degree rather than of kind, and the boundaries between approaches are fuzzy: When does an on-line experiment turn into a computational analysis, and how do Facebook status updates really differ from self-reports? Nevertheless, the term computational methods is useful to make us realize that new datasets and processing techniques offer us possibilities beyond just scaling up our previous work; and to alert us to the potential challenges, pitfalls, and required expertise in using these methods.

This Special Issue originates from the first set of panels organized by the Computational Methods Interest Group of the International Communication Association. The purpose of the issue, and of this introduction in particular, is to provide an overview of the exciting work that is being done to study communication using computational methods, and highlight the advantages and challenges of this methodology. To start, in the next section we will review the potential benefits offered by computational methods. This is followed by a discussion of key limitations and challenges facing scholars using computational methods. We end with an overview of the articles published in this volume and pointers for the future direction of our field.

Opportunities offered by computational methods

If computational methods simply allowed us to use our existing methodologies at greater speed, scale, or ease of use it would be welcomed, but it would hardly be revolutionary. Instead, we argue that computational methods allow us to analyze social behavior and communication in ways that were not possible before and have the potential to radically change our discipline at least in four ways.

From self report to real behavior

Digital traces of online social behavior can function as a new behavioral lab available for communication researchers. These data allow us to measure actual behavior in an unobtrusive way rather than self-reported attitudes or intentions (e.g., Araujo, Wonneberger, Neijens, & de Vreese, 2017;

Dovidio, 1992). This can help overcome social desirability problems, and more importantly it does not rely on people's imperfect estimate of their own desires and intentions.

Digital traces on social media are bundled with important features that empower communication researchers to examine human communication phenomena with new perspectives. Specifically, the structural perspective has become more and more prominent in computational research with various social and interactive relations documented on social media platforms. The rapid advancement of network modeling techniques makes it feasible to study the intricate interplay between individuals and the local or global social structures they are embedded in (cf. Barabási, 2016; Diesner, Frantz, & Carley, 2005; Westlake & Bouchard, 2016). With voluminous time-stamped data on social media, it is methodologically viable to unravel the dynamics underlying human communication and disentangle the interdependent relationships between multiple communication processes (Monge & Contractor, 2003).

This can also help overcome the problems of linking content data to survey data. This a mainstay of media effects research but is problematic because of bias in media self-reports (Kobayashi & Boase, 2012; Scharkow & Bachl, 2017) and because news consumers nowadays often cherry-pick articles from multiple sites, rather than relying on a single source of news (Costera Meijer & Groot Kormelink, 2015). Using special-purpose mobile apps and browser extensions, we can now trace news consumption in real-time and combine it with survey data to get a more sophisticated measurement of news consumption and effects (Bodo et al., 2017; Guess, Nyhan, & Reifler, 2018; Kobayashi, Boase, Suzuki, & Suzuki, 2015).

From lab experiments to studies of the actual social environment

A second advantage is that we can observe the reaction of persons to stimuli in their actual environment rather than in an artificial lab setting. In their daily lives, people are exposed to a multitude of stimuli simultaneously, and their reactions are also conditioned by how a stimulus fits into the overall perception and daily routine of people. Moreover, we are mostly interested in social behavior, and how people act strongly depends on their (perception of) actions and attitudes in their social network (Barabási, 2016).

The emergence of social media substantially facilitates the design and implementation of experiment research. First, crowdsourcing platforms on social media lowers the obstacles in research subject recruitment. Traditionally, many communication researchers counted on student subjects of small or modest size in experiment studies. Nowadays, it is no longer difficult to recruit thousands or even millions of diverse or specialized subjects from crowdsourcing platforms (e.g., Amazon Mechanical Turk and Volunteer Science) to participate in an experiment at low or zero costs.

However, the implementation of experimental design on social media is not an easy task. Social media companies will be very selective on their collaborators and on research topics. As Wallach (2016) observed, the fear of losing reputation will probably cause social media companies to be more reluctant to share data in the future after the fallout of studies such as the Facebook mood manipulation study (Kramer, Guillory, & Hancock, 2014). The coordination of experiments on social media can also be extremely time-consuming. In a recently published study, it took the authors about five years to coordinate an experiment on social media (King, Schneer, & White, 2017). Furthermore, how to adequately address ethical concerns involved in online experiments has become a pressing ethical issue in scientific community.

From small-N to large-N

Simply increasing the scale of measurement can also enable us to study more subtle relations or effects in smaller subpopulations than possible with the sample sizes normally available in communication research (Monroe et al., 2015). For example, the Facebook "voting study" showed that a stimulus message to vote also affects close friends of the people who received the message, but this effect was so small that it was only significant because of the half a million subjects—but given the small margins in (American) elections even such a small effect can be decisive (Bond et al., 2012). Similarly, by measuring messages and behavior in real time rather than in daily or weekly (or yearly) surveys, much more fine-grained time series can be constructed, alleviating the problems of simultaneous correlation and making a stronger case for finding causal mechanisms.

In order to leverage the more complex models afforded by larger data sets we need to change the way we build and test our models. As argued by Hindman (2015), it is useful to consider techniques developed in machine learning research for model selection and model shrinkage such as penalized (lasso) regression and cross-validation which are aimed at out-of-sample prediction rather than within-sample explanation. Such techniques estimate more parsimonious models and hence alleviate the problems of overfitting that can occur with very large data sets. Additionally, methods such as Exponential Random Graph Modeling (ERGM; An, 2016) or Relational Event Modeling (Pilny, Schecter, Poole, & Contractor, 2016) can dynamically model network and group dynamics.

From solitary to collaborative research

Currently, most empirical scholars in communication science gather, clean, and analyze their own data, either individually or as a group. Moreover, in many cases the tools and scripts used for data processing are also developed locally. Digital data and computational tools make it easier to share and reuse these resources. The increased scale and complexity also make it almost necessary to do so: it is very hard for any individual researcher to possess the skills and resources needed do do all the steps of computational research him or herself (Hesse, Moser, & Riley, 2015). An increased focus on sharing data and tools will also force us to be more rigorous in defining operationalizations and documenting the data and analysis process, furthering transparency and reproducibility of research.

A second way in which computational methods can change the way we do research is by fostering the interdisciplinary collaboration needed to deal with larger data sets and more complex computational techniques (Wallach, 2016). For example, measurements and analysis methods from neuroscience are being increasingly used in analyzing communication processes (Falk, Cascio, & Coronel, 2015; Weber, Mangus, & Huskey, 2015). Agent-based modeling uses computer models and empirical data to facilitate theory building (Palazzolo, Serb, She, Su, & Contractor, 2006). By offering a chance to zoom in from the macro level down to the individual data points, digital methods can also bring quantitative and qualitative research closer together, allowing qualitative research to improve our understanding of data and build theory, while keeping the link to large-scale quantitative research to test the resulting hypotheses (O'Brien, 2016).

Challenges and pitfalls in computational methods

As argued above, computational methods offer a wide range of possibilities for communication researchers to explore new research questions and re-examine classical theories from new perspectives. By observing actual behavior in the social environment, and if possible of a whole network of connected people, we get a better measurement of how people actually react, rather than of how they (report or intent to) react in the artificial isolation of the lab setting; and the scale at which this is possible allows more complex or subtle causal relations to be tested and discovered. Large-scale exploratory research can help formulate theories and identify interesting cases or subsets for further study, while at the same time smaller and qualitative studies can help make sense of the results of big data research (cf. O'Brien, 2016). Similarly, "big data" confirmatory research can help test whether causal relations found in experimental studies actually hold in the "wild", i.e., on large populations and in real social settings (Monroe et al., 2015).

Using these new methods and data sets, however, creates a new set of challenges and pitfalls, some of which will be reviewed below. Most of these challenges do not have a single answer, and require continued discussion about the advantages, disadvantages, and best practices in computational communication science. To contribute to this discussion, we pose a number of key questions about computational methods below, and give pointers to the relevant literature to understand the problems and possible solutions.

How do we keep research datasets accessible?

Is it ironic or naive to ask about getting research datasets in the age of big data? Our answer is no. Although the volume, variety, velocity, and veracity of big data has been repeatedly bragged in both news reports and scholarly writings, it is a hard truth that many of the "big data" sets are proprietary ones which are highly demanding to access for most communication researchers (Boyd & Crawford, 2012; Lazer et al., 2009; Wallach, 2016). The privileged access to big data by a small group of researchers will make researchers with the access "enjoy an unfair amount of attention at the expense of equally talented researchers without these connections" (Huberman, 2012, p. 308). Moreover, studies conducted by researchers connected to these actors are generally based only on a single platform (e.g., Twitter or Facebook), which makes it challenging to develop a panoramic understanding of users behavior on social media as a holistic ecosystem and increases generalizability problems (Wallach, 2016). More importantly, such privileged access to big data will thwart the reproducibility of computational research which serves as the minimum standard by which scientific claims are judged (Peng, 2011).

Samples of big data on social media are made accessible to the public either in its original form (data collected via Twitter public API) or in aggregate format (e.g., data from Google Trends). Moreover, as explicated by Matthew Weber (2018), external parties also create accessible archives of web data. However, the sampling, aggregation, and other transformation imposed on the released data is a black box, which poses great challenges for communication researchers to evaluate the quality and representativeness of the data and then assess the external validity of their findings derived from such data.

We need to make sure our data is open and transparent, and to make sure that research is not reserved to the privilleged few who have the network or resources to acquire data sets. To do this, is is vital that we stimulate sharing and publishing data sets. Where possible these should be fully open and published on platforms such as dataverse, where needed for privacy or copyright reasons the data should be securely stored but accessible under clear conditions. A corpus management tool like AmCAT (Van Atteveldt, 2008) can help alleviate copyright restrictions by allowing data to be queried and analysed even if the full text of the data set cannot be published. Additionally, we should work with funding agencies and data providers such as newspaper publishers and social media platforms to make standardized data sets available for all researchers.

Is "big" data always good data?

With the increasing ease-of-use of computational algorithms, communication researchers themselves can retrieve megabytes or terabytes of digitized data from social media or other online sources. Both the nature of the new types of digital trace and social media data and the relative convenience in collecting such data are more appealing to communication researchers, in comparison to the time-consuming field work, relatively small sample, decreasing response rate, and heavily criticized biases in survey research. Do communication researchers need to bother with small-sample survey data when it is easy and cheap to get "big data" from social media? Big data, however, is not a panacea for all methodological problems in empirical research, and it has its obvious limitations despite its widely touted advantages.

First, big data is "found" while survey data is "made" (Taylor, 2013). Most of the big data are secondary and intended for other primary uses most of which have little relevance to academic research. On the other side, most of the survey data are "made" by researchers who design and implement their studies and questionnaires with specific research purposes in mind. The big data is "found" and then tailored or curated by researchers to address their own theoretical or practical concerns. The gap between the primary purpose intended for big data and the secondary purpose found for big data will pose threat to the validity of design, measurement, and analysis in computational communication research.

Secondly, that data is "big" does not mean that it is representative for a certain population (Boyd & Crawford, 2012; Hargittai, 2015; Wallach, 2016). As Hargittai (2015) has shown based on representative survey data, people do not randomly select into social media platforms, and very limited information is available for communication researchers to assess the (un)representativeness of big data retrieved from social media. As Hazel Kwon and her colleagues point out in this volume, "specialized" actors on social media, such as issue experts, professionals, and institutional users, are over-represented while the ordinary publics are under-represented in computational research, which leads to a sampling bias to be carefully handled in empirical studies.

This also means that p-values are less meaningful as a measure of validity. There is a lively debate about the use and abuse of p-values and null-hypothesis significance testing (NHST; see, e.g., Leek & Peng, 2015; Vermeulen et al., 2015; Vidgen & Yasseri, 2016; Wasserstein & Lazar, 2016) and the leading political methodology journal *Political Analysis* decided to stop reporting p-values altogether (Gill, 2018). Especially for very large data sets, where representativeness and selection and measurement biases are a much greater threat to validity than small sample sizes, p values are not a very meaningful indicator of effect (Hofmann, 2015).

In general, we should recognize that size of data is neither a sign of validity nor of invalidity of the conclusions. Especially for big data studies, we should focus more on substantive effect size and validity than mere statistical significance, for example by showing confidence intervals and using simulations or bootstrapping to show the estimated real effects of the found relations.

Are computational measurement methods valid and reliable?

The unobtrusiveness of social media data makes them less vulnerable to traditional measurement bias, such as instrument bias, interviewer bias, and social desirability bias. However, this does not imply that they are free of measurement errors.

Measurement errors can be introduced when text mining techniques are employed to identify semantic features in user-generated content, whether using dictionaries, machine learning, or unsupervised techniques (Boumans & Trilling, 2016; Yang, Adomavicius, Burtch, & Ren, 2018) and when social and communication networks are constructed from user-initiated behavior. For example, Soroka, Young, and Balmas (2015) found that different sentiment dictionaries capture different underlying phenomena and highlight "the importance of tailoring lexicons to domains to improve construct validity" (p. 108). In the same volume, González-Bailón and Paltoglou (2015) also observe the lack of correlation between sentiment dictionaries, and similarly argue for the need for domain adaptation of dictionaries. Similar to techniques like factor analysis, unsupervised methods such as topic modelling require the researcher to interpret and validate the resulting topics, and although quantitative measures of topic coherence exist these do not always correlate with human judgments of topic quality (Chang, Gerrish, Wang, Boyd-Graber, & Blei, 2009).

However, it should be noted that classical methods of manual content analysis are also no guarantee of valid or reliable data. Referring to the "myth of the trained coder", Rene Weber and co-authors in this volume show that using trained manual coders to extract subjective features such as moral claims can lead to overestimation of reliability and argue that untrained (crowd) coders can actually be better at capturing intuitive judgments.

The errors can introduce systematic biases in subsequent multivariate analysis and threaten the validity of statistical inference. This means that we need to emphasize the validity of measurements of social media and other digital data. (see e.g. De Choudhury et al., 2010; Newman, 2017; Paul & Dredze, 2011; Yang et al., 2018). The validity of a method or tool is dependent on the context in which it is used, so even if a researcher uses an existing off-the-shelf tool with published validity results it is vital to show how well it performs in a specific domain and on a specific task. Additionally, a culture of sharing and reusing tools and methods and publishing the source code and validation sets of tools helps foster continuous and collaborative improvements to the measurement tools we all use.

What is responsible and ethical conduct in computational communication research?

What responsible and ethical conduct should be adopted is another challenge in computational communication research. With the publication of several controversial large-scale experiments on social media (e.g., Bond et al., 2012; Kramer et al., 2014), the scientific community and the general public have expressed growing concern on ethical (mis)conduct in computational social science.

Such concerns can exist in different steps of computational communication research (Boyd & Crawford, 2012; Kosinski, Matz, Gosling, Popov, & Stillwell, 2015). For instance, in field experiments on social media, how can researchers get informed consent from the subjects? When users of a social media platform accept the terms of service of the platform, can researchers assume that the users have given an explicit or implicit consent to participate in any types of experiments conducted on the platform? As most of the datasets in computational communication research are directly produced by individuals, to what extent should the data be anonymized and sanitized for the sake of privacy protection, how can we achieve a balance between protecting individual privacy and advocating reproducible research? How do we deal with the findings that our digital traces can reveal a lot of very personal traits (Kosinski, Stillwell, & Graepel, 2013) and that there are techniques to de-anonymize supposedly "anonymized" data (Narayanan & Shmatikov, 2008)?

There are no unambiguous answers to all these questions, but we do not have the luxury of ignoring these problems and (further) losing the trust of the general public. This calls for a collective effort from the whole community to set up a responsible conduct of research in computational communication research.

How do we get the needed skills and infrastructure?

Reaping the benefits of computational methods requires that as a scientific community we need to invest in skills, infrastructure, and institutions (Jagadish et al., 2014; Wallach, 2016). As we expect more and more research to include (some) computational aspects, it is increasingly important that as practitioners we are skilled at dealing with data and computational tools. As pointed out by Shah et al. (2015), many digital traces and other "big" data are textual rather than the numerical data most communication scholars are trained for and used to, and will require us to "hone [our] skills in natural language processing" (p. 21).

Of course, we can and should collaborate as much as possible with researchers in fields like computer scientists, computational linguists, and artificial intelligence. However, collaboration requires research that is innovative and challenging to both sides, and in many cases what we need is a good programmer to help us gather, clean, analyze, and visualize data rather than a computer scientist to invent a new algorithm. While the bigger (or richer) groups can afford to hire such programmers, many (young) scholars do not have these resources and, moreover, it is very difficult to select, supervise, and motivate a programmer without some computational skills.

Thus, we expect that doing research in communication science will increasingly demand at least some level of computational literacy. Not everyone can (or should) become a programmer, but modern computer languages, libraries, and toolkits have made it easier than ever to achieve useful results, and with a relatively limited investment in computing skills one can quickly become more productive at data driven research and better at communicating with programmers or computer scientists. We think it is vital that we make computational methods more prominent in our teaching to make sure the new generation of communication scientists and practitioners are stimulated and facilitated to learn computational skills such as data analytics, text processing, or web scraping, as applicable.

Second, it is important to invest in research infrastructure and to move to a culture of sharing and reusing tools and data. One person or group cannot hope to master all skills and tools needed to gather, clean, process, and analyze data using innovative computational methods. Bigger teams have more skills and resources, of course, but there is no need for all steps of the process to be taken within the same team or project, and in many cases the value of data or tools are much greater than the context within which they were originally developed.

Finally, we need to make sure that our institutional arrangements stimulate scholars to invest in and share computational skills, methods, and data. Thus, it is important that researchers and institutions give credit to development and sharing of tools and data (cf. Crosas, King, Honaker, & Sweeney, 2015). As long as the basic "coins" in academia remain publications and citations, we need to make sure that data and tools can be published and cited, and that these publications and citations are valued. Especially important here is to also stimulate the maintenance and documentation of tools and data. A new tool can be published in a journal article, but it can be difficult to get credit for a new version or better documentation of a tool, especially for contributions to tools originally developed by another scholar. This stimulates a fragmentation of the ecosystem, even though it can be more useful for the community to have fewer but well-documented and well-maintained tools than to have many tools or data sets that lack documentation or maintenance. We also need to understand and appreciate the relative effort that goes into tools development and interdisciplinary research, where there is often a long lag before research becomes fully productive.

Contents of this volume

The articles in this special issue covers a wide range of computational methods relevant to communication research, including text mining, network modeling, and the validity and provenance of big data sets.

On automatic text analysis, Daniel Maier and his colleagues review the topic modeling literature and discuss the advantages, challenges, and best practices in applying LDA in communication research. Their discussion of reliability and validity in topic modeling is of particular relevance to communication research. Rene Weber and co-authors describe how crowd coding can be an indispensable tool for extracting moral claims and other subjective information from text. They argue that the more intuitive judgments of (multiple) untrained crowd coders might actually yield a better measurement than expert coders, who can be influenced by group biases that cloud the intercoder reliability measures. Elena Rudkovsky and her colleagues use word embeddings to improve automatic sentiment analysis on Austrian newspapers. Finally, Damian Trilling and Jeroen Jonkman propose and discuss four criteria that a framework for automated content analysis should fulfill, including scalability, free and open source, adaptability, and accessibility via multiple interfaces.

On network analysis, Alina Lungeanu and her colleagues move beyond a dyadic person-to-person framework to construct social networks and adopt a hypergraph approach to account for the nesting of individuals in groups and the patterns of interlocks among groups. They discuss the conceptual innovation of the hypergraph approach and demonstrate how to address the methodological challenges in such a hypergraph approach by applying it to examine the assembly of scientific collaboration teams.

The last two authors discuss the challenges in obtaining valid "big" data sets. Matthew Weber gives an overview of the possibilities and challenges in using web archives for communication research. Web archives are an important and frequently used source of information on historical trends in Internet use, and by showing how issues of noise and representativeness can be addressed Weber paves the way for a more robust use of these resources in our field. Hazel Kwon and her colleagues address sampling biases in digital research and demonstrate how supervised machine learning can reduce sampling bias induced from "proxy-population mismatch" on Twitter.

Together, these authors describe and apply a range of different computational methods and data sets, with a focus on critically assessing the utility and validity of computational methods for studying communication. They show how computational methods can be used to accelerate the pace of discovery in communication science, provided that we can tackle the challenges of conducting valid, open, and ethical research. In particular, we think that it is vital that as a community we move forward on at least three fronts: (1) build the infrastructure, skills, and institutional incentives required to use and maintain computational methods and tools; (2) work toward open, transparent, and collaborative research, with sharing and reusing datasets and tools the norm rather than the exception; and (3) continue developing, validating, and critically discussing computational methods in the context of substantive communication science questions. By producing this special issue, we hope to have contributed toward reaching these goals and to the further development and dissemination of computational methods.

ORCID

Wouter van Atteveldt http://orcid.org/0000-0003-1237-538X
Tai-Quan Peng http://orcid.org/0000-0002-2588-7491

References

Alvarez, R. M. (Ed.). (2016). *Computational social science: Discovery and prediction*. Cambridge, UK: Cambridge University Press.

An, W. (2016). Fitting ERGMs on big networks. *Social Science Research*, 59, 107–119. doi:10.1016/j.ssresearch.2016.04.019

Araujo, T., Wonneberger, A., Neijens, P., & de Vreese, C. (2017). How much time do you spend online? understanding and improving the accuracy of self-reported measures of internet use. *Communication Methods and Measures*, 11(3), 173–190. doi:10.1080/19312458.2017.1317337

Barabási, A. (2016). *Network science*. Cambridge, UK: Cambridge University Press.

Blei, D. M., Ng, A. Y., & Jordan, M. I. (2003). Latent dirichlet allocation. *The Journal of Machine Learning Research*, 3, 993–1022.

Bodo, B., Helberger, N., Irion, K., Zuiderveen Borgesius, F., Moller, J., van de Velde, B., ... de Vreese, C. (2017). Tackling the algorithmic control crisis-the technical, legal, and ethical challenges of research into algorithmic agents. *Yale JL & Technical*, 19, 133.

Bond, R. M., Fariss, C. J., Jones, J. J., Kramer, A. D., Marlow, C., Settle, J. E., & Fowler, J. H. (2012). A 61-million-person experiment in social influence and political mobilization. *Nature*, 489(7415), 295. doi:10.1038/nature11421

Boumans, J. W., & Trilling, D. (2016). Taking stock of the toolkit: An overview of relevant automated content analysis approaches and techniques for digital journalism scholars. *Digital Journalism*, 4(1), 8–23. doi:10.1080/21670811.2015.1096598

Boyd, D., & Crawford, K. (2012). Critical questions for big data: Provocations for a cultural, technological, and scholarly phenomenon. *Information, Communication & Society*, 15(5), 662–679. doi:10.1080/1369118X.2012.678878

Chang, J., Gerrish, S., Wang, C., Boyd-Graber, J. L., & Blei, D. M. (2009). *Reading tea leaves: How humans interpret topic models*. Advances in neural information processing systems (pp. 288–296). New York, NY: Curran Associates.

Colleoni, E., Rozza, A., & Arvidsson, A. (2014). Echo chamber or public sphere? predicting political orientation and measuring political homophily in twitter using big data. *Journal of Communication*, 64(2), 317–332. doi:10.1111/jcom.2014.64.issue-2

Collingwood, L., & Wilkerson, J. (2012). Tradeoffs in accuracy and efficiency in supervised learning methods. *Journal of Information Technology & Politics*, 9(3), 298–318. doi:10.1080/19331681.2012.669191

Costera Meijer, I., & Groot Kormelink, T. (2015). Checking, sharing, clicking and linking: Changing patterns of news use between 2004 and 2014. *Digital Journalism*, 3(5), 664–679. doi:10.1080/21670811.2014.937149

Crosas, M., King, G., Honaker, J., & Sweeney, L. (2015). Automating open science for big data. *The ANNALS of the American Academy of Political and Social Science*, 659(1), 260–273. doi:10.1177/0002716215570847

De Choudhury, M., Lin, Y.-R., Sundaram, H., Candan, K. S., Xie, L., & Kelliher, A. (2010). How does the data sampling strategy impact the discovery of information diffusion in social media? *Icwsm*, 10, 34–41.

Diesner, J., Frantz, T. L., & Carley, K. M. (2005). Communication networks from the enron email corpus "it's always about the people. enron is no different". *Computational & Mathematical Organization Theory, 11*(3), 201–228. doi:10.1007/s10588-005-5377-0

Dovidio, J. F. (1992). New technologies for the direct and indirect assesment of attitudes. In J. Tanur (Ed.), *Questions about questions: Inquiries into the cognitive bases of surveys* (pp. 204–237). New York, NY: Russell Sage Foundation.

Falk, E. B., Cascio, C. N., & Coronel, J. C. (2015). Neural prediction of communication-relevant outcomes. *Communication Methods and Measures, 9*(1–2), 30–54. doi:10.1080/19312458.2014.999750

Gill, J. (2018). Comments from the new editor. *Political Analysis, 26*(1), 1–2. doi:10.1017/pan.2017.41

González-Bailón, S., & Paltoglou, G. (2015). Signals of public opinion in online communication: A comparison of methods and data sources. *The ANNALS of the American Academy of Political and Social Science, 659*(1), 95–107. doi:10.1177/0002716215569192

Grimmer, J. (2016). Measuring representational style in the house: The tea party, obama, and legislators' changing expressed priorities. In R. M. Alvarez (Ed.), *Computational social science: Discovery and prediction* (p. 307). Cambridge, UK: Cambridge University Press.

Guess, A., Nyhan, B., & Reifler, J. (2018). *Selective exposure to misinformation: Evidence from the consumption of fake news during the 2016 U.S. Presidential campaign.* Retrieved from https://www.dartmouth.edu/~nyhan/fake-news-2016.pdf

Hargittai, E. (2015). Is bigger always better? potential biases of big data derived from social network sites. *The ANNALS of the American Academy of Political and Social Science, 659*(1), 63–76. doi:10.1177/0002716215570866

Hesse, B. W., Moser, R. P., & Riley, W. T. (2015). From big data to knowledge in the social sciences. *The Annals of the American Academy of Political and Social Science, 659*(1), 16–32. doi:10.1177/0002716215570007

Hindman, M. (2015). Building better models: Prediction, replication, and machine learning in the social sciences. *The ANNALS of the American Academy of Political and Social Science, 659*(1), 48–62. doi:10.1177/0002716215570279

Hofmann, M. A. (2015). Searching for effects in big data: Why p-values are not advised and what to use instead. Proceedings of the 2015 winter simulation conference (pp. 725–736). New York, NY: IEEE Press.

Huberman, B. A. (2012). Sociology of science: Big data deserve a bigger audience. *Nature, 482*(7385), 308. doi:10.1038/482308d

Jacobi, C., Van Atteveldt, W., & Welbers, K. (2016). Quantitative analysis of large amounts of journalistic texts using topic modelling. *Digital Journalism, 4*(1), 89–106. doi:10.1080/21670811.2015.1093271

Jagadish, H., Gehrke, J., Labrinidis, A., Papakonstantinou, Y., Patel, J. M., Ramakrishnan, R., & Shahabi, C. (2014). Big data and its technical challenges. *Communications of the ACM, 57*(7), 86–94. doi:10.1145/2622628

Jungherr, A. (2014). The logic of political coverage on twitter: Temporal dynamics and content. *Journal of Communication, 64*(2), 239–259. doi:10.1111/jcom.2014.64.issue-2

King, G., Schneer, B., & White, A. (2017). How the news media activate public expression and influence national agendas. *Science, 358*(6364), 776–780. doi:10.1126/science.aao1100

Kobayashi, T., & Boase, J. (2012). No such effect? The implications of measurement error in self-report measures of mobile communication use. *Communication Methods and Measures, 6*(2), 126–143. doi:10.1080/19312458.2012.679243

Kobayashi, T., Boase, J., Suzuki, T., & Suzuki, T. (2015). Emerging from the cocoon? revisiting the tele-cocooning hypothesis in the smartphone era. *Journal of Computer-Mediated Communication, 20*(3), 330–345. doi:10.1111/jcc4.2015.20.issue-3

Kosinski, M., Matz, S. C., Gosling, S. D., Popov, V., & Stillwell, D. (2015). Facebook as a research tool for the social sciences: Opportunities, challenges, ethical considerations, and practical guidelines. *American Psychologist, 70*(6), 543. doi:10.1037/a0039210

Kosinski, M., Stillwell, D., & Graepel, T. (2013). Private traits and attributes are predictable from digital records of human behavior. *Proceedings of the National Academy of Sciences, 110*(15), 5802–5805. doi:10.1073/pnas.1218772110

Kramer, A. D., Guillory, J. E., & Hancock, J. T. (2014). Experimental evidence of massive-scale emotional contagion through social networks. *Proceedings of the National Academy of Sciences, 111*(24), 8788–8790. doi:10.1073/pnas.1320040111

Lazer, D., Pentland, A. S., Adamic, L., Aral, S., Barabasi, A. L., Brewer, D., ... Alstyne, M. V. (2009). Life in the network: The coming age of computational social science. *Science (New York, NY), 323*(5915), 721. doi:10.1126/science.1167742

Leek, J. T., & Peng, R. D. (2015). Statistics: P values are just the tip of the iceberg. *Nature News, 520*(7549), 612. doi:10.1038/520612a

Lungeanu, A., Carter, D. R., DeChurch, L., & Contractor, N. (2018). How Team Interlock Ecosystems Shape the Assembly of Scientific Teams: A Hypergraph Approach. *Communication Methods and Measures, 12*(2–3), 175–199. doi:10.1080/19312458.2018.1430756

Maier, D., Waldherr, A., Miltner, P., Wiedemann, G., Niekler, A., Keinert, A., ... Adam, S. (2018). Applying LDA topic modeling in communication research: Toward a valid and reliable methodology. *Communication Methods and Measures, 12*(2–3), 93–118. doi:10.1080/19312458.2018.1430754

Monge, P. R., & Contractor, N. S. (2003). *Theories of communication networks.* New York, NY: Oxford University Press.

Monroe, B. L., Pan, J., Roberts, M. E., Sen, M., & Sinclair, B. (2015). No! formal theory, causal inference, and big data are not contradictory trends in political science. *PS: Political Science & Politics, 48*(1), 71–74.

Narayanan, A., & Shmatikov, V. (2008). *Robust de-anonymization of large sparse datasets.* Security and privacy, 2008. sp 2008. ieee symposium on (pp. 111–125). New York, NY: IEEE Press.

Newman, M. (2017). *Measurement errors in network data.* arXiv preprint arXiv:1703.07376.

Nie, N. H., Bent, D. H., & Hull, C. H. (1970). *Spss: Statistical package for the social sciences.* New York, NY: McGraw-Hill.

O'Brien, D. T. (2016). Using small data to interpret big data: 311 reports as individual contributions to informal social control in urban neighborhoods. *Social Science Research, 59,* 83–96. doi:10.1016/j.ssresearch.2016.04.009

Odijk, D., Burscher, B., Vliegenthart, R., & de Rijke, M. (2013). Automatic thematic content analysis: Finding frames in news. In Jatowt, A. et al. (eds.), *Social informatics,* SocInfo 2013. Lecture Notes in Computer Science, vol 8238. Cham: Springer.

Palazzolo, E. T., Serb, D. A., She, Y., Su, C., & Contractor, N. S. (2006). Coevolution of communication and knowledge networks in transactive memory systems: Using computational models for theoretical development. *Communication Theory, 16*(2), 223–250. doi:10.1111/comt.2006.16.issue-2

Parks, M. R. (2014). Big data in communication research: Its contents and discontents. *Journal of Communication, 64*(2), 355–360. doi:10.1111/jcom.2014.64.issue-2

Paul, M. J., & Dredze, M. (2011). You are what you tweet: Analyzing twitter for public health. *Icwsm, 20,* 265–272.

Peng, R. D. (2011). Reproducible research in computational science. *Science, 334*(6060), 1226–1227. doi:10.1126/science.1213847

Pilny, A., Schecter, A., Poole, M. S., & Contractor, N. (2016). An illustration of the relational event model to analyze group interaction processes. *Group Dynamics: Theory, Research, and Practice, 20*(3), 181. doi:10.1037/gdn0000042

Roberts, M. E., Stewart, B. M., Tingley, D., Lucas, C., Leder-Luis, J., Gadarian, S. K., … Rand, D. G. (2014). Structural topic models for open-ended survey responses. *American Journal of Political Science, 58*(4), 1064–1082. doi:10.1111/ajps.12103

Rudkowsky, E., Haselmayer, M., Wastian, M., Jenny, M., Emrich, S., & Sedlmair, M. (2018). More than Bags of Words: Sentiment Analysis with Word Embeddings. *Communication Methods and Measures, 12*(2-3), 140–157. doi:10.1080/19312458.2018.1455817

Russell Neuman, W., Guggenheim, L., Mo Jang, S., & Bae, S. Y. (2014). The dynamics of public attention: Agenda-setting theory meets big data. *Journal of Communication, 64*(2), 193–214. doi:10.1111/jcom.2014.64.issue-2

Scharkow, M., & Bachl, M. (2017). How measurement error in content analysis and self-reported media use leads to minimal media effect findings in linkage analyses: A simulation study. *Political Communication, 34*(3), 323–343. doi:10.1080/10584609.2016.1235640

Shah, D. V., Cappella, J. N., & Neuman, W. R. (2015). Big data, digital media, and computational social science: Possibilities and perils. *The ANNALS of the American Academy of Political and Social Science, 659*(1), 6–13. doi:10.1177/0002716215572084

Soroka, S., Young, L., & Balmas, M. (2015). Bad news or mad news? sentiment scoring of negativity, fear, and anger in news content. *The ANNALS of the American Academy of Political and Social Science, 659*(1), 108–121. doi:10.1177/0002716215569217

Stone, P. J., Dunphy, D. C., Smith, M. S., Ogilvie, D. M. (1966). *The general inquirer: A computer approach to content analysis.* Cambridge, MA: MIT Press.

Tan, C., Niculae, V., Danescu-Niculescu-Mizil, C., & Lee, L. (2016). *Winning arguments: Interaction dynamics and persuasion strategies in good-faith online discussions.* Proceedings of the 25th international conference on world wide web (pp. 613–624). ACM Digital Library, New York, NY.

Taylor, S. J. (2013). *Real scientists make their own data.* Retrieved from https://seanjtaylor.com/post/41463778912/real-scientists-make-their-own-data

Trilling, D. (2017). Big data, analysis of. In *The J. Matthes, C. S. Davis, R. F. Potter (Eds.), international encyclopedia of communication research methods.* New York, NY: Wiley Online Library.

Tucker, J. A., Nagler, J., MacDuffee, M., Metzger, P. B., Penfold-Brown, D., & Bonneau, R. (2016). Big data, social media, and protest. In R. M. Alvarez (Ed.), *Computational social science: Discovery and prediction* (p. 307). Cambridge, UK: Cambridge University Press.

Van Atteveldt, W. (2008). *Semantic network analysis: Techniques for extracting, representing, and querying media content* (dissertation). Charleston, SC: BookSurge.

Van Atteveldt, W., Sheafer, T., Shenhav, S., & Fogel-Dror, Y. (2017). Clause analysis: Using syntactic information to automatically extract source, subject, and predicate from texts with an application to the 2008–2009 Gaza War. *Political Analysis, 25*(2), 207–222. doi:10.1017/pan.2016.12

Vermeulen, I., Beukeboom, C. J., Batenburg, A., Avramiea, A., Stoyanov, D., van de Velde, B., & Oegema, D. (2015). Blinded by the light: How a focus on statistical "significance" may cause p-value misreporting and an excess of p-values just below. 05 in communication science. *Communication Methods and Measures*, 9(4), 253-279. doi:10.1080/19312458.2015.1096333

Vidgen, B., & Yasseri, T. (2016). P-values: Misunderstood and misused. *Frontiers in Physics*, 4, 6. doi:10.3389/fphy.2016.00006

Wallach, H. (2016). Computational social science: Towards a collaborative future. In R. M. Alvarez (Ed.), *Computational social science: Discovery and prediction* (p. 307). Cambridge, UK: Cambridge University Press.

Wasserstein, R. L., & Lazar, N. A. (2016). The ASA's statement on p-values: Context, process, and purpose. *The American Statistician*, 70(2), 129-133. doi:10.1080/00031305.2016.1154108

Weber, M. (2018). Methods and Approaches to Using Web Archives in Computational Communication Research. *Communication Methods and Measures*, 12(2-3), 200-215. doi:10.1080/19312458.2018.1447657

Weber, R., Mangus, J. M., & Huskey, R. (2015). Brain imaging in communication research: A practical guide to understanding and evaluating fmri studies. *Communication Methods and Measures*, 9(1-2), 5-29. doi:10.1080/19312458.2014.999754

Westlake, B. G., & Bouchard, M. (2016). Liking and hyperlinking: Community detection in online child sexual exploitation networks. *Social Science Research*, 59, 23-36. doi:10.1016/j.ssresearch.2016.04.010

Wu, S., Hofman, J. M., Mason, W. A., & Watts, D. J. (2011). *Who says what to whom on twitter*. Proceedings of the 20th international conference on world wide web (pp. 705-714). ACM Digital Library, New York, NY.

Xu, P., Wu, Y., Wei, E., Peng, T.-Q., Liu, S., Zhu, J. J., & Qu, H. (2013). Visual analysis of topic competition on social media. *IEEE Transactions on Visualization and Computer Graphics*, 19(12), 2012-2021. doi:10.1109/TVCG.2013.221

Yang, J., & Leskovec, J. (2010). *Modeling information diffusion in implicit networks*. Data mining (icdm), 2010 IEEE 10th international conference on (pp. 599-608). New York, NY: IEEE Press.

Yang, M., Adomavicius, G., Burtch, G., & Ren, Y. (2018). Mind the gap: Accounting for measurement error and misclassification in variables generated via data mining. *Information Systems Research*, 29, 4-24. doi:10.1287/isre.2017.0727

Applying LDA Topic Modeling in Communication Research: Toward a Valid and Reliable Methodology

Daniel Maier, A. Waldherr, P. Miltner, G. Wiedemann, A. Niekler, A. Keinert, B. Pfetsch, G. Heyer, U. Reber, T. Häussler, H. Schmid-Petri, and S. Adam

ABSTRACT
Latent Dirichlet allocation (LDA) topic models are increasingly being used in communication research. Yet, questions regarding reliability and validity of the approach have received little attention thus far. In applying LDA to textual data, researchers need to tackle at least four major challenges that affect these criteria: (a) appropriate pre-processing of the text collection; (b) adequate selection of model parameters, including the number of topics to be generated; (c) evaluation of the model's reliability; and (d) the process of validly interpreting the resulting topics. We review the research literature dealing with these questions and propose a methodology that approaches these challenges. Our overall goal is to make LDA topic modeling more accessible to communication researchers and to ensure compliance with disciplinary standards. Consequently, we develop a brief hands-on user guide for applying LDA topic modeling. We demonstrate the value of our approach with empirical data from an ongoing research project.

Introduction

Topic modeling with latent Dirichlet allocation (LDA) is a computational content-analysis technique that can be used to investigate the "hidden" thematic structure of a given collection of texts. The data-driven and computational nature of LDA makes it attractive for communication research because it allows for quickly and efficiently deriving the thematic structure of large amounts of text documents. It combines an inductive approach with quantitative measurements, making it particularly suitable for exploratory and descriptive analyses (Elgesem, Steskal, & Diakopoulos, 2015; Koltsova & Shcherbak, 2015).

Consequently, LDA topic models are increasingly being used in communication research. However, communication scholars have not yet developed good-practice guidance for the many challenges a user faces when applying LDA topic modeling. Important methodological decisions must be made that are rarely explained at length in application-focused studies. These decisions relate to at least four challenging questions: (a) How does one pre-process unstructured text data appropriately? (b) How does one select algorithm parameters appropriately, e.g., the number of topics to be generated? (c) How can one evaluate and, if necessary, improve reliability and interpretability of the model solution? (d) How can one validate the resulting topics?

These challenges particularly affect the approach's reliability and validity, both of which are core criteria for content analysis in communication research (Neuendorf, 2017), but they have, nevertheless, received little attention thus far. This article's aim is to provide a thorough review and discussion of these challenges and to propose methods to ensure the validity and reliability of topic models. Such scrutiny is necessary to make LDA-based topic modeling more accessible and applicable for communication researchers.

This article is organized as follows. First, we briefly introduce the statistical background of LDA. Second, we review how the aforementioned questions are addressed in studies that have applied LDA in communication research. Third, drawing on knowledge from these studies and our experiences from an ongoing research project, we propose a good-practice approach that we apply to an empirical collection of 186,557 web documents. Our proposal comprises detailed explanations and novel solutions for the aforementioned questions, including a practical guide for users in communication research. In the concluding section, we briefly summarize how the core challenges of LDA topic modeling can be practically addressed by communication scholars in future research.

Statistical background of LDA topic modeling

LDA can be used to identify and describe latent thematic structures within collections of text documents (Blei, 2012). LDA is but one of several statistical algorithms that can be used for topic modeling; however, we are concentrating on LDA here as a general and widely used model. Blei, Ng, and Jordan (2003) introduced LDA as the first approach that allows for modeling of topic semantics entirely within the Bayesian statistical paradigm.

The application of LDA is based on three nested concepts: the text collection to be modelled is referred to as the *corpus*; one item within the corpus is a *document*, with words within a document called *terms*. Thus, documents are nested within the corpus, with terms nested within documents (see Figure 1, left side).

The aim of the LDA algorithm is to model a comprehensive representation of the corpus by inferring latent content variables, called *topics*. Regarding the level of analysis, topics are heuristically located on an intermediate level between the corpus and the documents and can be imagined as content-related categories, or clusters. A major advantage is that topics are inferred from a given collection without input from any prior knowledge. Since topics are hidden in the first place, no information about them is directly observable in the data. The LDA algorithm solves this problem by inferring topics from recurring patterns of word occurrence in documents.

In their seminal paper, Blei et al. (2003, p. 996) propose that documents can be "represented as random mixtures over latent topics, where each topic is characterized by a distribution over words." Speaking in statistical terms, the document collection (corpus) can equally be described as a distribution over the latent topics, in which each topic is a distribution over words. In linguistic theories, topics can be

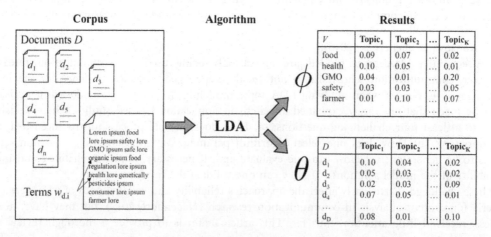

Figure 1. Application of LDA to a Corpus. *Note.* LDA = latent Dirichlet allocation.

seen as factors that consist of sets of words, and documents incorporate such factors with different weights (Lötscher, 1987). Topic models draw on the notion of distributional semantics (Turney & Pantel, 2010) and particularly make use of the so-called *bag of words* assumption, i.e., the ordering of words within each document is ignored. To grasp the thematic structure of a document, it is sufficient to describe its distribution of words (Grimmer & Stewart, 2013).

Although it appears fairly obvious what a *topic* is at first glance, there exists no clear-cut established definition of *topics* in communication research (Günther & Domahidi, 2017, p. 3057). Following Brown and Yule (1983, p. 73), Günther and Domahidi (2017, p. 3057) conclude that a "topic" can only vaguely be described as "what is being talked/written about". In the context of LDA topic modeling, the concept of a topic also takes on an intuitive and rather "abstract notion" of a topic (Blei et al., 2003, p. 995). However, what *topic* actually means in theoretical terms remains unclear. The meaning of a topic in an LDA topic model must be assessed empirically instead (Jacobi, Van Atteveldt, & Welbers, 2015, p. 91) and defined against the background of substantive theoretical concepts, such as "political issues" or "frames" (Maier, Waldherr, Miltner, Jähnichen, & Pfetsch, 2017).

LDA's core: the data-generating process

LDA relies on two matrices to define the latent topical structure: the word-topic assignment matrix ϕ and the document-topic assignment matrix θ (see Figure 1, right side). The word-topic assignment matrix ϕ has two dimensions, K and V, in which K is a numerical value defining the number of proposed topics in the model (which must be determined by the researcher), and V is the total number of words in the vocabulary of the corpus. Thus, any value of $\phi_{w,k}$ signifies the conditional probability with which the word $w = 1, \ldots, V$ is likely to occur in topic $k = 1, \ldots, K$. Analogously, θ has two dimensions, K and D, in which K, again, describes the number of proposed topics, and D is the number of documents in the corpus. Each value of $\theta_{d,k}$ discloses the conditional probability with which a topic k is likely to occur in a given document $d = 1, \ldots, D$ (see Figure 1, right side). In practice, the two resulting matrices are guiding the research process and enabling interpretation regarding content. For instance, from ϕ, researchers can identify the most salient, and thereby most characteristic, terms defining a topic, which facilitates the labeling and interpretation of topics. From θ, researchers can read the probability of the topics' appearance in specific documents; thus, documents may be coded for the presenceby Blei et al. (2003) of salient topics.

The computational core challenge is to estimate the two matrices, ϕ and θ. To master this challenge, Blei et al. (2003) designed a hypothetical statistical generative process within the Bayesian framework that tells us how documents are created and how words from unobserved topics find their way into certain places within a document.

Before we explicate this process, it is important to know that in Bayesian statistics, theoretically reasonable distributions are assigned to unknown variables, such as ϕ and θ. These distributions are called *prior distributions*, as they are assigned prior to data analysis and define their initial state. Here, two prior distributions are needed, one for ϕ and one for θ. LDA models use probability distributions from the Dirichlet family of distributions.[1] Each of the two Dirichlet priors is governed by the number of its dimensions K (the number of topics, which is equal for ϕ and θ) and an abstract (prior) parameter. As there are two prior distributions, there are also two prior parameters, which are sometimes also referred to as hyperparameters, i.e., α for θ and β for ϕ. In essence, α and β influence the shape and specificity of the word-topic and topic-document distributions. While the assignment of the prior parameters is included in the first two steps of the data-generating process, the remainder represents the stochastic core of the model.

What does the data-generating process by Blei et al. (2003) look like?

(1) We assume that each document, d, in a corpus can be described as a probability distribution over topics. This distribution, called θ_d (the topic distribution of document d), is drawn from a Dirichlet distribution with prior parameter α (which must be chosen by the researcher).

(2) Thus, each topic can be defined as a probability distribution over the entire corpus vocabulary, i.e., all the different words that appear in the documents. More technically, for each topic k, we draw ϕ_k, a distribution over the V words of the vocabulary from a Dirichlet distribution with prior parameter β (which must be chosen by the researcher).

(3) Within each document ($d = 1, \ldots, D$) and for every word in that document ($i = 1, \ldots, N_d$), in which i is the index count for each word in document d and N_d is the total length of d, we sample:
  (a) a topic ($z_{d,i}$) from the respective topic distribution in the document (θ_d), and
  (b) a word ($w_{d,i}$) from the respective topic's word distribution ϕ_k, in which k is $z_{d,i}$, the topic we sampled in the previous step.

The core concept of the model implies a statistical creation of a document as a process of randomly drawing topics (3a), then randomly drawing words associated with these topics (3b). This process has a crucial function: It explicates the dependency relationship between the observed variables (words in documents $w_{d,i}$) and the unobserved variables (word-topic distribution ϕ and document-topic distribution θ), thereby paving the way for the application of statistical inference (Griffiths & Steyvers, 2004).

Although the inference procedures cannot be addressed here in detail, it is essential to understand that the statistical theory sketches a joint-probability distribution of the observed *and* latent variables altogether (see Blei, 2012, pp. 79–80). From this joint-probability distribution, defined by the generative process, the *conditional probability distribution of the latent variables* ϕ and θ can be estimated (see Blei, 2012, pp. 79–80) using variational inference (Blei et al., 2013) or Gibbs sampling (see Griffiths & Steyvers, 2004). Therefore, for application on an empirical corpus, the algorithm makes use of the generative process and inverts the aforementioned steps. LDA starts with a random initialization, i.e., it randomly assigns term probabilities to topics (i.e., the initial state of ϕ) and topic probabilities to documents (i.e., the initial state of θ). The algorithm then aims to maximize joint likelihood of the model by iteratively adapting values of the word-topic distribution matrix ϕ and document-topic distribution matrix θ.

Advantages, limitations, and challenges of applying LDA

In summary, LDA models draw on an abstract hypothetical probabilistic process that implies different assumptions. It has proved to be a powerful approach to quickly identify major thematic clusters in large text corpora and model topics as latent structures in a text corpus. Compared with simple co-occurrence analysis, a topic model can reveal a latent semantic connection between words, even if they never actually occurred in a document together. Compared with other topic-clustering methods, a further advantage of LDA topic modeling is its *mixed membership* approach (Grimmer & Stewart, 2013, p. 18), i.e., one document can contain several topics, which is a useful assumption.

Another condition is the aforementioned bag-of-words assumption. In the context of topic modeling, it proves useful and efficient to explore global and general topic clusters in document collections, which is a frequent task in communication research. However, by discarding word order, specific local context information on semantic relations between words is lost, which otherwise might help interpret deeper meanings and solve ambiguities (Lenci, 2008, p. 21). Therefore, some researchers developed variations on topic modeling that consider word order (Wallach, 2006). Another limitation is that LDA assumes topics are independent of each other; thus, correlations between topics or hierarchical structures in terms of meta-topics and sub-topics are not part of the analysis. For this purpose, Blei and Lafferty (2007) developed the Correlated Topic Model (CTM), which also models relations between topics.

When applying LDA, it is important to keep in mind that the model results are not deterministic. Instead, the results are affected by the researcher's choices about the input parameters and the built-in stochastic processes. Reliability and validity cannot be taken for granted. In the remainder of this article, we highlight four challenges with LDA topic modeling and propose guidelines as to how to deal with them.

(1) Before a topic model can even be estimated for an empirical corpus, the text collection must be sanitized of undesirable components and further pre-processed. Cleaning and pre-processing affect the input vocabulary and the documents included in the modeling process. Until now, little is known about the impact of preprocessing on reliability, interpretability, and validity of topic models. However, recent studies (e.g., Denny & Spirling, 2017) suggest that preprocessing strongly affects all these criteria. We provide suggestions on how text data can be cleaned, which pre-processing steps are reasonable to include, and in which order these steps should be applied.

(2) Three model parameters must be selected (K, α, and β), which affect the dimensions and a priori defined distribution of the target variables, ϕ and θ. All three parameters (i.e., K, α, and β) are of substantial importance for the resulting topic model. Thus, the selection of appropriate prior parameters and the number of topics is crucial to retrieve models that adequately reflect the data and can be meaningfully interpreted. Thus far, there is no statistical standard procedure to guide this selection; thus, this remains one of the most complicated tasks in the application of LDA topic modeling. Our proposal suggests a two-step approach: In the first step, the prior parameters are calibrated along the mean intrinsic coherence of the model, i.e., a metric focused on the interpretability (Mimno, Wallach, Talley, Leenders, & McCallum, 2011) to find appropriate candidate models with different numbers for the K proposed topics. In the second step, a qualitative investigation of these candidates follows, which aims to match the models' results with the theoretical concept under study.

(3) The random initialization of the model and the sequence of multiple random processes are integral parts of LDA. The fact that topical contexts are manifested by combining certain words throughout multiple documents will guide the inference mechanism to assign similar topics to documents containing similar word distributions. Inference, itself, is also governed by stochastic random processes to approach a maximum joint probability of the model based on the evidence in the data. Due to both random initialization and stochastic inference, the results from topic models are not entirely deterministic. This calls for reliability checks that indicate the robustness of the topic solutions. We provide an easy-to-calculate reliability metric (Niekler & Jähnichen, 2012) and show that random initialization is a weakness in the LDA architecture. It is clearly inferior to non-random initialization methods, which, as we demonstrate, can improve the reliability of an LDA topic model.

(4) Most importantly, topics are latent variables composed of word distributions. We agree with DiMaggio, Nag, and Blei (2013, p. 586), who write "[P]roducing an interpretable solution is the beginning, not the end, of an analysis." To draw adequate conclusions, the interpretation of the latent variables must be substantially validated. We advise researchers to use systematically structured combinations of existing metrics and in-depth investigation to boost the significance of the validation process.

The four challenges are not independent of each other. Having a clean text corpus and finding a parameter setting that generates interpretable topics are important prerequisites for valid interpretation. Just as well, reliability of the topic solution is an essential precondition for validity.

Literature review

In this section, we systematically review how communication-related research has responded to these challenges so far. We performed keyword searches in *EBSCO Communication Source* and *Web of*

Science (SSCI).[2] The search yielded 61 unique results, which two authors classified as focusing on communication research or other fields of study. Articles were considered further if they applied the LDA algorithm and set out to answer a question of communication research, or used mass-communication data (e.g., newspaper articles, public comments, tweets). Some studies have a substantive thematic research focus, while many others referred to methodological issues. Of the latter studies, only those that demonstrate the application of topic modeling with a sample corpus were included in our review, while general descriptions and discussions of the method were ruled out (e.g., Griffiths, Steyvers, & Tenenbaum, 2007; Günther & Quandt, 2016).

We completed our retrieval of relevant and recent studies by checking *Google Scholar* and also revisiting basic literature on topic modeling (e.g., Blei, 2012; Blei et al., 2003). The final collection of research articles contained 20 publications in communication research (listed in Appendix A), with 12 studies focusing on the method and only 8 studies dealing with thematic research questions. We reviewed all 20 studies for solutions regarding their approach to (a) preprocessing, (b) parameter selection, (c) reliability, and (d) validity.

Data cleaning and preprocessing of unstructured text data

All studies under review addressed the issue of data cleaning and preprocessing, but they differed in the level of detail used to describe the process. The process of cleaning text data is contingent on the research question and the type of data used. For instance, if a study's focus is on one language only, a language filter is used (e.g., Parra et al., 2016). In the case of web documents or tweets, boilerplate content, such as uniform resource locators (URLs) or hypertext markup language (HTML) markups, need to be removed prior to data analysis (e.g., Ghosh & Guha, 2013; Parra et al., 2016). Other studies consider the aggregation of distinct text elements necessary to obtain larger documents. These mergers are necessary, either because the text elements are too short for LDA to extract substantive topics, as in the case of tweets (Guo, Vargo, Pan, Ding, & Ishwar, 2016, pp. 9–10), or to facilitate analysis, e.g., when comparing topics on a monthly basis (Puschmann & Scheffler, 2016).

The standard procedures of language pre-processing include tokenization (breaking documents down into term components), discarding punctuation and capitalization of words, filtering out stop-words and highly frequent and infrequent terms (relative pruning), and stemming and/or lemmatizing. Stemming and lemmatizing are used to make inflected words comparable to each other. While stemming reduces each word to its stem by stripping "its derivational and inflectional suffixes" (Lovins, 1968, p. 22) (e.g., "contaminating" and "contamination" become "contamin"), lemmatizing converts them to their lemma form/lexeme (e.g., "contaminating" and "contamination" become "contaminate") (Manning & Schütze, 2003, p. 132). Recent work suggests that not only the pre-processing procedures as such, but also their ordering, significantly influence the results of subsequent (supervised and unsupervised) text-analysis techniques, including topic modeling (Denny & Spirling, 2017). These findings are reasonable because the various pre-processing steps depend on each other.

Choosing the number of topics and prior parameters

When specifying a topic model, several parameters, such as the number of topics, K, must be defined. With this parameter, the granularity of the topic model can be adjusted. Generally, the more topics we accept, the more specific and narrow the resulting topics are. However, accepting too many topics might result in similar entities that cannot be distinguished in a meaningful way (e.g., Grimmer, 2010, pp. 12–13). At the same time, too few topics might lead to very broad entities combining different aspects that should be separated (Evans, 2014, p. 2).

To determine an adequate number of topics, researchers usually run several candidate models with varying numbers of topics. Subsequently, the resulting models are compared for significant differences and interpretability (e.g., Biel & Gatica-Perez, 2014; Elgesem et al., 2015). Since the objective is to find substantive topics, this approach also has been termed a *substantive search* (Bonilla & Grimmer, 2013, p. 656). Because the overall goal is to generate a topic solution that can be validly interpreted, some researchers also draw on further external and internal validation criteria (discussed below) to choose between different candidate models (Baum, 2012; Evans, 2014).

There are also different metrics used to inform the process of model selection. The most widely applied is the measure of *perplexity* (used by, e.g., Ghosh & Guha, 2013; Jacobi et al., 2015). The perplexity metric is a measure used to determine the statistical goodness of fit of a topic model (Blei et al., 2003). Generally, it estimates how well a model produced for the major part of the corpus predicts a held-out smaller portion of the documents.

Another strategy is to run a non-parametric topic model, such as a Hierarchical Dirichlet Process (HDP) topic model (see Teh, Jordan, Beal, & Blei, 2006) in which K does not need to be defined in advance. Instead, a statistically appropriate number of topics is estimated from the data (Bonilla & Grimmer, 2013). However, for such a model, other even more abstract parameters must be defined in advance, so that the problem about the model's granularity is not solved, but merely shifted to yet another parameter.

The choice of the prior parameters α and β is rarely discussed in current studies. Ghosh and Guha (2013) apply default values that are set in the *R topicmodels* package by Grün and Hornik (2011). Biel and Gatica-Perez (2014) refer to standard values proposed by Blei et al. (2003). Evans (2014) uses an optimization procedure offered by the *MALLET* software package (McCallum, 2002) to iteratively optimize the Dirichlet parameter for each topic at regular intervals.

Reliability of topic solution

While reliability is usually not regarded as a major concern with computer-based content-analysis techniques, the random processes in the LDA algorithm make robustness in the sense of retest reliability of a topic model an important issue. However, few researchers ensure that the obtained topics are robust across multiple runs of the model, with the same parameter set (but different random seeds) (DiMaggio et al., 2013; Levy & Franklin, 2014). More researchers are examining whether the identified topics are reproducible across several runs of the topic model with different parameters, most often varying the number of topics (e.g., Levy & Franklin, 2014; Van Atteveldt, Welbers, Jacobi, & Vliegenthart, 2014). Biel and Gatica-Perez (2014) have checked whether they can replicate the model's topics with smaller samples of the dataset.

Topic interpretation and validity

The most straightforward approach of most studies regarding valid interpretation of the resulting topics is to review the words with the highest probabilities for each topic (top words) and try to find a label describing the substantive content of the topic. Often, researchers also read through a sample of documents featuring high proportions of the respective topic (e.g., Elgesem, Feinerer, & Steskal, 2016; Jacobi et al., 2015; Koltsova & Shcherbak, 2015). These strategies are applied to ensure *intra-topic semantic validity* of topics as the most crucial aspect of semantic validity (Quinn, Monroe, Colaresi, Crespin, & Radev, 2010).

Additionally, some researchers use quantitative diagnostic metrics, such as topic coherence (e.g., Evans, 2014) or mutual information measures (e.g., DiMaggio et al., 2013). While (intrinsic) topic coherence measures how frequently the top words of a topic co-occur (Mimno et al., 2011), mutual information aims to identify which of the top words contributes the most significant information to a given topic (e.g., Grimmer, 2010). To ascertain whether topics are sufficiently distinct from each other (inter-topic validity) or to find patterns of semantics among topics, hierarchical clustering can be applied (e.g., Marshall, 2013; Puschmann & Scheffler, 2016).

In various studies, we also noticed strategies for external validation. External criteria can include expert evaluations (Levy & Franklin, 2014), manual codings, and code systems (e.g., Guo et al., 2016;

Jacobi et al., 2015). Some studies also checked whether the temporal patterns of topics corresponded with events that occurred in the study's time frame (e.g., Evans, 2014; Newman, Chemudugunta, Smyth, & Steyvers, 2006).

Summarizing our review, we agree with Koltsova and Koltcov (2013, p. 214) that "the evaluation of topic models is a new and still underdeveloped area of inquiry." While in the past few years, a range of strategies for testing the validity of topic models has been established, a standard methodology for ensuring the reliability of the topics has yet to be developed in communication research.

Toward a Valid and reliable methodology for LDA topic modeling

In this section, we propose our methodological approach to topic modeling with respect to cleaning and preprocessing, model selection, reliability, and valid interpretation of identified topics. We illustrate the soundness of our approach by using empirical data from an ongoing research project in which we investigate online communication of civil-society actors concerning the issue of food safety. The theory we drew on originates from political agenda-building research (Cobb & Elder, 1983). Hence, we are interested in exploring the spectrum of "political issues" discussed by civil-society organizations concerned about food safety on the Web. In political communication, the term "issue" is used to denote a contentious matter of dispute, with the potential of "groups taking opposing positions" (Miller & Riechert, 2001, p. 108).

Building and preprocessing the corpus

To identify websites on the Internet that are concerned with the issue of food safety, we collected hyperlink networks, i.e., websites connected by hyperlinks, on a monthly basis from June 2012 to November 2014 (30 months), starting with eight websites involving U.S.-based civil-society actors.[3] The networks were collected using the web-based software *Issue Crawler*.[4] Altogether, 575,849 webpage documents were identified in these networks, of which—for both technical and practical reasons—we downloaded only those pages that included (a combination of) issue-specific search terms (see Waldherr, Maier, Miltner, & Günther, 2017, p. 434), resulting in a collection of 344,456 webpages.

The web-crawling procedure resulted in a heterogeneously structured set of webpages. Since we were interested in analyzing substantive text only, the crawled webpages had to be further processed to remove so-called boilerplate content, such as navigation bars, page markups, ads, teasers, and other items regarded as irrelevant.

In the first step, we deleted the HTML-markups using the content-extraction library *Apache Tika*. Second, the text files were passed through the *openNLP* toolkit for sentence separation. The text of each page was separated into sentence candidates temporarily stored in separate lines. So far, candidates included navigation elements, teasers, or copyright information. We filtered out the boilerplate text and selected only valid sentences among all sentences on each page with a rule-based approach using *regular expressions* (see Manning & Schütze, 2003, p. 121).

The resulting main texts from each webpage were classified further using a language-detection algorithm to distinguish between documents written in English or German (the project languages), and other languages. Language detection was necessary for subsequent pre-processing steps. Since removal of boilerplate content from pages could reveal that an extracted document was not thematically relevant for our analysis, we filtered again for relevant content by only including those documents containing the (combination of) issue-specific key terms. These procedures resulted in a massive reduction of content. The final corpus included 186,557 documents stored in a database for further analysis.

In the final step, we ran a duplicate detection algorithm (Rajaraman & Ullman, 2011) on the filtered document set to identify near-duplicates in very large datasets efficiently. Documents were marked as duplicates if their similarity, defined by the Jaccard index on their word set, was above a threshold of .95. For each duplicate, a reference to the first occurrence of that document was stored to allow for queries, including or excluding duplicates in the resulting set. Altogether, 87,692 documents were marked as being unique.

Generally speaking, we deem rigorous data cleaning to be necessary and suggest that text documents should be relieved of boilerplate content, such as ads, side bars, and links to related content. If boilerplate content either is not randomly distributed across all the documents in the corpus—which would be a naive assumption for most empirical corpora—or the documents are not cleaned extensively enough, the LDA algorithm could be distorted and uninterpretable, as messy topics could emerge.

Corpus cleaning is only the first step. Automated content-analysis procedures, such as topic modeling, need further specific preprocessing of textual data. "Preprocessing text strips out information, in addition to reducing complexity, but experience in this literature is that the trade-off is well worth it" (Hopkins & King, 2010, p. 223). As we pointed out in the literature review, many LDA studies have reported using a range of seemingly standard pre-processing rules. However, most studies fail to emphasize that these consecutively applied rules depend on each other, which implies that their ordering matters (see also Denny & Spirling, 2017). Although a single correct pre-processing chain cannot be defined, the literature provides reasons for proceeding in a specific order.

Thus, we suggest that after data cleaning, the documents should be divided into units, usually word units, called tokens. Hence, this step is called tokenization (Manning & Schütze, 2003, p. 124). After tokenization, all capital letters should be converted to lowercase, which should be applied for the purpose of term unification. After that, punctuation and special characters (e.g., periods, commas, exclamation points, ampersands, white-space, etc.) should be deleted. While punctuation may bear important semantic information for human readers of a text, it is usually regarded as undesirable and uninformative in automatic text analyses based on the bag-of-words approach (e.g., Scott & Matwin, 1999, p. 379). However, following Denny and Spirling (2017, p. 6), some special characters, such as the hashtag character, might be informative in specific contexts, e.g., modeling a corpus of tweets, and should be kept in such cases. The next step is to remove stop-words, which are usually functional words such as prepositions or articles. Their removal is reasonable because they appear frequently and are "insufficiently specific to represent document content" (Salton, 1991, p. 976). While lowercasing and removal of punctuation and special characters can be done in any order after tokenization, they should be done before the removal of stop-words to reduce the risk that stop-word dictionaries may be unable to detect stop-words in the corpus vocabulary. Unification procedures, such as lemmatization and stemming, should be used only after stop-word removal. As mentioned above, both techniques are used for the purpose of reducing inflected forms and "sometimes derivationally related forms of a word to a common base form" (Manning, Raghavan, & Schütze, 2009, p. 32). However, we prefer lemmatization over stemming because stemming "commonly collapses derivationally related words, whereas lemmatization commonly only collapses the different inflectional forms of a lemma" (Manning et al., 2009, p. 32). Thus, interpreting word stems correctly can be tough, or even impossible. For example, while the word *organized* is reduced to its stem, *organ*, its lemma is *organize*.

In the very last step, relative pruning should be applied. Due to language-distribution characteristics, we can expect a vast share of very infrequent words in the vocabulary of a collection. In fact, roughly half of the terms of the vocabulary occur only once (Zipf's Law, e.g., Manning & Schütze, 2003, pp. 23–29). Thus, relative pruning is recommended to strip very rare and extremely frequent word occurrences from the observed data. Moreover, relative pruning reduces the size of the corpus vocabulary, which will enhance the algorithm's performance remarkably (Denny & Spirling, 2017) and will stabilize LDA's stochastic inference. In our empirical study, relative pruning was applied, removing all terms that occurred in more than 99% or less than .5% of all documents (Denny & Spirling, 2017; Grimmer, 2010; Grimmer & Stewart, 2013).

If the unification of inflected words is not applied before relative pruning, chances are high that semantically similar terms such as *genetic* and *genetically* will be part of the vocabulary, i.e., if a user complies with the suggested ordering, the corpus vocabulary will be reduced, while still maintaining a great diversity of substantively different words. In our empirical case, we followed the proposed ordering of the pre-processing steps.

Model selection: reliability issues and choosing appropriate parameters

Model selection is the process of determining a model's parameters, i.e., the number of topics, K, and the prior parameters, α and β. The objective of this process is to find the parameter configuration that leads to the most appropriate model available for the data and the research interest alike. Evaluating how well a model fits the data and whether it appropriately serves its purpose always should be guided by a study's research question and the theoretical concepts of interest. We note that communication researchers working with content data generally aim to gain knowledge about the content and its substantive meaning. A topic model provides information about both, but the quality of the information depends on how well human researchers can interpret the model with respect to theory. Thus, interpretability must be regarded as a necessary precondition for a model's validity. Hence, we argue that the interpretability of the modeled topics should be the prime criterion in the model-selection phase. However, a parameter configuration that leads to interpretable solutions is worthless if it cannot be replicated. From this perspective, interpretability and reliability are intertwined and directly related to a model's validity.

In this section, we first introduce two metrics, reliability and intrinsic coherence, which enable users to provide information about the quality of a topic model. To enhance both criteria right away, the topic-modeling literature puts forth techniques that have been discussed under the term *regularization*. We briefly discuss the findings of the regularization literature in the second part of the section and provide an easy-to-implement regularization technique to boosting the reliability of topic models. We confirm this approach by providing evidence from experiments we conducted. The final part of the section concentrates on selecting the most appropriate model using what we call *substantive search in coherence-optimized candidates*.

Measuring reliability and interpretability of topic models

Reliability of a topic model can be measured in different ways. We implemented an approach following the intuition of comparing two models, i and j, for their similarities. For each topic from model i, the probability values of the N topics' top words were compared with the probabilities of each of the N topics' top words from all topics in model j. Two topics, one from each model, were counted as a matched pair if the cosine similarity of their top-word probabilities was at a maximum *and* above a defined threshold ($t = .7$). The proportion of topic matches from models i and j over all K topics was defined as a reliability score (Niekler, 2016). Reliability between more than two models can be computed as an average between all model pairs.

Regarding a model's quality in terms of interpretability, multiple metrics are available. The most frequently used statistical measures are *held-out likelihood* or *perplexity* (Blei et al., 2003). For their application, a model needs to be computed on one (major) part of a collection, e.g., 90% of all documents, then applied to the (smaller) 10% of collection documents not included in the modeling process. The model's goodness of fit (likelihood) is estimated by how well the model predicts the held-out smaller portion of the documents. Higher likelihood corresponds to a lower perplexity measure.

A method of systematic manual evaluation has been proposed by Chang, Boyd-Graber, Gerrish, Wang, and Blei (2009). For a tested topic, they used the list of the top N terms of a fitted model and inserted a random term with high probability from another topic of that model. If human subjects (users) can identify this false intruder, the topic may be considered coherent. Surprisingly, the study demonstrated in a large user study that the widely used evaluation metrics based on perplexity do not correspond well with human results of intrusion detection, and in some cases, they are even negatively correlated. Also, LDA variants—such as correlated topic models (CTM) (Blei & Lafferty, 2006), which reportedly achieve a higher model likelihood—turned out to be less coherent.

In response to these findings, topic-coherence measures were proposed based on the assumption that the more frequently top words of a single topic co-occur in documents, the more coherent the topic. Studies have shown that coherence measured with respect to data that is external (Newman, Lau, Grieser, & Baldwin, 2010) or internal to the corpus (Mimno et al., 2011) correlates with human judgment on topic interpretability. The latter is also referred to as intrinsic coherence.[5]

For both interpretability and reliability, different *regularization* techniques have been tested. In this regard, regularization of topic models describes a process that helps mitigate ill-posed mathematical problems and guides them toward a more favorable solution.

Enhancing interpretability and reliability with regularization techniques

The seminal model proposed by Blei et al. (2003) is based on the idea that the clustering effect of the algorithm works well, even if the initial assignments for θ and ϕ are set completely at random. Although the generative model consists of successive random processes, in theory, many allocation iterations will lead to similar models because the allocations depend on distributions dominated by the data. However, experiments conducted by Lancichinetti et al. (2015), and Roberts, Stewart, and Tingley (2016) point to serious issues of topic models regarding reliability.

While interpretability of topic models has been extensively studied, reliability has been a much less discussed issue thus far. Hence, we distinguish between approaches that raise the interpretability of a model and approaches that aim at higher topic reliability among repeated inferences on the same data.

For the issue of interpretability, two branches of research can be identified. The first branch develops regularization techniques that alter the inference scheme of the original LDA model (Newman, Bonilla, & Buntine, 2011; Sokolov & Bogolubsky, 2015). The second branch of regularization techniques solely alters the initialization of the model to guide the inference process toward a desired local optimum. For instance, word co-occurrence statistics are used in conjunction with clustering techniques to assign words to semantic clusters for initializing the model (e.g., Newman et al., 2011; Sokolov & Bogolubsky, 2015). Without exception, all these studies demonstrate a positive effect from regularization strategy on topic interpretability.

Regarding reliability, only a few studies are available that propose improving strategies. Reliability problems can emerge from two model settings: (a) random initialization of the two result matrices and (b) successive random processes. For the latter, Koltcov, Nikolenko, Koltsova, Filippov, and Bodrunova (2016) introduce a slight variation to the LDA Gibbs sampler as originally proposed by Griffiths and Steyvers (2004). When drawing a topic for a word, they force the neighboring words into the same topic. This results not only in better coherence, but also in higher reliability. Unfortunately, there is no publicly available implementation for this approach. Alternatively, Lancichinetti et al. (2015) extract K semantic term clusters based on word co-occurrence statistics to initialize the LDA model's K topics. They show that this procedure leads to perfect reproducibility of the topic model when running the inference process for one iteration after initialization.

In acknowledgement of this research, we aim for a solution that raises both interpretability and reliability. Moreover, we prefer to rely on freely available, well-established implementations of the original LDA model. Therefore, we opt for a regularization strategy that is compatible and relatively easy to implement, namely an initialization strategy in which semantically pre-clustered terms are provided as an input to the inference algorithm. In accordance with Roberts et al. (2016), who expect "advances in areas such as optimal initialization strategies," we decided to refine the Lancichinetti et al. (2015) idea. The major drawbacks of their approach are that they use an artificial corpus and run Gibbs sampling for only one single iteration after initialization. Although this leads to perfect reliability, the effect on interpretability remained untested. We assume that not running multiple iterations of sampling has a severe negative influence on topic quality in real-world applications. Therefore, we conducted an experiment in which we evaluate the effects of different initialization strategies across a varying number of inference iterations with respect to reliability and coherence as measures for model quality. To examine whether our findings generalize across corpora and topic resolutions, we ran the test for three different corpora (food-safety-related content from Germany, the U.K., and the U.S., which is the focal corpus of the empirical study), with different topic numbers K.[6]

As a baseline strategy, we tested the standard random initialization of LDA. As a second strategy, we fixed the random initialization with a specific seed value, but afterward, we reset the random-number generator. We ran this experiment to test the influence of random sampling during the inference algorithm, independent of initialization. As our own third strategy, we proposed a modification of clustered initialization from Lancichinetti et al. (2015). We also initialized the topics based on term-co-occurrence networks. In contrast to the original approach, which was tested on two highly artificial text collections, we observed that their proposed combination of significance measure (Poisson) and clustering algorithm (Infomap) does not perform well on real-world data to identify coherent semantic clusters. Thus, we selected alternatives to achieve a better pre-clustering of terms. For determining co-occurrence significance, we relied on Dunning's Log-Likelihood Ratio Test (LL) (Bordag, 2008). Subsequent semantic community detection is performed by applying the Partitioning-Around-Medoids (PAM) algorithm (see Kaufman & Rousseeuw, 1990).

Each experiment was repeated $n = 10$ times. Figure 2 displays the average reliability of the experiments over the progress of Gibbs sampling iterations. Confidence intervals for reliability are provided on the basis of $\frac{n*(n-1)}{2} = 45$ possible pairs for comparing models i and j. The results indicate that our cluster-initialization strategy significantly improves the reliability of the inference for all three corpora and leads to levels of reproducibility above 85% for the German and U.K. corpus, and above 75% for the U.S. corpus. The seeded initialization also outperforms the random standard initialization, but does not reach the performance of an initialization by semantic network clustering. From this result, we conclude that the stability of the inference algorithm itself actually can be quite high once it starts from the same position. We further conclude that providing semantic clusters of terms as a starting position leads to even more stable results in the inference process, thereby indicating why it is the preferred strategy to improve reliability.

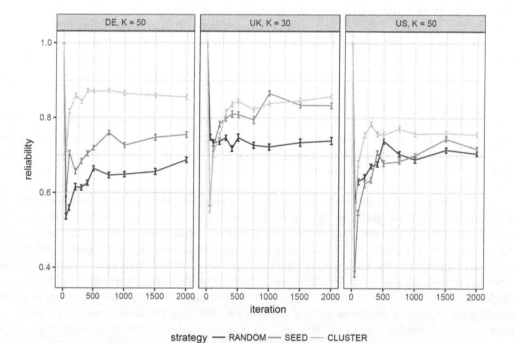

Figure 2. Reliability of topic models for three corpora (DE = Germany; UK = United Kingdom; US = United States) according to different initialization techniques (random = default random initialization; seed = fixed seed initialization; and cluster = semantic co-occurrence network initialization) and varying number of inference iterations; K = number of topics.

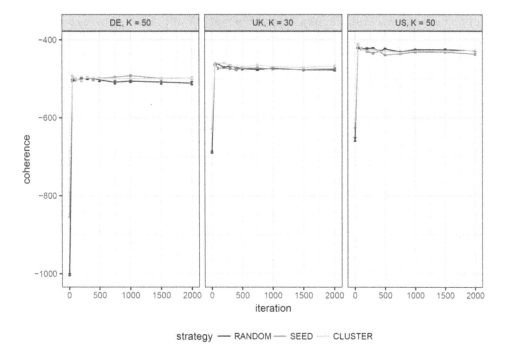

Figure 3. Mean coherence of topic models for three corpora (DE = Germany, UK = United Kingdom, US = United States) according to different initialization techniques (random = default random initialization; seed = fixed seed initialization; and cluster = semantic co-occurrence network initialization) and varying number of inference iterations; K = number of topics.

Figure 3 displays the average topic-model coherences of the ten repeated runs of our experiment, including their confidence intervals. Compared with the reliability check, the results are rather mixed. Although the cluster initialization usually performs very well, differences between all the strategies are not very pronounced. The most important finding from this part of the experiment is that topic coherence is drastically lowered if sampling runs for only one iteration. Although it guarantees perfect reliability, the results of such an early stopped process cannot be used in a practical scenario. We conclude that to further improve interpretability, the process also needs to run for some time until the topic composition stabilizes. We recommend at least 1,000 iterations. Running only one iteration, as proposed in Lancichinetti et al. (2015), trades reliability for interpretability and appears to be a bad choice in practical scenarios.

Selecting the model: substantive search in coherence-optimized candidate models

In general, finding the *optimal* parameter set is not an easy task in an unsupervised, data-driven scenario. There is no gold standard to evaluate model results, as in a supervised scenario, and the best solution cannot be ensured by a single criterion independent of the research interest. The literature on natural language processing (NLP) provides various methods and evaluation metrics for topic models that can be utilized to find the optimal parameters. But it is still highly likely that solutions optimized along single metrics do not comply with the analytical requirements in communication research, such as the desired topic granularity necessary to obtain meaningful results. For this reason, we suggest avoiding the use of only one numerical optimization procedure for parameter selection, and instead combine different measures with intersubjective qualitative human judgment.

Like the procedure described by Marshall (2013, p. 709), we applied a systematic approach for the choice of the number of topics, K, and the prior parameters, α and β. Instead of using default suggestions, which often do not yield optimal results, we systematically varied different combinations for K (30, 50, and 70) and α (.01, .05, .1, .2, .5, 1). As the combinatorial set expands with the number of parameters included, we fixed the value of β at $1/K$, the default value as proposed by the widely used topic model library *gensim* (Řehůřek & Sojka, 2010). The prior for the topic-document matrix α was found to be of greater importance for the quality of the topic model (e.g., Wallach, Mimno, & McCallum, 2009), which was the reason to fix β and let α vary. The model was run with 1,000 iterations. We calculated 6 different models (i.e., all possible combinations of α) for each of the three values in K (resulting in 18 models, see Appendix B) and chose the single best model for each K regarding the mean intrinsic topic coherence for further investigation. We refer to these three models as our candidate models.

Instead of using the whole corpus for the model creation, in this phase, we took a random sample of 10,000 non-duplicate documents (out of 87,692 unique documents) to calculate these models. Whether a document sample is representative "depends on the extent to which it includes the range of linguistic distributions in the population" (Biber, 1993, p. 243). Thus, for topic-modeling purposes, a valid sample must catch the variety of word co-occurrence structures in the document population. Random sampling can be regarded a valid procedure for topic modeling of very large document collections. Due to the characteristic distribution of language data, we can expect a huge share of very infrequent words in the vocabulary of a collection. This is also the reason why the pruning of infrequent vocabulary is a recommended and valid pre-processing step. In other words, applying relative pruning to the full corpus yields a very similar vocabulary, as would applying relative pruning to a random sample of 10% of the corpus. In both cases, document content is reduced to a very similar vocabulary. Thus, it is reasonable to expect that co-occurrence structures of these terms in a large-enough random sample would be very similar to those in the entire corpus.

Still, the size of the sample must be big enough to draw valid conclusions about which parameter configurations yielded solid models. Scholars from corpus linguistics (e.g., Hanks, 2012) argue that sample size is the most important criterion to consider in covering the thematic diversity of the corpus. As a rule of thumb for domain-specific corpora, we recommend using at least a two-digit fraction (10% minimum) of the overall corpus size. In our empirical case, we drew a random sample of 10,000 documents, or 11.4% (10,000/87,692) of the document total. However, it is important to note that it cannot be guaranteed that this technique will work well for corpora containing significantly smaller sized and/or more heterogeneous documents. In our view, the validity of this technique crucially depends on whether the sample size is big enough to capture the heterogeneity of the corpus vocabulary. In this regard, future research needs to figure out valid guidelines for sampling strategies and sample sizes.

The 10,000 sampled documents are used only for purposes of model creation and selection. Inference is conducted for the complete corpus. The separation of model creation and inference enables us to directly use the model that we created on the basis of the random sample and successively infer the topic composition of the remaining documents.

A group of four researchers discussed the three best topic models in terms of their mean coherence metric, one for each value in K. For the collaborative investigation of the three models, the LDA visualization software *LDAvis* was used (Sievert & Shirley, 2014). The question that was guiding the qualitative investigation of the group was: *Which topic model most suitably represents the contentious matters of dispute, i.e., the "issues," of the food-safety discourse in civil society on the Web?* The discussion and interpretation were based on the models' ϕ matrices, i.e., word-topic distributions, and also considered varying orders of the top words using Sievert and Shirley (2014) relevance metric (explained in the next section). The group discussion led to a consensus within the research group. The model with $K = 50$ offered the most reasonable topic solution to interpret the theoretical concept of "political issues," which was the focus of our research. While setting $K = 70$ led to too many topics that could easily be traced back to arguments put forth by single websites, minor events, or remaining boilerplate, $K = 30$ obfuscated and blurred issues that would otherwise be treated separately by the research group. We decided in favor of the model with the parameters $K = 50$, $\alpha = .5$, and $\beta = 1/K = .02$. This solution deserved further investigation in validity checks.

Topic validity and labeling

We regard interpretability as a necessary, but not a sufficient prerequisite for validity. With some exceptions (e.g., DiMaggio et al., 2013), interpretation, validity, and successive labeling of topics become blended and blurred in application-focused studies. We want to gain awareness that good interpretability of a topic's top-word list is not equivalent to its validity. Referring to Neuendorf (2017, p. 122), "validity is the extent to which a measuring procedure represents the intended – and only the intended – concept." To uncover whether the modeled topics represent the concept under study, such as the issue-concept, we developed a three-step procedure. First, we summarized the most important quantitative information from the model. Second, all topic models created for non-artificial text corpora will contain a fraction of uninterpretable topics, which cannot be valid by definition and thus must be excluded. The third step is an in-depth investigation that includes a close reading of documents and the labeling of the topics.

Summarizing topics

To summarize the topics, we used several auxiliary metrics to better understand the semantics of the topics' word distributions. Specifically, we used the following four metrics.

(1) *Rank-1*: The Rank-1 metric (see Evans, 2014) counts how many times a topic is the most prevalent in a document. Thus, the metric can help identify so-called background topics, which usually contribute much to the whole model, but their word distribution is not very specific. In the case of a high topic share in the entire collection being accompanied by a low Rank-1 value, we can make a reasonable guess that a topic occurs in many documents, but rarely can be found as the dominant topic of a document. The empirical example presented below contains several background topics, such as *economy, politics*, and *health care*, all of which constitute the setting in which the food-safety debate among civil-society actors takes place.

(2) *Coherence*: This metric, developed by Mimno et al. (2011, p. 264), already was used for model-selection purposes. However, applied to single topics, it also helps guide intuition and may help identify true topics in which a researcher might not see a coherent concept at first glance.

(3) *Relevance*: The word distributions within any topic of the model are based on the word probabilities conditioned on topics. However, provided that a given word, e.g., *food*, occurs frequently in many documents, it is likely to have a high conditional probability in many topics and thereby occurs frequently as a top-word. In this case, such a word does not contribute much to the specific semantics of a given topic. Sievert and Shirley (2014, pp. 66–67) developed the so-called *relevance metric*, which is used to reorder the top words of a topic by considering their overall corpus frequency. The researchers can decide how much weight should be ascribed to corpus frequencies of words by manipulating the weighting parameter λ, which can have values ranging from 0 to 1. For $\lambda = 1$, the ordering of the top words is equal to the ordering of the standard conditional word probabilities. For λ close to zero, the most specific words of the topic will lead the list of top words. In their case study, Sievert and Shirley (2014, p. 67) found the best interpretability of topics using a λ-value close to .6, which we adopted for our own case.

(4) Sources and *concentration*: In our empirical dataset, we selected sources of topics by asking which websites were promoting certain topics and how much a topic was concentrated in the potential sources. Therefore, we assessed the average source distribution of topics by computing the Hirschman-Herfindahl Index (HHI) as a *concentration* measure. The HHI ranges from 1/*number of sources* to 1. An HHI = 1 signifies maximum concentration, i.e., the topic is pronounced by only one source. A very low HHI value, conversely, indicates that a topic can be found in many sources.

For the interpretation of our topics, we summarized the aforementioned metrics on a single overview sheet, one for each topic in the model (see Appendix C for an example topic).

Exclusion of topics

After summarizing the topics in this manner, two researchers reviewed all the topic sheets independently from each other. By relying on both the metrics and their expert knowledge about food safety, they (independently) judged whether the topics should still be included for further investigation or not. More specifically, topics whose top-word lists were hard to interpret and which came with low values in Rank-1 and coherence while showing low prevalence and high concentration were excluded. If one author had judged that a topic deserved in-depth investigation, the topic was kept. In the case that both authors came to the conclusion that a topic should be discarded it was discarded. In other words, we kept a topic if there was at least one indication that it contained a meaningful, coherent concept.

Another peculiarity of topic models are boilerplate topics. Although we extensively cleaned the corpus (see the *Building and preprocessing the corpus* section), boilerplate content still showed up in some topics. Boilerplate topics are common phenomena in topic models (Mimno & Blei, 2011). They have no substantive meaning, but their emergence sharpens other meaningful topics "by segregating boilerplate terms in a distinct location" (DiMaggio et al., 2013, p. 586). Most often, the identified boilerplate topics coincide with the most unreliable and least-salient topics (see also Mimno et al., 2011).

After discussing the results of the separate investigations we made a consensual decision using the aforementioned criteria. The authors decided that 13 topics should be removed because they showed no indication of being either meaningful or coherent. The remaining 37 topics were subject to the final validation and labeling step.

In-depth validation of topics and topic labeling

We investigated two criteria for topic validity explained by Quinn et al. (2010), i.e., *intra-topic semantic validity* and *inter-topic semantic validity*.

To evaluate intra-topic semantic validity, we reviewed the document-topic distributions from θ for the remaining topics. Ten randomly sampled documents were read, all containing relatively large proportions of the respective topic ($\theta_{d,k} > .5$).[7] For the sampled topics, brief summary descriptions of their content were written, and suggestions about the topic labels were proposed. Subsequently, the researchers deliberately decided in a discussion (a) whether a topic was semantically coherent and, thus, a valid topic in theoretical terms and (b) what label should be given to the topic. For our empirical case, the guiding question regarding (a) was: *Do the topics depict a contentious matter of discourse in the food-safety debate?* Regarding (b) we asked: *Which aspects of the sampled documents describe the issue most comprehensively?* Thus, the label is the product of determining what catches the notion of the underlying concept, in our case the "issues," most concisely.

In this phase of in-depth investigation, eight of the remaining 37 topics were further discarded because they either did not reveal a coherent semantic meaning or solely represented contents from a single website unconnected to aspects of the debate about food safety. Thus, 29 validated, manually labeled "issues" in the food-safety debate remained.

In a second step, we also investigated inter-topic semantic validity, i.e., the relationship between topics by using hierarchical cluster analysis (see Puschmann & Scheffler, 2016). More specifically, the top 30 words of the validated "issues" (from the ϕ_k matrix) were clustered using the cosine-similarity measure and the "complete" clustering method, as implemented in the "hclust" function in *R*. The resulting dendrogram served as an auxiliary guideline for grouping topics that are similar, according to their top words, into higher-order categories. However, clustering results need to be complemented with the results of the in-depth investigation. Relying on the clustering alone could lead to false conclusions because two topics might be distinct according to their top words, although they are semantically related.

Presentation and interpretation of the selected topic model

The valid topics of our empirical case are described in Table 1. For a more comprehensive presentation, we grouped the topics into six categories. The topics in the categories *Agriculture* and *Consumption and Protection* define core issues of food safety. The agricultural topics are especially concerned with economization trends, such as the use and consequences of genetically modified food and the overuse of antibiotics in industrial livestock farming. Consumer-protection topics deal with negative effects of contaminated food. Contamination can be caused by toxic chemicals (e.g., in packaging), as well as pathogenic bacteria such as salmonella, causing food-borne infections.

Another important topical aspect of food safety is visible in the category *Science and Technology*, in which topics deal with new knowledge and innovative means for making food production more efficient and safe. The *Environment* category demonstrates a dual capacity. On one hand, environmental damage can endanger food and water safety, e.g., when chemicals utilized for fracking natural gas out of the soil contaminate drinking water. On the other hand, food-production practices also can have negative consequences for the environment, e.g., the impact of the use of pesticides on bee populations. Another less-political, but still very important component of the food-safety debate concerns the category *Personal Health and Wellbeing*. Topics within this category include diets, which supposedly keep people healthy. Additionally, from the identified *Background Topics* category, it clearly can be induced that food safety in our empirical text corpus is a political and contentious issue, touching economic, legal, and health care issues alike.

Table 1. Validated topic model for the online text corpus about food safety in the U.S.

K	Label	Share % M (SD)	HHI M (SD)	Top-5 Words
Agriculture				
25	GM Food	3.94 (0.90)	0.04 (0.01)	food, label, genetically, monsanto, gmo
9	Organic Farming	2.58 (0.37)	0.02 (0.00)	organic, food, farm, farmer, agriculture
20	Livestock	2.55 (0.18)	0.03 (0.00)	meat, food, animal, beef, milk
10	Antibiotics	2.21 (0.46)	0.10 (0.02)	antibiotic, animal, health, drug, human
Consumption and Protection				
22	Foodborne Diseases	4.06 (1.34)	0.06 (0.02)	food, outbreak, salmonella, illness, report
8	FS Regulation	3.48 (0.40)	0.04 (0.01)	food, fda, safety, product, consumer
7	Contaminated Food	2.77 (0.63)	0.04 (0.01)	safety, recall, produce, fda, outbreak
29	Food Consumption	2.26 (0.14)	0.03 (0.01)	product, company, consumer, store, sell
27	Restaurant Inspection	2.14 (0.98)	0.09 (0.04)	food, restaurant, safety, health, inspection
16	Tap Water	1.53 (1.03)	0.22 (0.23)	water, food, public, protect, watch
39	BPA-packaging	1.50 (0.83)	0.15 (0.11)	chemical, bpa, safe, toxic, health
Science and Technology				
6	Health Reports	3.48 (0.25)	0.02 (0.00)	health, report, public, risk, datum
19	Chemicals	2.28 (0.28)	0.02 (0.00)	study, chemical, level, health, human
37	GM Technology	1.84 (0.12)	0.02 (0.00)	research, test, science, article, study
Environment				
44	Bees and Pesticides	3.14 (1.90)	0.41 (0.28)	bee, pesticide, epa, food, center
43	Environment	1.41 (0.28)	0.05 (0.02)	read, fish, salmon, environment, specie
50	Fracking	1.37 (0.30)	0.04 (0.02)	energy, gas, oil, water, environmental
31	Climate Change	1.34 (0.22)	0.03 (0.01)	climate, change, report, world, warm
Personal Health and Wellbeing				
21	(Un)healthy Diet	2.32 (0.44)	0.04 (0.01)	food, fat, sugar, diet, health
35	Health and Nutrition	2.31 (0.24)	0.01 (0.01)	program, community, work, education, child
38	Recipes	2.26 (0.41)	0.03 (0.01)	cook, eat, meat, make, recipe
1	School Food	2.00 (0.52)	0.17 (0.08)	food, school, pew, safety, project
12	Dietary Therapy/Prevention	1.42 (0.18)	0.03 (0.01)	cancer, disease, woman, blood, child
42	Medical Information	1.29 (0.39)	0.07 (0.08)	doctor, medicine, take, day, skin
Background Topics				
14	Politics	2.65 (0.28)	0.03 (0.01)	bill, state, obama, law, house
11	Economy	2.50 (0.29)	0.02 (0.01)	company, market, country, million, u.s.
24	Law and Order	2.20 (0.34)	0.02 (0.00)	report, year, police, official, court
2	Infectious Diseases	2.03 (0.62)	0.06 (0.02)	health, coli, pet, animal, case
48	Health Care	1.07 (0.46)	0.13 (0.11)	drug, health, care, medical, patient

Note. HHI = Hirschman-Herfindahl-Index; GM = genetically modified; BPA = Bisphenol A; FS = food safety; K = index of the topic.

In our view, a comprehensive presentation of a topic model also should encompass some of the most important measures, such as the salience of a topic and a fraction of the top-words (see Table 1). Top-word presentation is important to give readers insight into topics.

Conclusion: a good practice guide for communication researchers

The goal of this article is to make LDA-based topic modeling more accessible and applicable for communication researchers. Therefore, it focused on four challenging methodological questions: (a) appropriate pre-processing of unstructured text collections; (b) selection of a parameter set that ensures interpretability of the topic model; (c) evaluating and improving the reliability of a topic model, while at the same time keeping interpretability high; and (d) validation of resulting topics. The following paragraphs briefly recap our recommendations for communication scholars who want to apply LDA-based topic modeling in their research.

Pre-processing

LDA does not just work for "nice" and "easy" data. As our technically challenging case exemplifies, elaborate data cleaning is necessary, especially for unstructured text collections. Additionally, researchers may not only rely on a seemingly standard procedure for successively applied pre-processing steps. Instead, it is important to consider the specifics of the text corpus, including theoretical implications, as well as the proper ordering of pre-processing steps. For instance, the removal of some special characters, such as hashtag-symbols, might be reasonable for the analysis of newspaper article-collections, but not for tweet collections. Regarding proper ordering, we suggest proceeding in the following order: 1. tokenization; 2. transforming all characters to lowercase; 3. removing punctuation and special characters; 4. Removing stop-words; 5. term unification (lemmatizing or stemming); and 6. relative pruning. We prefer lemmatizing over stemming, because a word's lemma is usually easier to interpret than its stem.

Model selection

Also, the proposed model-selection process can be costly and time-consuming, but it will yield more reliable topic models with enhanced interpretability. We propose three considerations.

First, our approach suggests a two-step procedure for model selection that aims to optimize the human interpretation of topic models. In our view, interpretability should be the prime criterion in selecting candidate models. Communication researchers working with content data aim to gain knowledge about content characteristics and the substantive meaning of the text collection. Thus, the success of LDA applications for both objectives depends on how well the resulting model can be interpreted by human researchers. Therefore, we suggest first calculating candidate models with varying granularity levels (i.e., different values for K) and different combinations of prior parameters α and β. Then, choose one model for each K, in which the parameter configuration yields the best results regarding the intrinsic coherence metric. The chosen candidate models need to be further investigated in the second step with a substantive search in coherence-optimized candidate models. The purpose of the substantive search should be to select one of the candidates that matches the granularity level with the theoretical concept under study, such as *political issues* or *frames*. Substantive searches also may include qualitative techniques, such as group discussions, to ensure intersubjectivity. Software tools, such as *LDAvis* (Sievert & Shirley, 2014), proved to be extremely helpful to accomplish this task.

Second, if the size of a corpus is very extensive (e.g., $n > 50,000$ documents), large-enough samples (e.g., > 10% of the documents) can be used instead of the whole corpus to calculate the candidate models. It is clearly an intricate process to test various combinations of parameter settings, but using a significantly smaller random subset of the corpus turned out to be a viable approach for mastering this challenge. Using random samples will boost the algorithm's performance and enable researchers to test various parameter settings much faster. The separation of model creation and inference enabled us to directly use the model that we created on the basis of the random sample and successively infer the topic composition of the remaining documents. However, the validity of the sampling technique crucially depends on whether the sample size is big enough to capture the heterogeneity of the corpus vocabulary. Thus, we cannot guarantee that a sample of roughly 10% of the documents will work equally well for more heterogeneous corpora, and corpora containing significantly smaller sized documents (e.g., a corpus of tweets). Future research needs to address the question of valid guidelines regardless of corpus characteristics.

Third, a well-fitted model with meaningful interpretation is worthless if the results cannot be reproduced. To tackle this issue, we advanced the regularization technique of Lancichinetti et al. (2015) using a semantic-network initialization approach. The literature, as well as our experiments which included multiple corpora, provided evidence that available regularization techniques, such as ours, significantly enhances the reliability of topic models. However, because reliability cannot be guaranteed for topic models generally, we believe that reliability reporting for LDA models should become a disciplinary standard in communication research. We suggest using the metric proposed by Niekler (2016) for this purpose.

Validation

The sequential validation procedure approximates validity from different angles. The available metrics, which have different interpretations, are not treated as objective indicators for how well the model works or how good a topic is. Instead, our approach focuses on inter-individual interpretability using the metrics as a basis. Each step in the process involves deliberation among several researchers. Two criteria of validity were checked: intra-topic and inter-topic semantic validity (Quinn et al., 2010). Our case study teaches us that intra-topic semantic validity cannot be derived merely from a topic's word distribution. Several easy-to-calculate metrics definitely should be considered to sharpen the understanding of whether or not a topic refers to a coherent semantic concept. The most time-consuming, but indispensable, step is the manual check of documents with a high probability of containing a specific topic. This practice allows us to compare and check whether the notion that we sketch from the ϕ distribution matches the interpretation of several information-rich text documents. Labeling topics on the basis of broader context knowledge seems only fair.

Final thoughts

We emphasize that we do not propose a whole new method for topic modeling. Instead, we develop an approach to dealing with the methodological decisions one has to make for applying LDA topic modeling reliably and validly in communication research. With the exception of the regularization-technique which we demonstrated to work significantly better for multiple corpora, we used only a single corpus as a showcase for our explications. However, we deem our approach generalizable to other cases because every single component of our approach is either based on substantial existent studies and/or based on a theoretical rationale.

All in all, LDA topic modeling has proven to be a most promising method for communication research. At the same time, it does not work well with non-deliberate, arbitrary choices in model selection and validation. Our study proposes methods and measures to approximate and improve validity and reliability when using LDA. After all, we aim to provide a "good practice" example, bringing LDA into the spotlight as a method that advances innovation in communication research.

Notes

1. The Dirichlet distribution is a continuous multivariate probability distribution which is frequently used in Bayesian statistics.
2. EBSCO communication source (search in title OR abstract OR keywords; apply related words): "topic model", "topic modeling", "topic modelling", "latent Dirichlet allocation". Web of Science (only communication-related

categories: Sociology, Political Science, Psychology, Linguistics, Language Linguistics, Telecommunications, Communication, Social Science Interdisciplinary; search in Title, Abstract, Author Keywords, Keywords Plus): "topic model*", "latent Dirichlet allocation". The searches were run on 10.05.2016.

3. The websites were identified using a combination of a literature review, expert evaluations and Google searches; the starting URLs for the network collection were: http://www.centerforfoodsafety.org/, http://www.cspinet.org/foodsafety/, http://www.foodandwaterwatch.org/food/, http://www.organicconsumers.org/foodsafety.cfm, http://notinmyfood.org/newsroom, http://barfblog.foodsafety.ksu.edu/barfblog (until May 2013);http://barfblog.com (from June 2013), http://www.greenpeace.org/international/en/campaigns/agriculture/, http://www.pewhealth.org/topics/food-safety-327507.

4. For the gathering of the networks, we used the snowball procedure, with a crawling depth of 2 and a degree of separation of 1 (for detailed information see Waldherr et al. (2017, p. 432); for further, general information on the tool, please visit http://www.govcom.org/Issuecrawler_instructions.htm).

5. A topic's intrinsic coherence C of a topic t over the topic's M top-words ($V^{(t)} = (v_1^t, \ldots, v_M^t)$ is defined by Mimno et al. (2011, p. 265) as $C(t, V^{(t)}) = \sum_{m=2}^{M} \sum_{l=2}^{m-1} \log \frac{D(v_m^{(t)}, v_l^{(t)}) + 1}{D(v_l^{(t)})}$, where $D(v_l^{(t)})$ is the document frequency of word $v_l^{(t)}$ in the corpus and $D(v_m^{(t)}, v_l^{(t)})$ is the co-document frequency of the words $v_m^{(t)}$ and $v_l^{(t)}$.

6. For the U.K. corpus number of topics was set to $K = 30$, $K = 50$ for both the U.S. and Germany; we set $\alpha = .5$ and $\beta = .02$ for all models in this experiment. The data as well as the scripts of our experiments can be retrieved from: https://github.com/tm4ss/lda-reliability.

7. If no or not enough documents were available for $\theta_{d,k} > .5$, we set the threshold to $\theta_{d,k} > .3$.

Acknowledgement

The first author claims single authorship for subsection *Topic validity and labeling* and section *Presentation and interpretation of the selected topic model* including *Table 1* and *Appendix C*.

Funding

This publication was created in the context of the Research Unit "Political Communication in the Online World" (1381), subproject 7, which was funded by the Deutsche Forschungsgemeinschaft (DFG, German Research Foundation). The subproject was also funded by the Swiss National Science Foundation (SNF).

References

Baum, D. (2012). Recognising speakers from the topics they talk about. *Speech Communication*, 54(10), 1132–1142.
Biber, D. (1993). Representativeness in corpus design. *Literary and Linguistic Computing*, 8(4), 243–257.
Biel, J.-I., & Gatica-Perez, D. (2014). Mining crowdsourced first impressions in online social video. *Ieee Transactions on Multimedia*, 16(7), 2062–2074.
Blei, D. M. (2012). Probabilistic topic models. *Communications of the ACM*, 55(4), 77–84.
Blei, D. M., & Lafferty, J. D. (2006). Dynamic topic podels. Paper presented at the International Conference on Machine Learning, Pittsburgh, PA.
Blei, D. M., & Lafferty, J. D. (2007). A correlated topic model of science. *The Annals of Applied Statistics*, 1(1), 17–35.
Blei, D. M., Ng, A. Y., & Jordan, M. I. (2003). Latent Dirichlet Allocation. *The Journal of Machine Learning Research*, 3(4/5), 993–1022.
Bonilla, T., & Grimmer, J. (2013). Elevated threat levels and decreased expectations: How democracy handles terrorist threats. *Poetics*, 41, 650–669.
Bordag, S. (2008). A comparison of co-occurrence and similarity measures as simulations of context. *Proceedings of the 9th international conference on computational linguistics and intelligent text processing*, 52–63. doi: 10.1007/978-3-540-78135-6_5
Brown, G., & Yule, G. (1983). *Discourse analysis*. Cambridge, UK: Cambridge University Press.
Chang, J., Boyd-Graber, J., Gerrish, S., Wang, C., & Blei, D. (2009). *Reading tea leaves: How humans interpret topic models*. Paper presented at the Neural Information Processing System 2009.
Cobb, R. W., & Elder, C. D. (1983). *Participation in American politics: The dynamics of agenda-building*. Baltimore, MD: Johns Hopkins University Press.
Denny, M. J., & Spirling, A. (2017). *Text preprocessing for unsupervised learning: Why it matters, when it misleads, and what to do about it*. New York University. Retrieved from http://www.nyu.edu/projects/spirling/documents/preprocessing.pdf
DiMaggio, P., Nag, M., & Blei, D. M. (2013). Exploiting affinities between topic modeling and the sociological perspective on culture: Application to newspaper coverage of U.S. government arts funding. *Poetics*, 41, 570–606.

Elgesem, D., Feinerer, I., & Steskal, L. (2016). Bloggers' responses to the Snowden affair: Combining automated and manual methods in the analysis of news blogging. *Computer Supported Cooperative Work (CSCW)*, 25, 167–191.

Elgesem, D., Steskal, L., & Diakopoulos, N. (2015). Structure and content of the discourse on climate change in the blogosphere: The big picture. *Environmental Communication*, 9(2), 169–188.

Evans, M. S. (2014). A computational approach to qualitative analysis in large textual datasets. *PLoS One*, 9(2), 1–10.

Ghosh, D. D., & Guha, R. (2013). What are we 'tweeting' about obesity? Mapping tweets with topic modeling and Geographic Information System. *Cartography and Geographic Information Science*, 40(2), 90–102.

Griffiths, T. L., & Steyvers, M. (2004). Finding scientific topics. *Proceedings of the National Academy of Sciences*, 101(1), 5228–5235.

Griffiths, T. L., Steyvers, M., & Tenenbaum, J. B. (2007). Topics in semantic representation. *Psychological Review*, 114(2), 211–244.

Grimmer, J. (2010). A Bayesian hierarchical topic model for political texts: Measuring expressed agendas in Senate press releases. *Political Analysis*, 18(1), 1–35.

Grimmer, J., & Stewart, B. M. (2013). Text as data: The promise and pitfalls of automatic content analysis methods for political texts. *Political Analysis*, 1–31. doi:10.1093/pan/mps028

Grün, B., & Hornik, K. (2011). topicmodels: An R package for fitting topic models. *Journal of Statistical Software*, 40(13), 1–30.

Günther, E., & Domahidi, E. (2017). What communication scholars write about: An analysis of 80 years of research in high-impact journals. *International Journal of Communication*, 11, 3051–3071.

Günther, E., & Quandt, T. (2016). Word counts and topic models. *Digital Journalism*, 4(1), 75–88.

Guo, L., Vargo, C. J., Pan, Z., Ding, W., & Ishwar, P. (2016). Big social data analytics in journalism and mass communication: Comparing dictionary-based text analysis and unsupervised topic modeling. *Journalism & Mass Communication Quarterly*, 1–28. doi:10.1177/1077699016639231

Hanks, P. (2012). The corpus revolution in lexicography. *International Journal of Lexicography*, 25(4), 398–436.

Hopkins, D. J., & King, G. (2010). A method of automated nonparametric content analysis for social science. *American Journal of Political Science*, 54(1), 229–247.

Jacobi, C., Van Atteveldt, W., & Welbers, K. (2015). Quantitative analysis of large amounts of journalistic texts using topic modelling. *Digital Journalism*, 1–18. doi:10.1080/21670811.2015.1093271

Kaufman, L., & Rousseeuw, P. J. (1990). *Finding groups in data: An introduction to cluster analysis*. Hoboken, NJ: Wiley.

Koltcov, S., Nikolenko, S. I., Koltsova, O., Filippov, V., & Bodrunova, S. (2016). Stable topic modeling with local density regularization. In F. Bagnoli, A. Satsiou, I. Stavrakakis, P. Nesi, G. Pacini, Y. Welp, & D. DiFranzo (Eds.), *Internet science: Third international conference, INSCI 2016, Florence, Italy, September 12–14, 2016, Proceedings* (pp. 176–188). Cham, Switzerland: Springer International Publishing.

Koltsova, O., & Koltcov, S. (2013). Mapping the public agenda with topic modeling: The case of the Russian LiveJournal. *Policy & Internet*, 5(2), 207–227.

Koltsova, O., & Shcherbak, A. (2015). 'LiveJournal Libra!': The political blogosphere and voting preferences in Russia in 2011–2012. *New Media & Society*, 17(10), 1715–1732.

Lancichinetti, A., Sirer, M. I., Wang, J. X., Acuna, D., Körding, K., & Amaral, L. A. N. (2015). High-reproducibility and high-accuracy method for automated topic classification. *Physical Review*, 5(1). doi:10.1103/PhysRevX.5.011007

Lenci, A. (2008). Distributional semantics in linguistic and cognitive research. *Rivista Di Linguistica*, 20(1), 1–31.

Levy, K. E. C., & Franklin, M. (2014). Driving regulation: Using topic models to examine political contention in the U. S. trucking industry. *Social Science Computer Review*, 32(2), 182–194.

Lötscher, A. (1987). *Text und Thema. Studien zur thematischen Konstituenz von Texten. [Text and topic. Studies concerning thematical constituency of texts]*. Berlin, Germany: De Gruyter.

Lovins, J. B. (1968). Development of a stemming algorithm. *Mechanical Translation and Computational Linguistics*, 11(1–2), 22–31.

Maier, D., Waldherr, A., Miltner, P., Jähnichen, P., & Pfetsch, B. (2017). Exploring issues in a networked public sphere: Combining hyperlink network analysis and topic modeling. *Social Science Computer Review*, Advance online publication. doi:10.1177/0894439317690337

Manning, C. D., Raghavan, P., & Schütze, H. (2009). *An introduction to information retrieval*. Cambridge, UK: Cambridge University Press.

Manning, C. D., & Schütze, H. (2003). *Foundations of statistical natural language processing (6. print with corr.)*. Cambridge, MA: MIT Press.

Marshall, E. A. (2013). Defining population problems: Using topic models for cross-national comparison of disciplinary development. *Poetics*, 41(6), 701–724.

McCallum, A. K. (2002). *MALLET: A machine learning for language toolkit*. Retrieved from http://mallet.cs.umass.edu

Miller, M. M., & Riechert, B. P. (2001). The spiral of opportunity and frame resonance: Mapping the issue cycle in news and public discourse. In S. D. Reese, O. H. Gandy Jr., & A. E. Grant (Eds.), *Framing public life: Perspectives on media and our understanding of the social world* (pp. 107–121). Mahwah, NJ: Lawrence Erlbaum Associates.

Mimno, D., & Blei, D. M. (2011). Bayesian checking for topic models. *Proceedings of the 2011 Conference on Empirical Methods in Natural Language Processing*, 227–237.

Mimno, D., Wallach, H. M., Talley, E., Leenders, M., & McCallum, A. (2011). Optimizing semantic coherence in topic models. *Proceedings of the 2011 Conference on Empirical Methods in Natural Language Processing*, 262–272.

Neuendorf, K. A. (2017). *The content analysis guidebook* (2nd ed.). Los Angeles, CA: Sage.

Newman, D., Bonilla, E. V., & Buntine, W. (2011). Improving topic coherence with regularized topic models. *Proceedings of the 24th International Conference on Neural Information Processing Systems*, 496–504. Retrieved from http://dl.acm.org/citation.cfm?id=2986459.2986515

Newman, D., Chemudugunta, C., Smyth, P., & Steyvers, M. (2006). Analyzing entities and topics in news articles using statistical topic models. In S. Mehrotra, D. D. Zeng, H. Chen, B. Thuraisingham, & F.-Y. Wang (Eds.), *Intelligence and security informatics* (Vol. 3975, pp. 93–104). Berlin, Germany: Springer.

Newman, D., Lau, J. H., Grieser, K., & Baldwin, T. (2010). Automatic evaluation of topic coherence. *Proceedings of the 2010 Annual Conference of the North American Chapter of the ACL*, 100–108.

Niekler, A. (2016). *Automatisierte Verfahren für die Themenanalyse nachrichtenorientierter Textquellen*. [Automated approaches for the analysis of topics in news sources]. (PhD dissertation). University of Leipzig, Leipzig, Germany. Retrieved from http://www.qucosa.de/fileadmin/data/qucosa/documents/19509/main.pdf

Niekler, A., & Jähnichen, P. (2012). Matching results of latent dirichlet allocation for text. *Proceedings of the 11th International Conference on Cognitive Modeling (ICCM)*, 317–322.

Parra, D., Trattner, C., Gómez, D., Hurtado, M., Wen, X. D., & Lin, Y.-R. (2016). Twitter in academic events: A study of temporal usage, communication, sentimental and topical patterns in 16 computer science conferences. *Computer Communications, 73*, 301–314.

Puschmann, C., & Scheffler, T. (2016) Topic modeling for media and communication research: A short primer. *HIIG Discussion Paper Series* (No. 2016-05): Alexander von Humboldt Institut für Internet und Gesellschaft.

Quinn, K. M., Monroe, B. L., Colaresi, M., Crespin, M. H., & Radev, D. R. (2010). How to analyze political attention with minimal assumptions and costs. *American Journal of Political Science, 54*(1), 209–228.

Rajaraman, A., & Ullman, J. D. (2011). *Mining of massive datasets*. New York, NY: Cambridge University Press.

Rauchfleisch, A. (2017). The public sphere as an essentially contested concept: A co-citation analysis of the last 20 years of public sphere research. *Communication and the Public, 2*(1), 3–18.

Řehůřek, R., & Sojka, P. (2010). Software framework for topic modelling with large corpora. *Proceedings of the LREC 2010 Workshop on New Challenges for NLP Frameworks*, 45–50. Valletta, Malta: ELRA.

Roberts, M. E., Stewart, B. M., & Tingley, D. (2016). Navigating the local modes of big data: The case of topic models. In R. M. Alvarez (Ed.), *Analytical methods for social research. Computational social science: Discovery and prediction* (pp. 51–97). New York, NY: Cambridge University Press. doi:10.1017/CBO9781316257340.004

Salton, G. (1991). Developments in automatic text retrieval. *Science, 253*(5023), 974–980.

Scott, S., & Matwin, S. (1999). Featuring engineering for text classification. *Proceedings of the ICML-99*, 379–388. Bled, Slovenia.

Sievert, C., & Shirley, K. E. (2014). *LDAvis: A method for visualizing and interpreting topics*. Paper presented at the Workshop on Interactive Language Learning, Visualization, and Interfaces, Baltimore, MD.

Sokolov, E., & Bogolubsky, L. (2015). Topic models regularization and initialization for regression problems. *Proceedings of the 2015 Workshop on Topic Models: Post-Processing and Applications*, 21–27. doi:10.1145/2809936.2809940

Steyvers, M., & Griffiths, T. L. (2007). Probabilistic approaches to semantic representation. In T. K. Landauer, McNamara, S. Dennis, & W. Knitsch (Eds.), *Handbook of latent semantic analysis*, (pp. 424–440). Mahwah, NJ: Lawrence Erlbaum.

Teh, Y. W., Jordan, M. I., Beal, M. J., & Blei, D. M. (2006). Hierarchical dirichlet processes. *Journal of the American Statistical Association, 101*(476), 1566–1581.

Tsur, O., Calacci, D., & Lazer, D. (2015). *A frame of mind: Using statistical models for detection of framing and agenda setting campaigns*. Paper presented at the 53rd Annual Meeting of the Association for Computational Linguistics and the 7th International Joint Conference on Natural Language Processing, Beijing, China.

Turney, P. D., & Pantel, P. (2010). From frequency to meaning: Vector space models of semantics. *Journal of Artificial Intelligence Research, 37*, 141–188.

Van Atteveldt, W., Welbers, K., Jacobi, C., & Vliegenthart, R. (2014). *LDA models topics… But what are 'topics'?* Retrieved from http://vanatteveldt.com/wp-content/uploads/2014_vanatteveldt_glasgowbigdata_topics.pdf

Waldherr, A., Maier, D., Miltner, P., & Günther, E. (2017). Big data, big noise: The challenge of finding issue networks on the web. *Social Science Computer Review, 35*(4), 427–443.

Wallach, H. M. (2006). *Topic modeling: Beyond bag-of-words*. Paper presented at the 23rd International Conference on Machine Learning, Pittsburgh, PA.

Wallach, H. M., Mimno, D., & McCallum, A. (2009). Rethinking LDA: Why priors matter. In Y. Bengio, D. Schuurmans, J. D. Lafferty, C. K. I. Williams, & A. Culotta (Eds.), *Advances in neural information processing systems 22* (pp. 1973–1981). New York, NY: Curran Associates.

Zhao, W. X., Jiang, J., Weng, J., He, J., Lim, E.-P., Yan, H., & Li, X. (2011). *Comparing Twitter and traditional media using topic models*. Paper presented at the 33rd European Conference on IR Research, Dublin, Ireland.

Appendix A

Systematic review of studies in communication research, which uses LDA topic modeling

Reference	Type of Data	Preprocessing	Parameter Selection	Interpretability & Validity	Reliability
Studies with methodological focus					
Baum (2012)	Political speeches	Stemming Removing stop words *No specific sequence*	K (chosen after validation)	Review top words Review top documents Manual labeling External validation	—
Biel and Gatica-Perez (2014)	YouTube videos and comments	Removing punctuation and repeated letters Stemming *No specific sequence*	K (qualitative exploration), prior parameters (standard values)	Review top words Manual labeling Validation of topics via word intrusion tasks and topic intrusion tasks	Split sample test
DiMaggio et al. ((2013)	Newspaper articles	Removing stop words *No specific sequence*	K (qualitative exploration)	Review top words Review top documents Categorizing topics Statistical validation with mutual information (MI) criterion Internal validation via hand coding of sample texts External validation of topics with news events	Replication with variations of corpus, seeds and parameters
Evans (2014)	Newspaper articles	—	K (chosen after validation), prior parameters (optimization)	Review top words Manual labeling Quantitative metrics (topic coherence, etc.) External validation through qualitative domain knowledge	—
Ghosh and Guha (2013)	Tweets	1. Removing URLs and HTML entities 2. Removing punctuation and conversion to lowercase 3. Removing stop words 4. Stemming 5. Tokenization	K (quantitative metrics: perplexity); prior parameters (standard values)	Review top words Manual labeling External validation with political events	—
Guo et al. (2016)	Tweets	Stemming Removing punctuation, stop words, etc. *No specific sequence*	K (trial and error)	Review top words Manual labeling Comparison with manual coding	—
Jacobi et al. (2015)	News articles	1. Lemmatizing 2. Part of speech-tagging; Removing frequent and infrequent words; Removing terms with numbers/non-alphanumeric letters	K (qualitative exploration and quantitative metrics: perplexity)	Review top words Review top documents Review of co-occurrence of top words (topic coherence) Manual labeling Comparison with manual coding	—
Newman et al. (2006)	News articles	1. Tokenization; Removing stop words 2. Removing infrequent terms	K (no explanation)	Review top words and entities Manual labeling External validation of topics with news events	—
Puschmann and Scheffler (2016)	Newspaper articles	1. Removing numbers and punctuation, conversion in lower case 2. Removing stop words 3. Removing infrequent terms	K (quantitative metrics: perplexity and Euclidean distance)	Review top words Quantitative metrics (Euclidean distance) Manual evaluation Inter-topic semantic validation	—

(Continued)

(Continued).

Reference	Type of Data	Preprocessing	Parameter Selection	Interpretability & Validity	Reliability
Tsur, Calacci, and Lazer (2015)	Press releases and statements	—	K (qualitative exploration)	Review top words Manual labeling External validation by domain experts	—
Van Atteveldt et al. (2014)	News articles	Lemmatizing Removing frequent and infrequent words *No specific sequence*	K (high resolution)	Review top words Quantitative metrics (topic prevalence) Comparison with manual coding	Replication with different parameters
Zhao et al. (2011)	Tweets and newspaper articles	1. Removing stop words 2. Removing frequent and infrequent words 3. Removing tweets with less than three words/users with less than eight tweets	K (qualitative exploration)	Review top words Semi-automated topic categorization Manual labeling Manual judgement of interpretability	—
Studies with thematic research focus					
Bonilla and Grimmer (2013)	Newspaper articles and transcripts of newscasts	Stemming Removing punctuation and stop words *No specific sequence*	K (application of non-parametric topic model, qualitative exploration)	Review documents (random sample) Manual labeling Automated labeling (using mutual information)	Replication with varying number of topics
Elgesem et al. (2016)	Blog posts	—	K (qualitative exploration)	Review top words Review top documents Manual labeling	—
Elgesem et al. (2015)	Blog posts	—	K (qualitative exploration)	Review top words Review documents Manual labeling Quantitative metrics (mutual information, etc.)	—
Koltsova and Koltcov (2013)	Blog posts	Removing HTML tags, punctuation, etc. Lemmatization *No specific sequence*	K (quantitative metrics: perplexity)	Review top words Review top documents Manual labeling	—
Koltsova and Shcherbak (2015)	Blog posts	—	K (no explanation)	Review documents Manual labeling and evaluation	—
Levy and Franklin (2014)	Public comments	1. Stemming 2. Removing stop words 3. Removing terms with only single letters or numbers 4. Removing infrequent words	K (qualitative exploration)	Review top words External validation with expert evaluation	Replication with variations of corpus, seeds and parameters
Parra et al. (2016)	Tweets	Language filtering Removing stop words, special characters, URLs, words with less than three characters *No specific sequence*	K (qualitative exploration)	—	—
Rauchfleisch (2017)	Research articles	Removing stop words Removing numbers, replacing hyphens with space characters, conversion in lowercase Stemming *No specific sequence*	K (no explanation); parameters set according to Steyvers and Griffiths (2007)	Review top words Manual classification External validation	—

Note. K = number of topics. The ordering of pre-processing steps is numbered if the ordering was explicitly mentioned in the source.

Appendix B

Choice of candidate models from topic models with varying parameter sets

Nr.	K	α	β	Likelihood	Mean Coherence
1	30	0.01	0.033	−67464644.07	−399.49
2	30	0.05	0.033	−66324953.70	−399.60
3	30	0.10	0.033	−65740704.30	−401.30
4	30	0.20	0.033	−64822303.40	−393.80
5	30	0.50	0.033	−63435029.60	−396.90
6	30	1.00	0.033	−62317020.40	−393.30
7	50	0.01	0.020	−64835932.63	−423.18
8	50	0.05	0.020	−63182677.27	−421.18
9	50	0.10	0.020	−62079259.12	−421.67
10	50	0.20	0.020	−61058300.26	−427.59
11	50	0.50	0.020	−59290870.33	−404.24
12	50	1.00	0.020	−57956143.48	−405.92
13	70	0.01	0.014	−63164036.11	−438.95
14	70	0.05	0.014	−60895636.63	−426.21
15	70	0.10	0.014	−59579663.81	−422.07
16	70	0.20	0.014	−58399926.46	−423.43
17	70	0.50	0.014	−56628160.74	−404.67
18	70	1.00	0.014	−54896346.70	−411.50

Note. K = number of topics.

Appendix C

Summary statistics for the interpretation of a topic

Topic 22 — foodborne diseases

	Websites Top Websites	Share in %	Topwords $\lambda = 1$	$\lambda = 0.6$
1	fda.gov	14.40	food	outbreak
2	barfblog.com	11.40	outbreak	salmonella
3	cdc.gov	8.90	salmonella	illness
4	cspinet.org	4.20	illness	ill
5	notinmyfood.org	2.40	report	food
6	barfblog.foodsafety.ksu.edu	2.30	people	case
7	pewhealth.org	2.20	case	foodborne
8	foodsafety.gov	1.90	state	report
9	usatoday.com	1.60	eat	investigation
10	nytimes.com	1.50	ill	sick
11	organicconsumers.org	1.30	disease	contaminate
12	inspection.gc.ca	1.20	bacterium	people
13	bt.cdc.gov	1.10	contaminate	campylobacter
14	centerforfoodsafety.org	1.00	raw	bacterium
15	foodsafetytalk.com	0.80	foodborne	egg
16	eurosurveillance.org	0.80	infection	infection
17	foodsafetynews.com	0.80	investigation	raw
18	fsis.usda.gov	0.70	sick	hospitalize
19	oregonlive.com	0.70	chicken	strain
20	atwork.avma.org	0.60	egg	diarrhea

Rank1-Metric: Rank **26 out of 50**.
Coherence-Metric: Rank **18 von 50**.

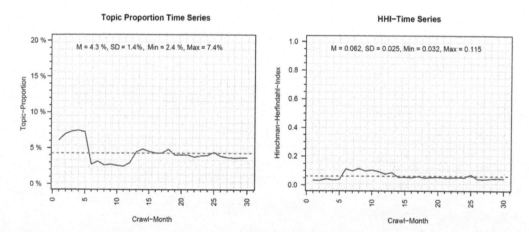

Note. The figure depicts a divided table and two time-series plots. The left side of the table shows the average most prevalent sources of the topic while the right side maps out the top-words according to two different relevance values ($\lambda = 1$ and $\lambda = .6$). Below the table the ranks of the Rank-1 and the coherence metrics are given. The left time series shows the salience of the topic over time, while the right plot gives a sense of how concentrated the topic was over the course of investigation.

Extracting Latent Moral Information from Text Narratives: Relevance, Challenges, and Solutions

René Weber, J. Michael Mangus, Richard Huskey, Frederic R. Hopp, Ori Amir, Reid Swanson, Andrew Gordon, Peter Khooshabeh, Lindsay Hahn, and Ron Tamborini

ABSTRACT
Moral Foundations Theory (MFT) and the Model of Intuitive Morality and Exemplars (MIME) contend that moral judgments are built on a universal set of basic moral intuitions. A large body of research has supported many of MFT's and the MIME's central hypotheses. Yet, an important prerequisite of this research—the ability to extract latent moral content represented in media stimuli with a reliable procedure—has not been systematically studied. In this article, we subject different extraction procedures to rigorous tests, underscore challenges by identifying a range of reliabilities, develop new reliability test and coding procedures employing computational methods, and provide solutions that maximize the reliability and validity of moral intuition extraction. In six content analytical studies, including a large crowd-based study, we demonstrate that: (1) traditional content analytical approaches lead to rather low reliabilities; (2) variation in coding reliabilities can be predicted by both text features and characteristics of the human coders; and (3) reliability is largely unaffected by the detail of coder training. We show that a coding task with simplified training and a coding technique that treats moral foundations as fast, spontaneous intuitions leads to acceptable inter-rater agreement, and potentially to more valid moral intuition extractions. While this study was motivated by issues related to MFT and MIME research, the methods and findings in this study have implications for extracting latent content from text narratives that go beyond moral information. Accordingly, we provide a tool for researchers interested in applying this new approach in their own work.

Introduction

Moral intuitions frequently motivate individuals' personal and political choices. There is mounting evidence that humans possess innate moral sensibilities which enable the understanding and enforcement of norms regarding what is best for society as a whole. A well-known conceptual framework supporting this view is Moral Foundations Theory (MFT; Graham et al., 2012; Haidt & Joseph, 2007), which contends that moral judgment and decision-making are built on a universal set of basic, intuitive moral foundations.[1] Advocates of MFT propose at least five moral foundations: (1) care/harm (an intuitive concern for the suffering of others); (2) fairness/cheating (an intuitive

---

Color versions of one or more of the figures in the article can be found online at www.tandfonline.com/hcms.

preference for reciprocity and justice); (3) loyalty/betrayal (an intuitive concern for the common good and bias against outsiders); (4) authority/subversion (an intuitive deference to dominance hierarchies); and (5) sanctity/desecration (an intuitive concern for purity, broadly defined, including pathogen avoidance). A sixth foundation—liberty/oppression (an intuition about the feelings of reactance and resentment people feel toward those who dominate them and restrict their liberty)—is currently under consideration (see http://moralfoundations.org). The relative salience of each foundation varies both across and within cultures, and the variation in individuals' moral intuition salience can be used to explain differences in attitudes and behaviors. Research has shown, for instance, that political conservatives tend to emphasize sanctity, loyalty, and authority (the binding foundations) more than liberals; conversely, liberals tend to place the greatest emphasis on care and fairness (the individualizing foundations; Graham, Haidt, & Nosek, 2009; Haidt & Graham, 2007).

Moral themes are latent in a wide range of media content, and a theoretical frame for understanding the impact of moral content embedded in mediated narratives is the Model of Intuitive Morality and Exemplars (MIME; Tamborini, 2013). The MIME suggests that, over time, consistent exposure to messages emphasizing the superiority of one moral foundation over another will increase the salience of that foundation among audiences and maintain its salience in the face of other influences (Tamborini, 2013). Furthermore, the MIME holds that insulation from value-inconsistent messages will foster polarized values within ideological groups and reduce openness to divergent views (Leidner & Castano, 2012; Moscovici, 1985). For example, both American Protestant fundamentalist (Ammerman, 1991) and Islamic fundamentalist groups (Armstrong, 2000) have isolated networks of interpersonal and mass-media communication in which individuals are exposed exclusively to messages consistent with group values.

The MIME's predictions regarding both differences in content produced for different sub-groups, as well as the effects of exposure to that content, have found substantial empirical support in recent years. For example, several studies have supported the predicted differences in media produced for sub-groups that differ by age (Lewis & Mitchell, 2014), political interest (Bowman, Lewis, & Tamborini, 2014), and culture (Mastro, Enriquez, Bowman, Prabhu, & Tamborini, 2012). Feinberg and Willer (2013, 2015)) have also shown that political messages are more persuasive when they are framed in terms of moral intuitions that align with the intuitions of the target population. Other studies have provided evidence in support of the MIME's predictions about the effect on intuition salience of both long-term exposure (e.g., Grizzard et al., 2016; Tamborini, Weber, Eden, Bowman, & Grizzard, 2010) and short-term exposure to moral intuitions embedded in narratives (e.g., Lewis, Grizzard, Mangus, Rashidian, & Weber, 2016).

MFT and MIME: previous moral intuition extraction from text

Many MFT- and MIME-related studies use latent moral information in narratives as an important variable. For example, researchers have coded for the presence of MFT foundations in content analyses of participants' text summaries about their moral acts throughout the day (Hofmann, Wisneski, Brandt, & Skitka, 2014), religious interviews (McAdams et al., 2008), tweets (Sagi & Dehghani, 2014), television programs for children (Lewis & Mitchell, 2014), and political YouTube videos and newspaper articles (Bowman et al., 2014; Feinberg & Willer, 2013). Researchers have also made use of the Moral Foundations Dictionary (MFD) provided by Graham and colleagues (2009) to code newspaper articles mentioning stem cell research (Clifford & Jerit, 2013) or religious sermons (Graham et al., 2009). Yet despite their common goal of extracting moral foundations, the coding procedures used in these studies vary considerably. Differences in the procedures and coder characteristics are summarized in Table 1. Notably, details of the coder training procedure are poorly documented in most cases, leaving open questions for researchers who might hope to replicate those procedures.

Compared to general MFT studies, research utilizing MIME-based coding schemes provides relatively more systematic coder training and uniform coding procedures for extracting moral

Table 1. Summary of coding procedures and interrater reliabilities for content analyses using an MFT and MIME rationale.

Study	Procedure	Coder Details	Range of Intercoder Reliability for Moral Foundations
MFT-Based Content Analyses			
Graham et al. (2009)	Word count software analyzed (n = 103) religious sermons for MFD words. Following this, human coders assessed the context surrounding each word in all sermons.	Linguistic Word Count Program; four coders blind to the study's hypotheses	N/A for the word count program; Krippendorff's alpha = .79, collapsed for all intuitions.
Hofmann et al. (2014)	Coders categorized each moral response (n = 3823) as it fit into one of the MFT foundations.	One rater (an author, Hofmann) coded participant responses (n = 3823) and one rater (a second author, Wisneski) coded 50% of this content.	Kappa = .85, collapsed for all intuitions.
Feinberg and Willer (2013)	In each study, coders indicated the extent to which each video (n = 51 videos; study 2a) or newspaper article (n = 232 articles; study 2b) was grounded in the 5 moral foundations on a 7-point scale ranging from 0 (not at all) to 6 (extremely).	Five coders blind to the study hypotheses (study 2a), and seven coders blind to the study hypotheses (study 2b).	Krippendorff's alpha = .73, collapsed for all intuitions for study 2a, and Krippendorff's alpha = .73 collapsed for all intuitions in study 2b.
McAdams et al. (2008)	Each interview (n = 128) being coded on a 5-point scale (1 = no concern; 5 = high concern) for each intuition.	Two coders—one of whom was blind to the hypotheses, and one of whom worked closely with an author to develop the rating system for each of the five intuitions	Alpha for care = .80; fairness = .76; loyalty = .82; authority = .82; purity = .86.
Clifford and Jerit (2013)	Coders identified: (1) MFD words associated with care, purity, and general moral words, (2) the contextual valence of the word, and (3) whether context associated with the moral word was being endorsed or rejected by the overall article.	One rater coded n = 3192 words from articles and one rater coded "a randomly selected subset of stories" (p. 664).	Krippendorff's alpha = .76, collapsed across care, purity, and general moral words.
MIME-Based Content Analyses			
Tamborini et al. (2017)	Coders identified (1) presence/valence of intuitions, (2) the extent to which these intuitions were rewarded or punished, and (3) whether the associated character was good or bad.	Four undergraduate coders coded n = 27 children's television episodes; a fifth rater acted as a referee to address disagreements.	Percent agreement was assessed for two sets of coders for care (74%, 75%), fairness (80%, 89%), loyalty, (93%, 90%), authority (90%, 90%), and purity (95%, 94%).
Hahn et al. (2017)	Same procedure as Tamborini et al. (2017) above, except that coders coded (1) only scenes which contained intuitions in conflict, and (2) the characters' choice in this conflict	Three undergraduate coders coded n = 40 conflict scenes identified in Tamborini et al.'s (2017) sample.	Krippendorff's alpha for care = .74, fairness = .94, loyalty = .73, authority = .93, purity = 1.
Lewis and Mitchell (2014)	Coders identified (1) scenes which contained intuitions in conflict and (2) what intuitions were in conflict.	Two undergraduate coders coded n = 30 popular children's television programs (this sample was used in Tamborini et al. (2017) and Hahn et al. (2017).	Krippendorff's alpha for care = .93, fairness = 1.00, loyalty = 1.00, authority = 0, purity = 0 (note: Alphas that are zero denote categories in which at least one of the coders marked "absent" for all units of analysis).

(Continued)

Table 1. (Continued).

Study	Procedure	Coder Details	Range of Intercoder Reliability for Moral Foundations
Bowman et al. (2014)	Coders identified (1) presence/absence (2) valence, and (3) intensity of intuitions.	Two female coders coded n = 401 headlines and n = 352 subheads of newspaper articles from sources based in U.S. counties	Krippendorff's alpha for presence/absence of loyalty = .98, fairness = 1, purity = .67; valence for loyalty = .89, fairness = .99; intensity for care = .71, fairness = .99.
Experimental MIME Studies that Include Content Analyses			
Tamborini et al. (2016)	Coders identified the extent to which experimental stimuli featured exemplars of any moral intuitions.	Three coders blind to the study's hypotheses rated a 40-min TV episode.	Krippendorff's alpha for care = 0.84, fairness = 0.91, loyalty = 0.90, authority = 0.85, purity = 0.92.
Tamborini, Lewis et al., (2016)	Coders identified the extent to which (1) experimental stimuli and (2) participant thought listings featured exemplars of any moral intuitions.	Three coders blind to the study's hypotheses rated (1) a 40-min TV episode and (2) participant thought listings (n = 173).	Stimuli: Krippendorff's alpha for care = 0.84, fairness = 0.91, loyalty = 0.90, authority = 0.85, purity = 0.92. Thought listings: Krippendorff's alpha for care = .78, fairness = .89, loyalty = .88, authority = .82, purity = .82.
Grizzard et al. (2016)	Coders identified the extent to which experimental stimuli featured exemplars of any moral intuitions.	Two coders (who were authors but blind to the hypotheses at the time of coding) coded (n = 10) movie plot summaries.	Krippendorff's alpha = .68 (81% agreement) for all coding categories combined.

intuitions from content. A typical procedure for MIME studies involves training coders for two to three months on definitions and examples of MFT foundations. In training sessions, coders code examples together, discuss the coding protocol aloud, and complete weekly assignments where they determine whether moral foundations are present in text and, if present, whether they are upheld or violated (e.g., Tamborini, Hahn, Prabhu, Klebig, & Grall, 2017). For instance, this procedure has been used in studies examining popular children's television programming. Tamborini et al. (2017) coded for the presence/absence of each moral foundation within a given episode. If a foundation was present, they then evaluated if it was in conflict with other foundations (e.g., should I choose to uphold care or fairness?; see also Hahn et al., 2017; Lewis & Mitchell, 2014). Although not content analytic research per se, three recent experimental studies have utilized a MIME-based coding scheme and procedure to assess the extent to which their stimuli feature moral foundations (Grizzard et al., 2016; Tamborini et al., 2016; Tamborini, Prabhu, Lewis, Grizzard, & Eden, 2016).

Although the extent of coder training for MIME-based studies may be relatively more uniform than other MFT content analyses, the procedures employed by MIME studies still varied in the examples used for coder training, the amount of in-person training coders received, and the characteristics of the coders themselves. Furthermore, a key difference in these studies is that they ask coders not to simply code explicit content, but instead to consider and classify how *latent* moral content activates their own subjective moral intuitions.

The current studies

Despite considerable heterogeneity in the procedures described in Table 1, reported reliabilities nonetheless vary from a low of 0.73 (Feinberg & Willer, 2013) to a high of 1.00 (Hahn et al., 2017). This range is surprisingly high considering the subjective nature of moral intuitions and, as discussed in detail below, we believe reliability may be artificially inflated at the expense of validity. And, while this article focuses only on MFT- and MIME-based coding procedures, it is possible that this concern may generalize to other studies focused on extracting latent content. Accordingly, the procedure described in this article offers a roadmap for researchers interested in evaluating other topics.

In this article, we subject different content extraction procedures to rigorous tests, underscore challenges by identifying a range of reliabilities each procedure is capable of producing, and provide solutions that maximize the reliability and validity of moral intuition extraction. In six content analytical studies we demonstrate that: (1) traditional content analytical approaches lead to rather low reliabilities when extracting moral content from news articles; (2) variation in coding reliabilities can be predicted by both text features and characteristics of the coders; (3) variation in coding reliabilities and coder agreement are largely unaffected by the intensity and detail of coder training—relying on a small group of highly trained and involved coders does not lead to substantially higher reliabilities than relying on a large group of coders with little training and involvement; and (4) a coding task with simplified training and a coding technique that treats moral foundations as the products of fast, spontaneous intuitions leads to plausible and acceptable inter-rater agreement. We discuss implications of these findings for future MFT and MIME research and suggest that the application of simplified coding techniques in a large crowd of coders leads to more valid extraction of latent moral information in text, and perhaps of latent information in general.

In this article, we focus our attention to a specific domain of latent information—moral intuitions in news narratives, which we consider an important and most difficult test case in communication studies. Beyond the extraction of latent moral information in news narratives, however, our methods and findings provide further recommendations and evidence for the usability of crowdsourcing for coding latent constructs in other domains such as in general political texts (Benoit, Conway, Lauderdale, Laver, & Mikhaylov, 2016; Lind, Gruber, & Boomgaarden, 2017). Lastly, our conclusions may also provide valuable methodological insights for coding and extracting more general frames in news using (human) supervised machine learning techniques (Burscher, Odijk, Vliegenthart, De Rijke, & De Vreese, 2014). Our discussion section considers these issues in greater detail.

Content analyses 1–4: setting the baseline

Coders

We conducted four separate content analyses using diverse human coder groups that differed in involvement and training time. The first coder group ($n_1 = 3$) consisted of undergraduate research assistants who participated for a total of two academic quarters at the University of California Santa Barbara. Using a small group of trained coders is a common procedure in traditional content analyses. This first group of coders received an initial training using a Web-based platform (see the "Procedures - Online Platform" section below) which lasted for about one hour. Subsequently, these coders attended weekly one-hour research meetings where issues were discussed and questions clarified. Our second and third coder groups $n_2 = 5$ and $n_3 = 14$ consisted of undergraduate students participating in separate year-long honors seminars at Michigan State University. These students were highly involved as the outcome of their coding was relevant for a presentation of their work at a university-wide undergraduate conference. At the same time, these students also received a high level of training on MFT and the MIME (3 semester-units of course credit) in addition to a training using the Web-based platform, weekly training meetings, and example items to code for weekly homework (taken together, ≈ 2.5 hr/wk) that were specific to the content analysis procedure. Finally, a sample from the undergraduate research pool ($n_4 = 223$) at UC Santa Barbara completed the 1 hr-long online platform training and coded articles for course credit. No additional training was provided and no additional incentives were issued to this last coder group.

Given the above, we understand these coder groups as follows: n_1 = high-involvement, medium training; n_2 = high-involvement, high-training; n_3 = high-involvement, high-training; and n_4 = low-

Table 2. Coder and coding statistics for content analyses 1–4.

Group	Coders	Pairs	Codings	Documents
High Involvement - Maximum Training	19	171	3,511	413
High Involvement - Medium Training	3	3	909	374
Low Involvement - Low Training	225	25,200	1,837	40

involvement, low-training. Table 2 summarizes the number of coders per group together with the number of coded articles.

Text materials

We collected articles published between 2013 and 2015 from four major news outlets: *The New York Times, Reuters, CBS News,* and *The Washington Post*. Once per day, the politics section of each source was automatically crawled using a Scrapy spider (http://scrapy.org) and the full text of each article was stored, along with relevant metadata, in a relational database. Additionally, named entities were automatically extracted using the Stanford Named Entity Recognition engine (http://nlp.stanford.edu/ Finkel, Grenager, & Manning, 2005), which provides a list of the people, locations, and organizations referenced in each article.

The Python Natural Language Toolkit (http://www.nltk.org/ Bird, Loper, & Klein, 2009) was used to tokenize and stem the text of each article, which was then subjected to a simple word-frequency analysis: using the MFD created by Graham and colleagues (2009), which associates certain words with particular moral foundations, we counted the number of words for each moral foundation. These word-count measures were used to help select articles for human coding, ensuring that articles contain some moral information and prioritizing articles with high variance in moral content. Within this pre-filtered set, assignments of documents to coder groups were made randomly. Each coder group coded a common set of at least ten articles, although, because some coders completed more codings than others, certain pairs of coders have many more articles in common.

Measures

Coders' moral and political views

We pre-tested our coders' political knowledge using a five-item index created by Delli Carpini and Keeter (1993). Coders' moral intuition salience was measured with the Moral Foundations Questionnaire (MFQ; Graham et al., 2009). To measure political views, we used the Society Works Best Index (SWB; Smith, Oxley, Hibbing, Alford, & Hibbing, 2011), which produces an additive index of liberalism/conservatism from subscales that reflect preferences for a society that takes care of its neediest members, has a tolerant approach to outgroups, promotes forgiveness of rule breakers, and favors egalitarian leadership practices with a flexible approach to moral codes of behavior. Participants also self-reported their political affiliation on an 11-point rating scale ("extremely liberal" to "extremely conservative").

Other coder characteristics

In addition to the measures above, we collected self-reported gender and age. System usage information was collected using a combination of client- and server-side logging in order to filter out low-quality participants, such as those who spent only a few seconds on training or coding pages.

Text difficulty

We computed three measures of text difficulty. First, because *ceteris paribus*, longer articles require more sustained attention and cognitive engagement to understand, the total word-count of an article served as a simple proxy for its difficulty. Second, we computed lexical diversity using the uncorrected type-token ratio (TTR). Articles with a higher TTR—i.e., a greater proportion of unique words to total words—exhibit greater lexical diversity and thus may be more difficult to read (however, although TTR has been widely-used for many decades, this relationship is not uncontroversial; see Vermeer, 2000). Finally, based on the notion that articles that reference many different actors may have more complex latent moral narratives, we treat the number of entities identified by the automated entity-recognition system as an indicator of text difficulty.

Procedures

Online coding platform and coder training

An online training platform, the Moral Narrative Analyzer (MoNA; https://mnl.ucsb.edu/mona), was developed to assist in coding moral content in news articles. We deliberately chose an online platform that manages both coder training and the coding procedure so as to minimize inconsistencies that might be introduced by subtle differences in face-to-face interactions. This choice allowed for the rigorous testing of different training and coding procedures. It also allows for easy sharing and modification which should allow other researchers to implement these procedures in their own work. Interested readers should email the corresponding author for access.

Upon registering with the system, coders completed basic demographic questions followed by the political knowledge, SWB, and MFQ scales. Coders were then required to complete an online training procedure before they were qualified to code articles. This procedure included reading detailed descriptions of each moral foundation, step-by-step guidelines for article coding (with examples), and practice articles that had already been coded. Coding instructions and the conceptual definitions of moral foundations followed established protocols in MIME content analyses that have been used to code a diverse set of narratives in fictional (e.g., movies) and non-fictional (e.g., news) media content (see Tamborini et al., 2017). Coders were then required to complete several comprehension checks designed to assess their understanding of each moral foundation and the coding procedure. Automated feedback was given when coders did not pass a comprehension check, and coders were unable to advance until they correctly passed all comprehension checks.

Coding procedure and units of analysis

After completing the training, coders began the coding process. Coders were presented with one article at a time to read and code. For each article, coders were required to specify which moral foundation was most salient overall (e.g., care/harm). Coders were also given the option to indicate that an article did not contain any moral content, which advanced the coder to the next article in their queue. For articles where an overall primary foundation was identified, coders were asked to identify the valence on a 5-point scale (e.g., completely care, mostly care, both care and harm, mostly harm, completely harm). This procedure was then repeated for the second-most-salient foundation within the article.

In addition, a given article may contain several moral actors who uphold or violate different moral foundations, thereby confounding attempts at article-level moral codings. Furthermore, long-standing traditions favoring balanced journalism tend to produce articles which avoid explicit moralizing despite describing morally relevant actions taken by the entities (e.g., people or organizations) discussed within an article. It is possible, then, that entities discussed within an article represent a more accurate unit of analysis for the assessment of moral content. If true, this suggests that reliabilities for codings at the article-level could end up being quite low, even if reliabilities for codings at the entity level are high. Accordingly, to test this premise, coders also coded morally-

Table 3. Coder-pairwise Krippendorff α by group, content analyses 1–4.

Group	Primary Only			Primary or Secondary		
	Mean	SD	Range	Mean	SD	Range
High-max	0.14	0.13	(−0.04, 0.17)	0.18	0.31	(−0.32, 0.48)
High-med	0.10	0.08	(−0.01, 0.19)	0.14	0.24	(−0.09, 0.39)
Low-low	0.11	0.25	(−0.55, 0.99)	0.17	0.36	(−0.95, 0.99)

Table 4. Coder-pairwise Cohen κ by group, content analyses 1–4.

Group	Document Primary Foundation			Entity-Specific Foundations		
	Mean	SD	Range	Mean	SD	Range
High-max	0.20	0.10	(−0.10, 0.37)	0.21	0.13	(−0.13, 0.55)
High-med	0.15	0.05	(0.09, 0.22)	0.14	0.09	(0.07, 0.26)
Low-low	0.13	0.24	(−1.00, 1.00)	0.09	0.24	(−1.00, 1.00)

relevant entities within the article. Entities detected by the Stanford NER algorithm were presented as a list from which coders could select up to four entities. Each selected entity was coded according to their most salient moral foundation and the valence of that foundation.

Finally, coders were asked to rate their overall confidence in their coding on an 11-point scale. Coders who rated their confidence below 7 were required to select at least one reason for their lack of confidence from a predefined list (e.g., "the article was too long").

Results

Reliabilities

We calculated corrected hit rates via Cohen's Kappa (Cohen, 1968) and Krippendorff's Alpha (Krippendorff, 2013) for all available coder pairs across three variables: article-wide primary moral foundation alone, article-wide primary and secondary moral foundations combined (liberally considering the pair to agree if either foundation matched), and the moral foundation assigned to any entities that were selected by both coders. Tables 3 and 4 summarize the results. Overall, reliabilities were quite low, ranging from 0.09–0.21, which is below generally accepted standards, and does not correspond to those reported in the MFT/MIME literature.

In addition to our general reliability analyses, we also reviewed the confusion matrices of many coder-pairs to assess trends in inter-rater agreement. Table 5 provides an example confusion matrix for one coder pair.

Overall, we found that the liberty and sanctity foundations are rarely used and often subject to substantial confusion when they do occur. We further noted that when the liberty foundation was selected as the primary foundation, coders were more likely to choose the midpoint of the moral valence scale (i.e., they were morally ambivalent). This result is consistent with the generally weak evidence for liberty as a distinct MFT foundation (e.g., Clifford, Iyengar, Cabeza, & Sinnott-Armstrong, 2015).

Table 5. Representative primary foundation confusion matrix for a pair in the high-max group (κ = 0.192).

Foundation	Authority	Fairness	Care	Liberty	Loyalty	Sanctity
Authority	4	9	7	1	4	0
Fairness	1	23	3	2	2	1
Care	2	10	20	1	4	0
Liberty	2	9	3	1	2	0
Loyalty	1	1	2	0	5	0
Sanctity	0	4	0	1	1	0

Table 6. Significant predictors of inter-coder reliabilities for content analyses 1–4.

Predictors	β	t	Sig.
Lexical diversity	−.273	−3.26	.001
Coding confidence	.134	12.85	.000
Society works best index	.118	10.93	.000
Gender	.043	4.37	.000
MFQ fairness	.031	2.90	.004
Political affiliation	.031	3.04	.002
Age	.025	2.46	.014

$R = .237$; $R^2 = .056$ (5.6%); $R^2_{adj} = .054$ (5.4%); $F(23, 9846) = 25.38$; $p < .001$

Predicting reliabilities

Next, we modeled pairwise reliability measures in a linear regression model with a number of coder-pair-specific qualities. Put differently, we analyzed whether pairwise reliabilities can be predicted by variables such as a coder pair's similarity (euclidean distance) in political views, the text difficulty of a coder pair's common article set, etc. (see the section "Measures" above). The analysis included $n = 9869$ coder pairs.

We found that text difficulty (as measured by lexical diversity) and—not surprisingly—coding confidence are the two strongest predictors of pairwise reliabilities. The more difficult the text material and the less confident coders are in their codings, the lower are their reliabilities (see Table 6). Furthermore, the analysis revealed that the more similar coders are in their SWB (Society Works Best attitudes) and self-reported political affiliation, the higher their reliabilities. Age and gender were also important predictors of pairwise coder reliabilities, with older coders and gender homogeneous coder pairs showing slightly higher reliabilities. A coder pair's similarity in terms of moral foundation salience was only a significant predictor in the fairness foundation; similarity in other foundations did not significantly predict coders' reliabilities. Likewise, all other measures, such as number of entities within a text, did not produce significant results. Notably, the number of care/harm, fairness/cheating, loyalty/betrayal, and authority/subversion words in a pair's common article set (as captured by the MFD) did not make a difference. Only a higher number of sanctity/desecration words predicted significantly higher reliabilities, which can be explained by the rather low number of articles of this type among our news articles.

Discussion

Our analyses show that our trained coder groups were—on average—not able to replicate the high levels of reliability and inter-coder agreement reported in the literature (see Table 1). In fact, even when evaluating the most highly trained coders using our most liberal metric, reliabilities do not meet the typical $α > 0.8$ threshold. Notably, while reliabilities increase slightly from the low-involvement, low-training to the high-involvement, maximum-training groups, the reliabilities do not differ substantially. Our pairwise reliability prediction model revealed that even when coders are extensively trained, text difficulty measures, coding confidence, political attitudes and affiliation, and even gender play an important role in explaining low reliabilities.

Overall, our results indicate that our human coder groups performed rather poorly on this type of (widely-used) moral foundation extraction procedure. There are several possible explanations for these findings. For instance, while consistent with previous content analytical paradigms, the decision to code moral information first at the article-level, and subsequently on entity level, makes several assumptions. Specifically, it assumes that an article contains just one or two overall moral foundations that are adhered to (e.g., a coder rates an article "completely/mostly care") or violated (e.g., a coder rates an article as "completely/mostly harm"), that coders are sensitive to these adherences/violations at both the article-level and entity level, and that coders can be trained in such a way that they interpret these adherences or violations in a systematic and reliable way. Despite the successes of previous content analyses, it is possible that these are untenable assumptions for news articles. However, some of the MFT content analyses which did code non-fictional news content (e.g., Feinberg & Willer, 2013) also report reliabilities above 0.7 (occasionally the human coding procedures for moral foundations were reduced to a simple "newspaper headline keyword find task" which also can explain a surprisingly high inter-coder reliability; see Bowman et al., 2014).

Drawing from our experiences with a number of pilot studies over a period of three years plus the four content analyses presented here, we think it is also possible that more fundamental assumptions about moral intuition extractions specifically, and about extracting latent information from text generally, may be flawed. In the following section, we explore the possibility that largely unchallenged assumptions made by traditional content analyses do not hold when applied to subjective, intuition-driven tasks like identifying latent moral information in text.

Myths of trained human codings?

Generations of social scientists have used traditional quantitative content analysis as a tool to collect intersubjective, reliable, and valid data that allow inferences about messages (e.g., Holsti, 1969). Those messages can be provided in different modalities, but are usually represented via text. In the early years of content analyses researchers focused largely on the manifest content of messages (e.g., Berelson, 1952), which all coders can be reasonably expected to understand in the same way. In contrast, contemporary content analyses include the measurement of latent information in messages (for an overview, see Riffe, Lacy, & Fico, 2005; Vlieger & Leydesdorff, 2011), which requires some form of subjective inference from coders during the coding task (for instance, inferring a character's intention within a narrative). Nevertheless, the quantitative content analyses used in social science research today predominantly emphasize: (1) a sound conceptual basis for all coding dimensions (both manifest and latent), (2) a methodical strategy for sampling and unitizing content, and (3) a detailed procedure for the selection and training of expert coders (Krippendorff, 2013). While there is little controversy regarding emphasis (1), the results of our four studies, as well as methodological innovations in the area of "big data social science" (see Lazer et al., 2009), challenge emphases (2) and (3).

Recent experimental research has shown that, despite the sophistication of the machine learning algorithms being applied to make sense of "big data," human codings must still be considered an essential benchmark for the extraction of latent information from text data. However, analytical techniques for making sense of those codings are largely based on the outdated ideal of a single correct ground-truth (Hsueh, Melville, & Sindhwani, 2009). More specifically, supported by evidence from a series of experiments, Aroyo and Welty (2015) set out to debunk a number of myths in traditional content analyses. Four of the myths they identify are of particular interest here: (1) there is one correct interpretation and coding of every coding unit (ground truth); (2) disagreement of coders (low inter-rater reliability) is inherently bad and ideally should be eliminated; (3) coder training reduces disagreement by constraining possible interpretations; and (4) expert coders with conceptual knowledge of the coding categories always provide more reliable and valid data. To refute these myths, Aroyo and Welty (2015) suggest a new theory of *crowd* truth which assumes that human codings are inherently subjective (despite any training attempts), and that "measuring annotations on the same objects of interpretation [...] across a crowd will provide a useful representation of their subjectivity and the range of reasonable interpretations" (p. 15).

Rejecting myth (1) in the context of moral intuition codings seems almost obvious. If moral intuition salience varies between individuals as MFT suggests, and intuitions represent a fast, mostly unconscious cognitive process that is largely unaffected by slow, conscious deliberations, then we should expect inter- and even intra-coder variation in evaluations of moral information in text. Furthermore, coder training, which focuses on conscious deliberation, should not be able to override intuitions substantially. Evidence for rejecting a ground-truth logic in other domains is plentiful (see, e.g., Sheng, Provost, & Ipeirotis, 2008). Myth (2) can be rejected on the basis of our reliability prediction analyses above. The fact that we were able to identify coder (e.g., political attitude) and text (e.g., lexical diversity) characteristics that explained a significant amount of variance in inter-coder reliability is a testament that disagreement does not exclusively represent noise, but signal. With this information it becomes possible, for instance, to identify text with high and low moral ambiguity (i.e., high or low inter-coder agreement) or to identify a group of coders with a specific political attitude profile that is the best group to code texts of different complexity (best in terms of agreement or disagreement). Similarly, our results in studies 1–4—surprisingly we must admit—suggest that myth (3) and (4) can be dismissed in moral intuition coding procedures. Our coder groups clearly differed in the amount of knowledge, training, and involvement in the coding task: from a group of undergraduate students who read only a few pages of instructions and received little credit, to a group of undergraduate students who were highly trained over a period of 10 weeks, attended an honors seminar on MFT and the MIME, and had a personal interest in best practice, highly reliable codings for their research projects. Our results in studies 1–4 (and in previous pilot studies not reported here in which we tested different versions of our coder trainings) have shown that coder training and expert knowledge do not make a substantial difference in our moral intuition coding procedure.

We might conclude that, when it comes to coding latent moral foundations, tasks that follow the guidelines of traditional content analysis are unlikely to meet common standards for inter-coder reliability (e.g., Krippendorff α > 0.8), yet the published literature seems to demonstrate just the opposite. In light of our findings in content analyses 1–4, one possible explanation is that the reported reliabilities might be inflated by methodological practices that reduce the independence of coders. Additionally, although interesting predictions have been made about latent moral frames in news content, we believe those frames to be far more difficult to reliably identify than the more explicit moral content found in fictional narratives. More broadly, we question the ground-truth coding logic that undergirds the bulk of prior work when extracting moral foundations represented in text; low reliabilities should not be mistaken for noise. With this in mind, we now turn to content analyses five and six, in which we test a moral intuition extraction procedure that is not constrained by traditional content-analytical methodology in that it: (1) accounts for the inherent subjective nature of the moral intuition concept; (2) applies new metrics for inter-rater agreement; and (3) allows the procedure to be implemented on crowdsourcing platforms using a large number of human coders.

Crowd content analyses 5–6: highlighting intuitions

For our fifth and sixth content analysis, we sought to radically redesign our coding procedure to capitalize on the crowd-truth paradigm discussed above. In doing so, we looked to other projects that developed simplified procedures for an otherwise-complex coding task. While a number of successful projects proved quite interesting (in fact, the Amazon Mechanical Turk platform was originally designed for exactly these sort of tasks), the EyeWire project (Kim et al., 2014) was most inspirational.

EyeWire is a large-scale coding project that simplifies the otherwise-complex task of tracing neurons in the retinae of mice. Historically, such a task required slow and painstaking work by highly trained specialists. The EyeWire project convincingly demonstrated that it is possible to break a complex project down into a series of small tasks that can be quickly and easily accomplished by a large number of minimally trained coders. The success of this project relied on some rather counterintuitive methods (at least according to traditional content analytical approaches). First, any single coding is not particularly useful. Codings were only useful in aggregate. Relatedly, codings for a given piece of content only provided useful data after a considerable number of coders had coded the same content. Contrary to the assumption behind myths 3 and 4 (presented above),

EyeWire analyses showed that an individual coder's coding quality was positively correlated with the number of codings completed; although the authors noted that such an outcome is uncommon in other crowd truth approaches. Accordingly, we set out to redesign the MoNA platform to allow for rapid training, highly modular coding tasks, the ability for coders to quickly code a multitude of articles, and scalability that allows for a large number of coders to code a substantial amount of news articles. We describe this revised procedure below.

Coders

A new and fifth coder group (n_5 = 227) was comprised of low-involvement/low-training students from the undergraduate research pool at UC Santa Barbara. These students received a simplified training procedure (see "Procedures" section below) and completed their article codings for course credit. No other training or incentives were provided.

In order to replicate findings in a larger, more heterogeneous crowd of human coders drawn from the general United States population, we used the Prolific Academic (https://www.prolific.ac/) platform and recruited 854 human coders, of which n_6 = 557 fully completed all assigned tasks. In contrast to other crowd platforms (e.g., Amazon's Mturk), the Prolific Academic platform offers higher levels of "workers' quality control" and provides a more heterogeneous and more motivated group of human coders, in part due to a significantly increased pay rate requirements (we paid approximately four times more than compared to Amazon's Mturk) and stronger pre-screening of participants; (see Necka, Cacioppo, Norman, & Cacioppo, 2016). We attempted to match our sample of coders to the US population in terms of political affiliation and gender as best as possible within the constraints of Prolific Academic sampling frame, which includes more Democrats than Republicans. The final sample consisted of 195 female democrats (35%), 187 male democrats (34%), 40 female republicans (7%), 84 male republicans (15%), 24 unaffiliated females (4%), and 27 unaffiliated males (5%). The reported mean age was 32.59 years (SD = 11.45). Political leaning was also assessed by using a single-item 11-point Likert scale ("Think about your personal political views. Where would you place yourself on a continuum ranging from very liberal to very conservative?," 0 = very liberal, 10 = very conservative), which had a mean of 3.26 (SD = 2.87), further indicating that our sample leans somewhat toward the political left (across all student samples for which we have collected this measurement, n = 656, mean = 3.39, SD = 2.25).

Text material and measures

For coder group five, the news articles were drawn from the database described for studies 1–4 above. We selected a subset of 20 articles which had relatively high levels of inter-rater agreement on the earlier coding task, with an equal number of articles for each moral foundation (as labeled by a plurality of coders in studies 1–4). Coder group six read articles that were more recent (published in 2016 or later) and from more politically diverse sources than previous groups. Articles were drawn from *The Washington Post, Reuters, The Huffington Post, The New York Times, Fox News, The Washington Times, CNN, Breitbart, USA Today,* and *Time*. We utilized metadata provided by the Global Database of Events, Language, and Tone (GDELT; Leetaru & Schrodt, 2013) to gather Uniform Resource Locators (URLs) of articles with at least 500 words. GDELT includes word-frequency scores for each moral foundation in the MFD. To make sure that our human coders received articles that included at least some moral content, we only selected articles which contained some MFD words. Using a purpose-built Python script, we attempted to scrape headlines and article text from those URLs, yielding a total of 8,276 articles. After applying a combination of text-quality heuristics and random sampling, 3,980 articles were selected for coding, of which 1,010 were coded by at least one participant. Compared with study 5, study 6 decreased the number of coders per article and increased the number of total articles. By capturing highlighted words (see below) from a wider variety of articles, more training data is available to develop a successor to the MFD (which tends to produce relatively low variance in news articles; Graham et al., 2009).

All coders for study 5 and 6 provided informed consent before completing the same MFQ, SWB, political knowledge, and demographics questions as coders in content analyses 1–4 did. Likewise, the conceptual definitions of moral foundations for coders followed the same protocols as in study 1–4 (see above).

Procedures

Online coding platform and coder training

We developed a fast, crowd-truth-driven coding task: for each article, coders were instructed to simply highlight portions of the text which they understood to be related to an assigned moral foundation. This new coding model was designed to be much simpler for users, thereby minimizing training time and time-per-coding while emphasizing the intuitive nature of moral judgments.

All coders received information about the background and purpose of the MoNA project, as well as text and a 7-min video explaining the general ideas behind MFT and each moral foundation. From there, coder training diverged with coders split into two groups: single-foundation coders and multi-foundation coders.[2] Single-foundation coders were tasked with learning about just *one* moral foundation (e.g., care/harm). This training included example images (e.g., a mother nursing a child, refugees in a war-torn country), a text-based description of the foundation, and detailed examples where the foundation was upheld or violated that were adapted from training materials used in previous content analyses (e.g., Tamborini et al., 2016, 2016). Multi-foundation coders were presented with the same materials, but for *all* (not just one) moral foundations. Subsequently, all coders (both single- and multi-foundation) were presented with text- and video-based training materials instructing them on how to complete the highlighting task (described below). Importantly, single-foundation coders were instructed to only code content pertaining to the specific moral foundation they were trained on. Multi-foundation coders were *also* tasked with coding an article according to just one moral foundation, however, the selected moral foundation differed for each article. This single- and multi-foundation coder strategy was adopted to empirically address an ongoing debate within the research team about whether a single-foundation coding strategy imposes too great of a restriction on user choice and potentially leads to lower coding validity (the "law of the instrument" argument—"give a small boy a hammer, and he will find that everything he encounters needs pounding"; Kaplan, 1964, p. 28).

Text highlighting procedure

Upon completion of the training procedure, coders were directed to the coding interface where they began to highlight articles one at a time. A "cheat-sheet" was provided with five simple rules for effective highlighting. Items included: "only highlight your specific foundation", "only highlight relevant content", "moral content often relates to an entity", "how much you highlight will change with each article", and "when in doubt, don't highlight". The interface was designed such that coders were provided with a toggle button that allowed for adding or removing highlights (see Figure 1). Single-foundation coder highlights were always in yellow. A color-coding scheme was adopted for multi-foundation coders where foundation-specific highlight colors were applied. In total, student coders in group five generated 12,653 text highlights; general U.S. population coders in group six generated 68,983 highlights.

Revised measurement of inter-coder agreement

Novel methods are required to evaluate the quality of our new coding procedure. Whereas many content analyses aim for categorical classification of discrete coding units pre-selected by the researchers, our highlight-based codings pre-assign a particular moral category and then allow coders to freely demarcate relevant units of information in the text. We adapted techniques from

Figure 1. A screen capture of the MoNA platform showing the document highlighting task.

natural language processing to assess inter-rater agreement as measured by the similarity of highlighted text, then pitched our empirical data against simulated random coding data to evaluate the effectiveness of our procedure for identifying moral content.

In order to evaluate inter-rater agreement, we need a measure of how similar the text highlighted by any given coder is to the text highlighted by other coders. We consider text highlighted by a coder as a judgment of that coder. Highlights for each article were preprocessed by tokenizing them into a list of words, filtering out the English stop words (e.g., "is" and "the") provided by the NLTK stopwords corpus, and applying the Porter (1980) algorithm to reduce words to their stems. We then evaluated shared information between highlights using a vector space model. This space has as many dimensions as there are unique word-stems in the collection of all highlights for a given article. Each highlight can be represented as a vector, which will contain non-zero values for all the words that occur in that highlight. As is common practice in text summarization procedures, the vector space was transformed using term frequency-inverse document frequency weighting (TF-IDF; see Leskovec, Rajaraman, & Ullman, 2014) to account for the fact that more frequently used words provide comparatively less information about the semantic differences between two selections of text.

The cosine similarity was measured between all possible pairs of highlight vectors for a given article, yielding a two-dimensional matrix with 1's on the diagonal such that the cell *similarity_matrix[i][j]* contains the cosine similarity between highlight *i* and highlight *j*. The mean value of row *i* in the matrix therefore represents the mean cosine similarity of highlight *i* to all other highlights. Row masks were generated to filter a row's values by assigned moral foundation; each highlight therefore has five mean-similarity scores, one for each moral foundation. When a coder is assigned to code content related to care, for example, each highlight should be more similar to other highlights for the care foundation than to highlights for any of the other moral foundations.

This technique was used to generate a data structure that is conceptually similar to a traditional confusion matrix used for categorical content analysis. The procedure is as follows.

(1) Start with a 5 × 5 matrix of 0's, one cell for each possible combination of moral foundations.
(2) For each highlight, find the moral foundation that has the highest mean-similarity score. For instance, if the assigned foundation is care, and care is also the foundation with the highest similarity score, then count this as a match and increment the care/care cell. If the assigned foundation is care but the foundation with the highest similarity score is fairness, then count this as a miss and increment the care/fairness cell.
(3) Once all highlights have been processed, divide each cell by the sum of its column to get a proportion. This allows us to know the proportion of highlights for which the assigned foundation was also the maximum-scoring foundation. If coders' codings are able to consistently distinguish between moral foundations, then the final matrix will have high values on the diagonal and low values off the diagonal.

Results

Inter-coder agreement - study 5 (student coders)

To compare foundation-assignment techniques, this procedure was run two separate times, once for single-foundation coders and again for multi-foundation coders. This data is summarized in Tables 7a and 7b below.

As expected, values are highest on the diagonal and exceed a naive baseline proportion of 0.2 for the within-foundation comparison. Furthermore, it seems that the multi-foundation group does a slightly better job in distinguishing between most foundations.

In order to evaluate whether these results are likely to have occurred by chance, we developed a simulated coding system to provide random highlights. The "robocoder" simulation was built such that the number of highlights per article and the number of words per highlight match the empirical distributions from our human coders. However, unlike our human coders, "robocoders" are naive to the semantic content of the text. Instead, each simulated highlight begins at a randomly selected word in the article and is associated with a randomly selected moral foundation. The result is a set of simulated highlights that match the formal elements of our empirical data (highlights per article and words per highlight) but should not distinguish moral foundations.

The "robocoder" procedure was used to generate 100 simulated datasets, each containing approximately the same number of highlights as the empirical sample, which were analyzed with the same procedure described above. The mean and standard deviation of the simulated results were used to standardize the values from Tables 7a and 7b. These standardized scores (z-values) are

Table 7a. Foundation-score proportions for the single-foundation coders in study 5. Columns are the assigned foundations; values are rounded.

Foundation	Authority	Care	Fairness	Loyalty	Sanctity
Authority	0.308	0.132	0.153	0.151	0.143
Care	0.130	0.285	0.195	0.202	0.222
Fairness	0.223	0.231	0.302	0.236	0.185
Loyalty	0.179	0.195	0.191	0.277	0.174
Sanctity	0.159	0.158	0.160	0.136	0.276

Table 7b. Foundation-score proportions for the multi-foundation coders in study 5. Columns are the assigned foundations; values are rounded.

Foundation	Authority	Care	Fairness	Loyalty	Sanctity
Authority	0.308	0.109	0.156	0.171	0.124
Care	0.129	0.317	0.169	0.190	0.235
Fairness	0.229	0.202	0.353	0.207	0.230
Loyalty	0.219	0.168	0.181	0.285	0.180
Sanctity	0.116	0.204	0.141	0.146	0.231

Table 8a. Z-scores for foundation-score proportions, single-foundation coders, study 5. Standardized based on a simulated random baseline. columns are the assigned foundations; values are rounded.

Foundation	Authority	Care	Fairness	Loyalty	Sanctity
Authority	7.10	−4.48	−3.11	−3.26	−3.73
Care	−4.58	5.57	−0.36	0.11	1.45
Fairness	1.50	2.01	6.73	2.34	−0.99
Loyalty	−1.36	−0.34	−0.61	5.04	−1.74
Sanctity	−2.67	−2.76	−2.65	−4.24	5.01

Table 8b. Z-scores for foundation-score proportions, multi-foundation coders, study 5. Standardized based on a simulated random baseline. columns are the assigned foundations; values are rounded.

Foundation	Authority	Care	Fairness	Loyalty	Sanctity
Authority	7.08	−5.96	−2.91	−1.88	−4.97
Care	−4.68	7.70	−2.03	−0.65	2.28
Fairness	1.89	0.12	10.09	0.47	1.97
Loyalty	1.25	−2.11	−1.26	5.61	−1.35
Sanctity	−5.53	0.25	−3.90	−3.55	2.07

presented in Tables 8a and 8b. The strong positive z-scores along the diagonal indicate that the mean pairwise similarity of highlights within each moral foundation are significantly higher than would be expected if highlights were made at random (all z's > 1.65, $p < 0.05$). Conversely, strongly negative z-scores indicate mean pairwise similarities that are significantly lower than would be expected if highlights were made at random, while scores close to zero indicate similarity that is roughly equivalent to what would be expected from a sample of random highlights. For instance, Table 8a shows that highlights from single-foundation coders assigned to authority are significantly similar to each other ($z = 7.10$, $p < 0.0001$), and significantly dissimilar from care coders' highlights ($z = -4.58$, $p < 0.0001$), when compared to the baseline similarity level of random highlights.

Inter-coder agreement - study 6 (general U.S. population coders)

Our results in study 5 were largely replicated in our sample of coders from the general U.S. population in study/coder group 6. We applied the same analytical procedure described for study 5 above; results, which exhibit the same general pattern as study 5, are summarized in Tables 9 and 10. Note that the primary motivation for study 6 was to collect data across a wide variety of articles, so each article was coded by at most 15 coders. Consequently, the raw data presented in Table 9

Table 9. Foundation-score proportions for study 6. Columns are the assigned foundation; rows are the maximally similar foundation; values are rounded.

Foundation	Authority	Care	Fairness	Loyalty	Sanctity
Authority	0.241	0.151	0.182	0.192	0.165
Care	0.165	0.251	0.195	0.177	0.203
Fairness	0.180	0.181	0.236	0.180	0.163
Loyalty	0.200	0.165	0.171	0.222	0.161
Sanctity	0.214	0.252	0.216	0.229	0.307

Table 10. Z-scores for foundation-score proportions, study 6. Standardized based on a simulated random baseline. columns are the assigned foundation; rows are the maximally-similar foundation; values are rounded.

Foundation	Authority	Care	Fairness	Loyalty	Sanctity
Authority	6.97	−5.14	−1.01	0.47	−2.91
Care	−2.55	6.66	0.86	−1.00	1.89
Fairness	−0.89	−0.95	5.24	−0.85	−2.89
Loyalty	1.30	−2.84	−2.01	3.27	−3.34
Sanctity	−4.87	0.38	−3.89	−2.91	6.34

must be interpreted carefully and the simulation-standardized results in Table 10 should be preferred. This is most noticeable in the inflated similarities for the sanctity foundation seen in Table 9. That trend is apparent in both the simulated and empirical data, suggesting it is an artifact of the analytical procedure. The simulation therefore naturally accounts for this inflation, since it applies an identical analysis procedure on equally sparse but randomly generated highlights, leading to z-values for sanctity in Table 10 which are relatively low compared to the raw proportions reported in Table 9.

Discussion

The results in our revised coding task demonstrate that our highlighting procedure greatly outperforms a random baseline in both a homogenous student group and more heterogeneous general population group of human coders. Furthermore, it seems that the multi-foundation coders are generally better able to distinguish between foundations compared to the single-foundation coders, although these differences are relatively small. We interpret these findings and their replication in a large independent group of human coders as good evidence that a highlighting procedure for moral intuition extraction from text does indeed produce consistent, non-random results while better accounting for the inherent latent and subjective nature of moral intuitions.

Overall discussion, limitations, and outlook

In our content analyses we found that traditional content-analytical approaches lead to moral intuition extraction from text narratives with highly variable but generally low reliabilities which can be predicted by both text and coder characteristics. We also found that this variation is largely unaffected by coder selection and coder training. In our section "Myths of Trained Human Codings?" above, we discuss the divide between current practices in traditional content analyses and evidence that refutes fundamental assumptions of trained human codings, which provided a theoretical basis for our reformed content analytical approach in studies 5 and 6. We understand the following *Myths of Human Annotations* (Aroyo & Welty, 2015) as especially noteworthy: the notion that there is one correct interpretation and coding of every coding unit; that disagreement of coders is inherently undesired; that coder training reduces coder disagreement; and that expert coders with conceptual knowledge of the coding categories provide more reliable and valid data. We interpret our findings as further evidence against these myths which seem especially prevalent in content analyses that focus on the extraction of latent information from text. Moral foundations, as represented in text, can be considered as latent information because human coders' perception and interpretation of moral information crucially depends on the salience of coders' individual moral intuitions. Furthermore, if moral intuitions follow largely a fast, spontaneous, subconscious cognitive process, then it is not surprising that deliberations (i.e., coder trainings) are mostly ineffective.

However, this does not necessarily mean that in traditional content-analytical approaches we should generally see much lower inter-coder reliabilities than reported in the literature. We believe that due to the typical setup of content analytical studies in communication research, in which coders are either part of the research team (frequently including the investigators as expert coders; see, e.g., Grizzard et al., 2016) or at least are able to communicate among each other during coder trainings and even during the actual coding to "clarify confusion" (see, e.g., Goranson, Ritter, Waytz, Norton, & Gray, 2017, a study with serious implications), those coders inadvertently adapt to each other's coding and potentially outcome expectations. This may be especially true when traditional content analysts report

> "spending months in training sessions with coders, during which time they refined categories, altered instructions, and revised data sheets until the coders felt comfortable with what was expected of them and the analysts

were convinced they were getting the data they needed. It is typical for analysts to perform reliability tests during the development of coding instructions until the reliability requirement is met as well" (Krippendorff 20, p. 130).

As communication science often aims for an understanding of how a broader, more diverse public, and not extensively trained human coders respond to media messages, a crowdsourcing content analytical approach may actually reflect a more ecologically valid procedure for the assessment of latent constructs embedded in media content (Lind et al., 2017).

The real issue here is then: Does the common logic that validity never trumps reliability still apply under these circumstances? (Potter & Levine-Donnerstein, 1999). Could it be that reliability in traditional moral foundation extraction procedures is inflated to the detriment of validity? These are difficult questions to address, as a thorough answer would require meta-analysis of a large number of published studies which employ diverse methods and multiple (theoretically) predicted outcomes in statistical models. Unfortunately, the field of MFT and MIME research is not developed enough yet to warrant such an investigation. Nevertheless, in our research we deliberately chose to develop MoNA as an online platform which standardizes and manages both coder training and the coding task itself. This decision made truly independent trainings and codings possible, which we believe is a major reason for the substantially lower reliabilities we have observed in our analyses compared to previous studies.

It is possible, of course, that compared to previous research, all 1,028 coders who were involved in our six content analyses and completed the task, from small, highly-trained, highly-involved groups of 3 coders, to a large, less-trained, less-involved group of 557 coders from the general U.S. population, were just poorly trained and produced by and large random codings. This is unlikely, however, for two main reasons: (1) If a generally inferior coding procedure is indeed responsible for the findings, then we should not be able to find coder groups with systematically higher reliabilities in our reliability prediction analyses. We did find, however, groups of coders with high inter-coder reliabilities when coders align in moral intuition salience and other characteristics. (2) Our research team has developed and tested numerous iterations of coder trainings and coding procedures with care and over a period of three years. In addition, at least five of the authors (RW, MM, RH, LH, and RT) have extensive experience in MFT and MIME related research and are well versed in the development of coder trainings. There is no plausible explanation why a generally inferior coding procedure has found its way into all six content analyses presented here but not into previous content analyses.

Possibly our most important finding for future MFT and MIME research, and perhaps for the extraction of latent content in general, is that a simplified, intuitive coding procedure using a large heterogeneous crowd of mildly trained coders leads to acceptable inter-coder agreement. Considering the increasing availability of crowdsourcing platforms such as Mechanical Turk (https://www.mturk.com), Prolific Academic (https://www.prolific.ac), and CrowdFlower (https://www.crowdflower.com), as well as intensifying research that studies the weighting and selection of high-quality coders in crowdsourcing tasks (e.g., Raykar & Yu, 2012; Sheng et al., 2008), we suggest a crowd truth approach in combination with computational methods for text preparation and selection, entity extraction, and reliability tests as presented in this article as a general and promising solution for future moral intuition extractions from text. This conclusion confirms and specifies recent findings in studies testing the usability of crowdsourcing for coding latent constructs in political texts (Benoit et al., 2016; Lind et al., 2017).

Limitations

As in all research, the studies reported in this manuscript are not without their limitations. A major limitation of our studies is that our content analyses presented here only include non-fictional, news narratives as text material. In line with early theorizing within moral foundation theory (Graham et al., 2009), we believe that analyzing news narratives with respect to moral information can be considered as "worst-case-scenario", because news narratives' primary goal is to deliver unbiased information rather than produce a dramatic narrative structure. It is plausible that moral intuition extraction procedures that use fictional, dramatic narratives, which are more likely to maximize the prevalence of moral information and moral conflict (e.g., Booker, 2004), do not suffer from the same limitations. In this sense, we believe that our findings represent a lower baseline of reliabilities and coder agreement for moral foundation extraction.

Outlook

The freely available, open source MoNA platform (http://mnl.ucsb.edu) which manages text selection, coder training, reliability tests, and moral intuition extraction based on a highlighting task, can be easily combined with crowdsourcing platforms. Furthermore, this new procedure has the additional benefit that the text highlight data can be processed with natural language processing algorithms and with the goal of creating new, crowd-sourced Moral Foundation Dictionaries (MFDs; i.e., extensions of Graham & Haidt, 2012) which are "less subject to the bias and oversight from dictionaries made by a small number of experts" (Schwartz & Unger, 2015, p. 81), but are instead based on methodical content analyses, are empirically tested, and can subsequently be used to improve the analysis of moral information in large amounts of text data (e.g. global online news, see http://gdeltproject.org). A promising approach for extending MFDs is to identify words and phrases that are highly discriminative of particular MFT categories based on our text highlights in content analyses 5 and 6. For instance, pointwise mutual information (PMI) is a generalized measure of correlation that is often used in natural language processing applications to identify word collocations and automatically extract dictionaries from textual documents (Manning & Schuetz, 1999). The creation of the extended MFD-E is currently underway.

Notes

1. The terms "moral foundations" and "moral intuitions" are sometimes used interchangeably in the literature. We use the term "foundations" to refer to the conceptual dimensions of MFT, i.e., the *universal dimensions* that categorize moral judgments. We use the term "intuitions" to refer to the *experiential, subjective processes* of moral judgment.
2. We only used multi-foundation coders in coder group six.

Acknowledgments

This research would not have been possible with the help of our research assistants at the University of California Santa Barbara (Mitch Grimes, Brandon Mims, Rachel Glikes, Douglas Keith, Sierra Scott, Cathy Chen, and Dane Asto) and at Michigan State University (Brandon Walling, Kathryn Hollemans, Erica Lydey, Maryssa Mitchell, Anna Young, Erika Lentz, Ellen Grimes, Kristin Barndt, Tyler Lawrence, Allison Aigner, Riley Hoffman, Elizabeth Paulson, Sierra Richards, Savannah Jenuwine, Pooja Dandamundi, Will Marchetti, and Abagail Johnson).

Funding

Contract grant sponsors: US Army Research Laboratory (to R.W.), contract grant number: W911NF-15-2-0115.

ORCID

René Weber http://orcid.org/0000-0002-8247-7341
Richard Huskey http://orcid.org/0000-0002-4559-2439
Lindsay Hahn http://orcid.org/0000-0002-0039-9782

References

Ammerman, N. T. (1991). North American fundamentalism. In M. E. Marty, & R. S. Appleby (Eds.), *Fundamentalisms observed* (pp. 1–65). Chicago, IL: University of Chicago.
Armstrong, K. (2000). *The battle for God: Fundamentalism in Judaism, Christianity, and Islam*. New York, NY: Knopf.

Aroyo, L., & Welty, C. (2015). Truth is a lie: Crowd truth and the seven myths of human annotation. *AI Magazine, 36* (1), 15–24. doi:10.1609/aimag.v36i1.2564

Benoit, K., Conway, D., Lauderdale, B. E., Laver, M., & Mikhaylov, S. (2016). Crowd-sourced text analysis: Reproducible and agile production of political data. *American Political Science Review, 110*(2), 278–295. doi:10.1017/S0003055416000058

Berelson, B. R. (1952). *Content analysis in communication research.* New York: Free Press.

Bird, S., Loper, E., & Klein, E. (2009). *Natural language processing with python.* Sebastopol, CA: O'Reilly.

Booker, C. (2004). *The seven basic plots.* New York: Continuum.

Bowman, N. D., Lewis, R. J., & Tamborini, R. (2014). The morality of May 2, 2011: A content analysis of US headlines regarding the death of Osama bin Laden. *Mass Communication and Society, 17,* 639–664. doi:10.1080/15205436.2013.822518

Burscher, B., Odijk, D., Vliegenthart, R., De Rijke, M., & De Vreese, C. H. (2014). Teaching the computer to code frames in news: Comparing two supervised machine learning approaches to frame analysis. *Communication Methods and Measures, 8*(3), 190–206. doi:10.1080/19312458.2014.937527

Clifford, S., Iyengar, V., Cabeza, R., & Sinnott-Armstrong, W. (2015). Moral foundations vignettes: A standardized stimulus database of scenarios based on moral foundations theory. *Behavior Research Methods, 47*(4), 1178–1198. doi:10.3758/s13428-014-0551-2

Clifford, S., & Jerit, J. (2013). How words do the work of politics: Moral foundations theory and the debate over stem cell research. *The Journal of Politics, 75,* 659–671. doi:10.1017/S0022381613000492

Cohen, J. (1968). Weighted kappa: Nominal scale agreement with provision for scaled disagreement or partial credit. *Psychological Bulletin, 70*(4), 213–220. doi:10.1037/h0026256

Delli Carpini, M. X., & Keeter, S. (1993). Measuring political knowledge: Putting first things first. *American Journal of Political Science, 37*(4), 1179–1206. doi:10.2307/2111549

Feinberg, M., & Willer, R. (2013). The moral roots of environmental attitudes. *Psychological Science, 24*(1), 56–62. doi:10.1177/0956797612449177

Feinberg, M., & Willer, R. (2015). From gulf to bridge: When do moral arguments facilitate political influence. *Personality and Social Psychology Bulletin, 41*(12), 1665–1681.

Finkel, J. R., Grenager, T., & Manning, C. (2005). Incorporating non-local information into information extraction systems by Gibbs sampling. *Proceedings of the 43nd Annual Meeting of the Association for Computational Linguistics (ACL 2005),* 363–370.

Goranson, A., Ritter, R. S., Waytz, A., Norton, M. I., & Gray, K. (2017). Dying is unexpectedly positive. *Psychological Science,* 1–12. doi:10.1177/0956797617701186

Graham, J., & Haidt, J. (2012). The moral foundations dictionary. Retrieved from http://moralfoundations.org/othermaterials

Graham, J., Haidt, J., Koleva, S., Motyl, M., Iyer, R., Wojcik, S., & Ditto, P. H. (2012). Moral foundations theory: The pragmatic validity of moral pluralism. *Advances in Experimental Social Psychology, 47,* 55–130.

Graham, J., Haidt, J., & Nosek, B. A. (2009). Liberals and conservatives rely on different sets of moral foundations. *Journal of Personality and Social Psychology, 96,* 1029–1046. doi:10.1037/a0015141

Grizzard, M., Shaw, A. Z., Dolan, E. A., Anderson, K. A., Hahn, L., & Prabhu, S. (2016). Does repeated exposure to popular media strengthen moral intuitions?: Exploratory evidence regarding consistent and conflicted moral content. *Media Psychology,* 1–27. doi:10.1080/15213269.2016.1227266

Hahn, L., Tamborini, R., Prabhu, S., Klebig, B., Grall, C., & Pei, D. (2017). The importance of altruistic versus egoistic motivations: A content analysis of conflicted motivations in children's television programming. *Communication Reports,* 1–13. doi:10.1080/08934215.2016.1251602

Haidt, J., & Graham, J. (2007). When morality opposes justice: Conservatives have moral intuitions that liberals may not recognize. *Social Justice Research, 20*(1), 98–116. doi:10.1007/s11211-007-0034-z

Haidt, J., & Joseph, C. (2007). The moral mind: How five sets of innate intuitions guide the development of many culture-specific virtues, and perhaps even modules. In P. Carruthers, S. Laurence, & S. Stich (Eds.), *The innate mind* (Vol. 3, pp. 367–391). New York: Oxford University Press.

Hofmann, W., Wisneski, D. C., Brandt, M. J., & Skitka, L. J. (2014). Morality in everyday life. *Science, 345,* 1340–1343. doi:10.1126/science.1251560

Holsti, O. R. (1969). *Content analysis for the social sciences and humanities.* Reading, MA: Addison-Wesley.

Hsueh, P., Melville, P., & Sindhwani, V. (2009). *Data quality from crowdsourcing: A study of annotation selection criteria.* Proceedings of the NAACL HLT Workshop on Active Learning for Natural Language Processing (pp. 27–35), Boulder, CO: Association for Computational Linguistics.

Kaplan, A. (1964). *The conduct of inquiry. Methodology for behavioral science.* San Francisco, CA: Chandler Publishing Company.

Kim, J. S., Greene, M. J., Zlateski, A., Lee, K., Richardson, M., Turaga, S. C., ... Seung, H. S. (2014). Space-time wiring specificity supports direction selectivity in the retina. *Nature, 509*(7500), 331–336. doi:10.1038/nature13240

Krippendorff, K. (2013). *Content analysis. An introduction to its methodology.* Thousand Oaks, CA: Sage.

Lazer, D., Pentland, A. S., Adamic, L., Aral, S., Barabasi, A. L., Brewer, D., ... Jebara, T. (2009). Life in the network: The coming age of computational social science. *Science, 323*(5915), 721–723. doi:10.1126/science.1167742

Leetaru, K., & Schrodt, P. A, (2013). GDELT: Global Data on Events, Location and Tone, 1979-2012. Paper presented at the International Studies Association Meeting, San Francisco. CA, April 2013. Retrieved from http://data.gdeltproject.org/documentation/ISA.2013.GDELT.pdf

Leidner, B., & Castano, E. (2012). Morality shifting in the context of intergroup violence. *European Journal of Social Psychology, 42*(1), 82-91. doi:10.1002/ejsp.v42.1

Leskovec, J., Rajaraman, A., & Ullman, J. D. (2014). *Mining of Massive Datasets*. Cambridge, UK: Cambridge University Press.

Lewis, R. J., Grizzard, M., Mangus, J. M., Rashidian, P., & Weber, R. (2016). Moral clarity in narratives elicits greater cooperation than moral ambiguity. *Media Psychology*, 1-24. doi:10.1080/15213269.2016.1212714

Lewis, R. J., & Mitchell, N. (2014). Egoism versus altruism in television content for young audiences. *Mass Communication and Society, 17*, 597-613. doi:10.1080/15205436.2013.816747

Lind, F., Gruber, M., & Boomgaarden, H. G. (2017). Content analysis by the crowd. Assessing the usability of crowdsourcing for coding latent constructs. *Communication Methods and Measures, 11*(3), 191-209. doi:10.1080/19312458.2017.1317338

Manning, C. D., & Schuetze, H. (1999). Collocations. In *Foundations of statistical natural language processing* (pp. 178-183). Cambridge, MA: MIT Press.

Mastro, D., Enriquez, M., Bowman, N. D., Prabhu, S., & Tamborini, R. (2012). Morality subcultures and media production: How Hollywood minds the morals of its audience. In R. Tamborini (Ed), *Media and the moral mind* (pp. 75-92). London, UK: Routledge.

McAdams, D. P., Albaugh, M., Farber, E., Daniels, J., Logan, R. L., & Olson, B. (2008). Family metaphors and moral intuitions: How conservatives and liberals narrate their lives. *Journal of Personality and Social Psychology, 95*(4), 978-990. doi:10.1037/a0012650

Moscovici, S. (1985). Innovation and minority influence. In S. Moscovici, G. Mugny, & E. Van Avermaet (Eds.), *Perspectives on minority influence* (pp. 9-51). Cambridge, UK: Cambridge University Press.

Necka, E. A., Cacioppo, S., Norman, G. J., & Cacioppo, J. T. (2016). Measuring the prevalence of problematic respondent behaviors among MTurk, campus, and community participants. *PloS One, 11*(6), 1-19. doi:10.1371/journal.pone.0157732

Porter, M. F. (1980). An algorithm for suffix stripping. *Program, 14*(3), 130-137. doi:10.1108/eb046814

Potter, W. J., & Levine-Donnerstein, D. (1999). Rethinking validity and reliability in content analysis. *Journal of Applied Communication Research, 27*(3), 258-284. doi:10.1080/00909889909365539

Raykar, V. C., & Yu, S. (2012). Eliminating spammers and ranking annotators for crowdsourced labeling tasks. *Journal of Machine Learning Research, 13*, 491-518.

Riffe, D., Lacy, S., & Fico, F. (2005). *Analyzing media messages: Using quantitative content analysis in research*. Mahwah, NJ: Lawrence Erlbaum.

Sagi, E., & Dehghani, M. (2014). Measuring moral rhetoric in text. *Social Science Computer Review, 32*(2), 132-144. doi:10.1177/0894439313506837

Schwartz, H. A., & Ungar, L. H. (2015). Data-driven content analysis of social media: A systematic overview of automated methods. *The ANNALS of the American Academy of Political and Social Science, 659*(1), 78-94. doi:10.1177/0002716215569197

Sheng, V. S., Provost, F., & Ipeirotis, P. H. (2008). *Get another label? Improving data quality and data mining using multiple, noisy labelers*. Proceedings of the 14th ACM SIGKDD International Conference on Knowledge Discovery and Data Mining (pp. 614-622), New York, NY: Association for Computing Machinery.

Smith, K. B., Oxley, D. R., Hibbing, M. V., Alford, J. R., & Hibbing, J. R. (2011). Linking genetics and political attitudes: Reconceptualizing political ideology. *Political Psychology, 32*(3), 369-397. doi:10.1111/pops.2011.32.issue-3

Tamborini, R. (2013). Model of intuitive morality and exemplars. In R. Tamborini (Ed.), *Media and the moral mind* (pp. 43-74). London, UK: Routledge.

Tamborini, R., Hahn, L., Prabhu, S., Klebig, B., & Grall, C. (2017). The representation of altruistic and egoistic motivations in children's television programming. *Communication Research Reports, 34*(1), 58-67. doi:10.1080/08824096.2016.1227312

Tamborini, R., Lewis, R. J., Prabhu, S., Grizzard, M., Hahn, L., & Wang, L. (2016). Media's influence on the accessibility of altruistic and egoistic motivations. *Communication Research Reports, 33*(3), 177-187. doi:10.1080/08824096.2016.1186627

Tamborini, R., Prabhu, S., Lewis, R. L., Grizzard, M., & Eden, A. (2016). The influence of media exposure on the accessibility of moral intuitions. *Journal of Media Psychology*, 1-12. doi:10.1027/1864-1105/a000183

Tamborini, R., Weber, R., Eden, A., Bowman, N. D., & Grizzard, M. (2010). Repeated exposure to daytime soap opera and shifts in moral judgment toward social convention. *Journal of Broadcasting & Electronic Media, 54*(4), 621-640. doi:10.1080/08838151.2010.519806

Vermeer, A. (2000). Coming to grips with lexical richness in spontaneous speech data. *Language Testing, 17*(1), 65-83. doi:10.1177/026553220001700103

Vlieger, E., & Leydesdorff, L. (2011). Content analysis and the measurement of meaning: The visualization of frames in collections of messages. *The Public Journal of Semiotics, 3*(1), 28-50.

🔓 OPEN ACCESS

More than Bags of Words: Sentiment Analysis with Word Embeddings

Elena Rudkowsky ⓘ, Martin Haselmayer ⓘ, Matthias Wastian, Marcelo Jenny ⓘ, Štefan Emrich, and Michael Sedlmair

ABSTRACT
Moving beyond the dominant bag-of-words approach to sentiment analysis we introduce an alternative procedure based on distributed word embeddings. The strength of word embeddings is the ability to capture similarities in word meaning. We use word embeddings as part of a supervised machine learning procedure which estimates levels of negativity in parliamentary speeches. The procedure's accuracy is evaluated with crowdcoded training sentences; its external validity through a study of patterns of negativity in Austrian parliamentary speeches. The results show the potential of the word embeddings approach for sentiment analysis in the social sciences.

Introduction

Sentiment analysis has become a major area of interest in communication research. Recent applications include analyses of media tone (Van Atteveldt, Kleinnijenhuis et al., 2008a; Haselmayer & Jenny, 2017; Hopkins & King, 2010; Soroka & McAdams, 2015; Soroka, Young, & Balmas, 2015; Young & Soroka, 2012), agenda setting (Ceron, Curini, & Iacus, 2016), framing (Burscher, Odijk, Vliegenthart, De Rijke, & De Vreese, 2014), election forecasting (Ceron, Curini, & Iacus, 2015, 2017), and candidate evaluations (Aaldering & Vliegenthart, 2016). These studies do automated text analysis with sentiment dictionaries (Aaldering & Vliegenthart, 2016; Haselmayer & Jenny, 2017; Young & Soroka, 2012) or use machine learning (Van Atteveldt, Kleinnijenhuis et al., 2008a; Burscher et al., 2014; Ceron et al., 2016; Hopkins & King, 2010) to get sentiment scores. What these studies share is a bag-of-words approach toward text data. In a nutshell, the bag-of-words representation of text treats words as independent units. Few studies attempt to include semantic or syntactic relations between words (van Atteveldt, Kleinnijenhuis et al., 2008b, 2017; Wueest et al., 2011).

The goal of this article is to move sentiment analysis in communication research forward by presenting a new approach that has become popular in natural language processing and computer science: the use of distributed word embeddings, (Al-Rfou, Perozzi, & Skiena, 2013; Le & Mikolov, 2014; Mikolov, Chen, Corrado, & Dean, 2013; Mikolov, Sutskever, Chen, Corrado, & Dean, 2013; Pennington, Socher, & Manning, 2014). Word embeddings represent (or embed) words in a continuous vector space in which words with similar meanings are mapped closer to each other. New words in application texts that were missing in training texts can still be classified through similar words (Goldberg, 2016; Mikolov et al., 2013), an advantage compared to the bag-of-words approach in which new words encountered in application texts are a nuisance.

Color versions of one or more of the figures in the article can be found online at www.tandfonline.com/hcms.

This is an Open Access article distributed under the terms of the Creative Commons Attribution-NonCommercial-NoDerivatives License (http://creativecommons.org/licenses/by-nc-nd/4.0/), which permits non-commercial re-use, distribution, and reproduction in any medium, provided the original work is properly cited, and is not altered, transformed, or built upon in any way.

We describe a procedure with word embeddings that enables us to estimate levels of negativity in parliamentary speeches and then apply it to a sample of 56,000 plenary speeches from the Austrian parliament. The procedure's accuracy is evaluated with the help of crowdcoded training sentences; its external validity by studying negativity in Austrian parliamentary speeches. The different levels of negativity that we find for speakers in different roles (minister, parliamentary party group leader, ordinary Member of Parliament) from government or opposition parties accord with common sense hypotheses about expected patterns. From these results we conclude that the word embeddings approach offers a lot of potential for sentiment analysis and, more generally, automated text analysis in the social sciences (Boumans & Trilling, 2016; Grimmer & Stewart, 2013; Lowe & Benoit, 2013; Lucas et al., 2015; Wilkerson & Casas, 2017).

Related work

Until recently, sentiment analysis in the social sciences almost exclusively relied on the *bag-of-words* approach. Mozetič, Grčar, and Smailović (2016) compare a variety of sentiment classification applications for Twitter data and find almost all of them using it. Researchers rely on existent sentiment dictionaries (Kleinnijenhuis, Schultz, Oegema, & Van Atteveldt, 2013) or create customized and context-sensitive dictionaries for their research questions (Aaldering & Vliegenthart, 2016; Haselmayer & Jenny, 2017; Young & Soroka, 2012). A third group of studies uses machine learning applications (Van Atteveldt, Kleinnijenhuis et al., 2008a; Burscher et al., 2014; Ceron et al., 2015, 2017; Hopkins & King, 2010). Some studies have reported good results for measuring sentiment at the level of articles or speeches (Hopkins & King, 2010), but the assumptions and simplifications that the bag-of-words approach entails, such as loss of grammatical structure or of context-dependent word meanings have been repeatedly pointed out (Grimmer & Stewart, 2013; Lowe & Benoit, 2013).

Semantic models offer an improvement as they take relationships between words into account, but they have been rarely used in communication research (van Atteveldt, Kleinnijenhuis et al., 2008b, 2017). This is surprising because Harris' (1954) distributional hypothesis that words occurring in the same or similar contexts tend to have similar meanings is old and well known to computational linguists. Such word context information can be fruitfully employed for sentiment analysis (e.g., Nasukawa & Yi, 2003).

Turney and Pantel (2010) provide an overview of earlier work on vector space models. The word embeddings approach gained significant attention after Mikolov and colleagues introduced a more efficient architecture for creating reusable word vector representations from large text corpora (Mikolov et al., 2013, 2013). A number of applications quickly followed (Le & Mikolov, 2014; Pennington et al., 2014; Tang et al., 2014).

Supervised sentiment analysis with word embeddings

Figure 1 presents a process pipeline of our embedding-based sentiment analysis procedure. In the upper half we see three databases: a corpus of text documents for which we want sentiment scores (labeled "application data"), a set of sentences whose sentiment scores have been established by human coders (training data), and a word embedding corpus that transforms these two data sources. The lower section depicts the steps needed to train the system and collect new sentiment scores. The depiction of processing units follow the Knowledge Discovery in Databases (KDD) framework for data mining applications (Fayyad, Piatetsky-Shapiro, & Smyth, 1996). Black arrows indicate input and output flows. Dashed arrows in light gray denote the training cycle for building a classification model from training data. Arrows in dark gray indicate the prediction phase that generates new sentiment scores for application data.

Let us look at the three data sets first. Training and application data are closely related and therefore should come from similar text sources. In principle, that does not apply for the transformation data set. Word embeddings represent word meaning based on their occurrence in a text corpus. If the text corpus is very large and diverse, the word embedding vectors will represent the

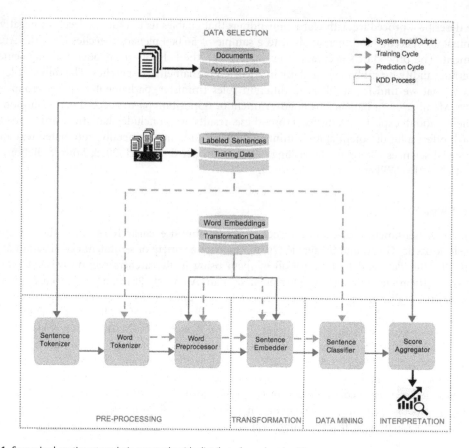

Figure 1. Supervised sentiment analysis approach with distributed word embeddings.

general (or dominant) meaning of a word, which should be useful in a variety of applications. Once the three data sets have been selected, the training cycle develops a classification model for the training data. Finding a good classification model usually requires multiple simulation runs with varying parameter settings. Evaluation of the model's accuracy with previously unseen samples from the training data follows. When it is considered satisfactory, it can be applied to new texts.

Application data: documents

The application data in Figure 1 represents the "data of interest" for which a researcher wants sentiment scores. The documents could be newspaper articles, transcribed speeches, or social media content. Our documents consist of about 56,000 German language speeches from the Austrian national parliament covering the period from 1996–2013 (Parliament Austria, 2013). The classifier unit predicts a sentiment score at the level of individual sentences. 578 MPs produced about 2.4 million sentences for which we want to obtain sentiment or, more specifically, negativity, scores aggregated to the level of individual speeches. Metadata about the documents are helpful to interpret and present the sentiment scores. In our application they include additional variables on speaker, party, and date of the speech.

Training data: labeled sentences

To train a classifier in a supervised machine learning application we need "ground truth" data. That ground truth comes from training data which should mimic the application data's vocabulary

(Haselmayer & Jenny, 2017; Young & Soroka, 2012). Asking humans to code the level of sentiment for complete parliamentary speeches appears extremely challenging. So we asked to them to code sentiment for single sentences. Sentences as coding units "tend to be efficient and reliable" (Krippendorff, 2013, p. 110).

We use training data comprising sentences from party press releases, transcripts of parliamentary speeches, and media reports (Haselmayer & Jenny, 2017). Hence, they contain very similar language.[1] Our training data consist of 20,580 sentences. Each sentence was labeled by at least ten German-speaking coders recruited from the crowdsourcing platform CrowdFlower. Codings range from not negative (0) to very negative (4) on a 5-point scale. Coders could also identify a sentence as uncodable. We cover only the neutral and negative parts of the sentiment scale. Psychological research has highlighted asymmetries between positive and negative evaluations of situations, persons, or events. People devote more attention and cognitive effort to negative information, which contributes more strongly to the overall impression (e.g., Baumeister, Bratlavsky, & Finkenauer, 2001; Rozin & Royzman, 2001).

Coders are asked to rate only the manifest content of the text.[2] A recent experimental study reports that partisan preferences of crowdcoders do not affect sentiment ratings at the aggregate level (Haselmayer, Hirsch, & Jenny, 2017). During the coding process, we monitor individual coder performance to identify cheating or spamming. We use test questions with predetermined correct answers and exclude contributors failing a 75% accuracy threshold on test questions. Recent studies demonstrate that crowdcoding political issues (Benoit, Conway, Lauderdale, Laver, & Mikhaylov, 2016) and sentiment strength of sentences produces valid results (Haselmayer & Jenny, 2017; Lind, Gruber, & Boomgaarden, 2017). To obtain a sentence score we compute the mean of all coders. This produces equal results as more complex aggregation measures according to recent crowdcoding studies (Benoit et al., 2016; Haselmayer & Jenny, 2017). We evaluate coding quality by comparing this with a "expert" mean coding by some of the authors. The Pearson correlation is 0.82 for a random sample of 200 sentences. In line with previous research, we find that a group of lay coders is able to replicate expert coding (e.g.,Benoit et al., 2016).

Transformation data: word embeddings

The third database in Figure 1, which we call transformation data, contains the word embeddings. This component is absent in bag-of-words models since they are built only from the words appearing in the training and application data. There are ready-to-use corpora with pre-trained word embeddings, for instance, Google's word2vec (Mikolov et al., 2013) or the GloVe embeddings (Pennington et al., 2014). We use a pre-trained German word embedding corpus from Polyglot (Al-Rfou et al., 2013), which is a natural language processing library for Python. These off-the-shelf embedding corpora can be used like dictionaries, but instead of translations or meanings, they return vector embeddings for the requested words. Therefore, the usage of pre-trained embeddings does not require any further computing time.

Supervised sentiment analysis tools are often trained on hundreds of thousands of training examples (Nobata, Tetreault, Thomas, Mehdad, & Chang, 2016; Wulczyn, Thain, & Dixon, 2016). Yet, gathering huge training datasets is not always possible: it is expensive, time-consuming, and thus often unaffordable. Our approach provides an affordable solution for large-scale text analysis that should be applicable to various languages and contexts. Such research may either draw on existing databases with labeled training data[3] or generate their own training data without too much effort. Our training data contain 20,580 sentences. Limited amounts of human-labeled training data lower the accuracy of the corresponding classification models. Word embeddings may increase the accuracy of classification models as they provide information (and vector representations) on words that are not or only scarcely represented in the training data based on their similarity with other words (Goldberg, 2016).

Figure 2 shows how sentiment can be reflected by word embeddings. This simplified example illustrates the mapping of sentiment to word embeddings. A distributed word embedding for the

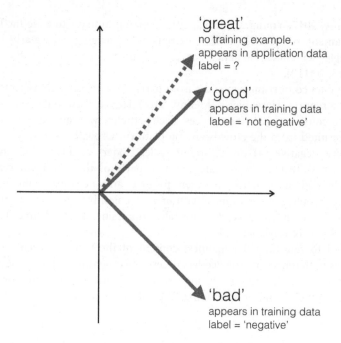

Figure 2. Illustrative example of mapping sentiment to word embedding dimensions.

word "good" reflects to some extent this word's relationship to other words—"good" is close to "great" and distant to "bad". If an embedding-based classification model is trained on sentences that contain the words "good" and "bad" it is later on able to perceive the word "great" as similar to "good" even though it has never seen that word before. In contrast, bag-of-words representations treat words as single independent units (one-hot representations). If a classifier is trained on the bag-of-words representation of the word "good", it is not able to perceive the word "great" as similar or the word "bad" as converse (unless it has been successfully trained on these words, too).

Polyglot's language-dependent word embeddings are trained on Wikipedia and represent the 100,000 most frequent words for each language. For German, those words cover 92% of the words in the German Wikipedia articles. Word coverage is significantly higher for languages using fewer morphological forms: 96% for English and 99.7% for Chinese (Al-Rfou et al., 2013). Each word embedding has 64 dimensions with each dimension being set to a floating point number. These dimensions correlate with language structure and meanings. In a well-trained embedding corpus arithmetic operations on word embeddings result in vectors that reflect underlying language patterns. A standard example to explain such relationships is that the embedding of the word "man" stands to "woman" as "king" stands to "queen". Another example is that the arithmetic vector operation on "Paris" – "France" + "Italy" results in a vector that is very close to "Rome" (Mikolov et al., 2013).

Sentence and word tokenization

The beginning of the processing pipeline in Figure 1 shows a sentence and a word tokenization component. The sentence tokenizer is necessary because our unit for training examples are sentences; therefore, we split the application data into natural sentences in the prediction phase.[4] We use the sentence tokenizer provided by Polyglot. An alternative is the Natural Language Toolkit (Loper & Bird, 2002) which also offers tokenizers at the level of sentences and words. We continue with splitting the sentences of training and application data further into single words or "tokens" using the word tokenizer of the Polyglot library. We keep punctuation since Polyglot's word embedding corpus comprises embeddings for punctuation as well. For sentiment analysis, exclamation or question marks can be useful for determining the negativity of a sentence.

Preprocessing

Preprocessing has tremendous consequences for the quality of automated text analysis. Recent studies demonstrate how preprocessing decisions impact on sentiment analysis (Haselmayer & Jenny, 2017) or dimensional scaling (Greene, Ceron, Schumacher, & Fazekas, 2016) results. Yet, the amount of necessary preprocessing also depends on the quality of the raw data. This is especially important here as the creation of sentence embeddings (see below) depends heavily on the retrieval of an embedding for each word in a sentence. Fewer matching word embeddings per sentence decrease the accuracy of sentiment prediction. As mentioned above, the Polyglot word embeddings cover the 100,000 most frequent words of Wikipedia. As the German language contains a lot of compound words, we have to deal with numerous context-specific compounds in our training data that are not covered by those 100,000 embeddings. Our training data further include entire sentences in uppercase, incorrectly hyphenated words (due to end-of-line hyphens) or "artificial" compound words (due to missing spaces). Using texts from similar, but not exactly the same sources introduces additional noise (Kandel et al., 2011).

In order to represent as many words per sentence as possible (by their corresponding word embedding), we apply various preprocessing techniques to words that have no match in the embedding corpus. We use lemmatization and stemming to find words that are not contained in their conjugated form. We lowercase or capitalize words to overcome the uppercase issue. We check multiple substring combinations to retrieve embeddings for substrings. We replace numbers by hashes (2018 = ####) to match Polyglot's fashion of representation of digits. These preprocessing steps reduce the number of unique words (i.e. strings separated from blanks) from roughly 40,000 to about 30,000 and increase prediction accuracy by 3 percentage points.

Sentence embedding

The sentence embedding unit of our approach averages all retrieved word embeddings per sentence by calculating the mean vector. This is a basic approach for building distributed sentence embeddings which does not take the ordering of words into account. We use this simple averaging approach as our main motivation is to introduce word embeddings for sentiment analysis to social scientists in general. Recent applications, such as the doc2vec approach, combine word and document embeddings for sentiment classification (Le & Mikolov, 2014) or generate "sentiment-specific" word embeddings (Tang et al., 2014).

Classification

After all sentences have been transformed into their corresponding embeddings a classification model is applied to determine their sentiment. Comparing several sentiment analysis applications Mozetič et al. (2016) state that: "A wide range of machine learning algorithms is used, and apparently there is no consensus on which one to choose for the best performance. Different studies use different datasets, focus on different use cases, and use incompatible evaluation measures" (Mozetič et al., 2016, p. 1). Moraes, Valiati, and Neto (2013) compare support vector machines and artificial neural networks for document classification tasks in various settings. Their experiments indicate that artificial neural networks produce superior results in many applications. Thus, we apply a neural network classifier using the Keras Python library (Chollet, 2015).

We use 10% of the training data as test data that the model does not see during the training cycle (illustrated by dashed arrows in light gray in Figure 1) to estimate an error rate for the application data after choosing the final model. To avoid any bias we generate ten random test samples. We build our model with the remaining training data and subsequently calculate the average accuracy for the previously unseen samples. The average accuracy is our estimate of the model's performance on unlabeled new data.

To identify the best model we test a variety of parameter settings. To compare their performance, we split off another 10% of the remaining 90% training data as our validation data. We use the categorical cross-entropy function for our model and a 3-dimensional output layer with a softmax activation function which creates three different categorical sentiment output labels. These are typical choices for classification problems which remain stable during the hyperparameter tuning. The hyperparameter tuning of the number of neurons on the first layer (64, 128), the number of hidden layers (1, 2), the number of neurons of the hidden layers (16, 32, 48), the dropout rates on the input or hidden layers (0, 0.1, 0.2, 0.3, 0.4), the optimizer used (stochastic gradient descent, Adam), and the learning rate (0.01, 0.001) relies on the grid search technique. The first layer of the best performing neural network has 64 neurons, a rectifier activation function and a dropout rate of 30%. This should prevent overfitting on the training data, which typically results in low accuracy on the unseen test data. Our final model applies a 32-dimensional second layer with the rectifier activation function and uses the Adam optimizer (Kingma & Ba, 2014).

Aggregation

The final aggregation and visualization component of the pipeline in Figure 1 is important to get insights from the calculated sentiment scores. Our approach produces sentiment scores at the sentence level. We further aggregate these scores to the level of speeches by calculating the mean sentiment score. We then analyze parliamentary debates using additional information on speakers, their party affiliation, the government status, or the date and the legislative period of a speech. We visualize differences between these categories using Tableau (Stolte, Tang, & Hanrahan, 2002) and present results on patterns of negativity in the "Case Study" section.

Evaluation

We present a two-fold evaluation of our approach. First, we measure the accuracy of our model on previously unseen training examples and compare its accuracy with a bag-of-words approach. Second, we test its external validity with several hypotheses on expected patterns of negativity in parliamentary speeches in the Austrian parliament.

Accuracy measures

Figure 3 shows the distribution of mean codings of the 20,580 sentences in our training data set. Sentences were coded on a scale ranging from 0 (not negative) to 4 (very negative). The color-coded sections indicate their allocation to three classes of negativity (not/slightly negative vs. negative vs. very negative).

Imbalanced class distributions of training examples can lead to biased and inaccurate results. To balance our training data we weight the sentence embeddings according to their class frequency during the training phase. With this setting we achieve an average accuracy of 58% on our 3 classes on previously unseen test data. The results are validated through multiple random sampling. A bag-of-words alternative with TF-IDF (Salton & McGill, 1986) and a multinomial Naive Bayes classifier achieved an average accuracy slightly below 55% on the same data. We chose a multinomial Naive Bayes classifier for the bag-of-words implementation because it performed better than a neural network classifier for our application (Raschka, 2014). Neural network toolkits typically perform less well with very high-dimensional, sparse vectors, such as bag-of-words representations, where every feature has its own dimension (Goldberg, 2016).

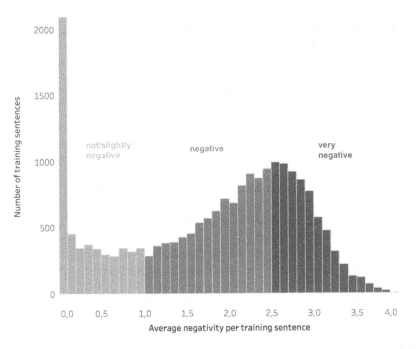

Figure 3. Negativity distribution of 20,600 training sentences ranging from 0 (not negative) to 4 (very negative), divided into three classes: not/slightly negative, negative and very negative.

A detailed evaluation comparison between the bag of words and the distributed words embeddings approach is shown in Tables 1 and 2. It can be easily seen that the word embeddings approach outperforms the bag of words approach with regard to the not/slightly negative, where the F1 score is substantially higher. For the very negative class, both approaches attain similar levels of accuracy. Regarding the negative class, the bag of words approach shows a substantially higher precision and a slightly lower recall due to the tendency of the bag of words approach to predict the middle class (negative). We suggest to interpret this evaluation also in a task-dependent way: for example, the tables tell us that if the bag of words model predicts a sentence to be not or slightly negative, we can trust this quite a bit (due to the relatively high recall). Yet, it misses a lot of correct not/slightly negative sentences (due to its low precision). The word embeddings model returns a lot more sentences classified as not/slightly negative, but due to its lower precision we cannot put as much trust in these decisions as in those made by the bag of words model. If, for example, it would be important to us to get all the not/slightly negative sentences and we wouldn't mind checking the suggested sentences manually, the word embeddings model would definitely be the model to go with. If we are not interested in getting all the not/slightly negative sentences, e.g.,

Table 1. Precision, recall, and F1 score for the bag of words approach.

	Actual	Predicted	Precision	Recall	F1 Score
not/slightly negative	524.3	205.6	0.33	0.83	0.47
negative	805.7	1188.7	0.71	0.48	0.57
very negative	730	665.7	0.53	0.58	0.56

Table 2. Precision, recall, and F1 score for the Word Embeddings approach.

	Actual	Predicted	Precision	Recall	F1 Score
not/slightly negative	522.4	575	0.65	0.59	0.61
negative	799.2	771.6	0.52	0.53	0.53
very negative	739.4	714.4	0.55	0.57	0.56

because we only want to present some examples, and we don't have a lot of time for checking the model output, the bag of words model could be superior. In fact, the different prediction behaviour of the two models could lead to a very promising model ensemble which is the focus of future work.

Socher et al. (2013) report benchmarks for binary and multiple classification tasks that put the performance of our approach into a broader perspective. In general, bag-of-words classifiers of longer documents work quite well even if they only rely on a few strong sentiment words. Accuracy for binary (positive vs. negative) sentiment classification at the sentence-level has remained quite stable at about 80% in recent years. For more difficult tasks, such as multiclass cases including a neutral category, accuracy is often below 60% (Socher et al., 2013, p. 3, Wang et al., 2012). Our word embedding approach is close to 60% accuracy for three classes. Yet, our implementation deals with degrees of negativity: not/slightly negative vs. negative vs. very negative. These classes are much harder to separate than a change of polarity from positive to neutral and from neutral to negative (which Socher et al., 2013 refer to as "multiclass"). In addition, we reach this level of accuracy analyzing German texts, which is more challenging than dealing with English language due to language complexity and the availability of tools for natural language processing (Haselmayer & Jenny, 2017). This also applies to the availability of domain-specific word embeddings. Hence, we would expect an increase in accuracy if we could have used word vectors for political communication, rather than relying on the rather general Polyglot corpus.

Case study: a validation of the procedure with patterns of negativity in Austrian parliamentary speeches

Sentiment analysis has increasingly turned to parliamentary debates as substantively interesting objects of study (e.g., Rheault, Beelen, Cochrane, & Hirst, 2016; Slapin & Proksch, 2014). A key component of what political opposition parties and their members do in parliaments of democratic systems is criticizing the government parties' policy ideas and the government ministers' work. Ministers transform policy ideas into bills introduced to parliament and they are responsible for their subsequent implementation. Members of government parties provide rhetorical support for the government's bills in parliamentary debates and the crucial votes for their passage. In this role they will criticize policy proposals of the opposition, but more often they will play defense for the government in a supporting role: "in parliamentary democracies the governing parliamentary party groups and the executive form a functional 'unit' which somewhat limits the functional independence of the majority parties and their visibility as independent players in the political process, the functions of the parliamentary opposition for the political system as a whole are often more, rather than less, tangible than that of the majority parliamentary party groups. Most authors consider the functional profile of the parliamentary opposition in parliamentary democracies to include the three tasks of criticising the government, scrutinising and checking governmental actions and policies, and representing a credible 'alternative government'" (Helms, 2008, 9).

Ministers are their bills' shepherds. To ensure smooth parliamentary passage a minister negotiates with members of the parliamentary opposition, accommodates a reasonable demand of an opposition party or incorporates a sensible idea in exchange for some praise, less public criticism or even additional "yes" votes (Müller, 1993; Müller et al., 2001; Russell & Gover, 2017). Ministers therefore usually refrain from issuing strong rhetorical attacks on the opposition. Such a task is more appropriate for the leader of the parliamentary party group or delegated to rhetorically talented MPs.

Some types of parliamentary debate are more confrontational by nature than others. Debates on bills vary widely. When a bill is passed by consensus there is no need for criticism by the opposition in the preceding debate. When a minister faces a no-confidence vote introduced by an opposition party the debate will be usually heated. A debate on a topic that an opposition party can impose on the government on short notice, as through the instrument of the Urgent Question Debate in the Austrian parliament, is also among the more confrontational ones. In the Urgent Question Debate a minister is forced to address an opposition party's criticism of his or her actions with a minimum time of preparation.

The typical roles of government ministers and MPs from government and opposition parties and the different types of parliamentary debates produce systematic variation that we will use to corroborate the external validity of our sentiment analysis procedure. We posit several hypotheses for these patterns that an observer of parliamentary politics should consider non-controversial or even "self-evident" statements.

We posit the following three hypotheses.

Hypothesis 1: Speakers from government parties exhibit less negativity than speakers from opposition parties.

Hypothesis 2: Parliamentary party group leaders are most likely to use negative statements, followed by ordinary MPs. Cabinet members are least likely to use negative statements.

Hypothesis 3: Urgent Question Debates exhibit higher levels of negativity than other parliamentary debates.

We validate these by applying our sentiment analysis approach to Austrian parliamentary speeches from 1996–2013. We include all speeches of MPs from the four parties that were constantly present in Parliament during that period.

H1 government vs. opposition

The first hypothesis expects speakers from government parties to exhibit less negativity than speakers from opposition parties. Figure 4 shows the negativity levels of the four parties that were present over the whole period. The dashed line indicates the overall trend for all parties. The negativity values are averaged per year and per party. Light gray lines indicate parties that remained either in government or in opposition during the entire period of our study. These parties are the ÖVP which was always part of the government and the Greens which remained in opposition. Parties that changed from opposition to government or the other way around during the period are visualized in darker gray. SPÖ switched from government to opposition and back to the government. The FPÖ followed the reverse pattern: opposition, government, back to opposition. The government coalitions are indicated at the bottom of the figure, each cabinet is further separated by a horizontal line. The BZÖ took part in one government coalition, but is excluded from this figure as it was only in parliament during a limited period.

With respect to our first hypothesis, the dashed trend line of all parties clearly indicates a party's status as being in (below the dashed trend line) or out (above the dashed line) of the ruling government coalition. The Greens (always in opposition) are above the trend line during the entire period and thus constantly exhibit a higher level of negativity. By contrast, the ÖVP (always in government) is constantly below the trend line with a lower level of negativity. The SPÖ was in government at the beginning and the end of our study. Its negativity level is similar to the ÖVP when in government, but the party's negativity increases sharply when the SPÖ became an opposition party in 2000. The Freedom party (FPÖ) exhibits the inverse trend: as opposition party, its negativity level is clearly above the trend line, similar to the Greens. The party apparently changed its rhetorical style once it became a government party (2000–2006). The premature ending of the Freedom Party's coalition with the ÖVP is followed by a substantive increase of negativity. Thus, there is support for our first hypothesis.

H2 parliamentary roles

Drawing on the differences of their political roles, Hypothesis 2 expects that parliamentary party group leaders are most likely to use negative statements, followed by ordinary MPs. Cabinet members are least likely to use negative statements. The period from 1996–2013 covers five legislative terms (five elections) in the Austrian National Parliament. Figure 5 illustrates role-based differences for each of these legislative

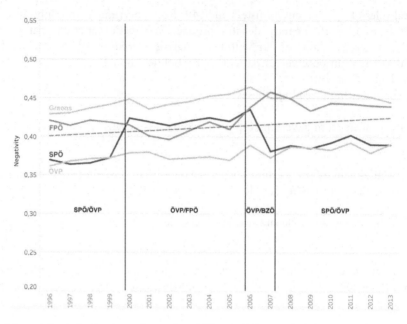

Figure 4. Negativity evolution in the Austrian parliament from 1996 to 2013 showing those four parties that were present over the whole period.

terms. The bar chart indicates mean negativity levels for all groups per term (20th–24th legislative period). We observe a robust pattern: Parliamentary party group leaders dole out stronger attacks than the ordinary Members of Parliament. Cabinet members exhibit even more rhetorical restraint.

H3 urgent question debates

Hypothesis 3 expects that negativity in Urgent Question Debates is higher than in other parliamentary debates. An opposition party typically requests an Urgent Question Debate to jump a surprising attack on the government or a government minister on a current topic, which leads us to expect that they should exhibit stronger levels of negativity than other plenary debates. Figure 6 shows the negativity level of debates following Urgent Questions compared to all other types of debates based on mean values per legislative term. Although differences are small, Urgent Question Debates on average exhibit a higher level of negativity compared to all other debates taken together.

Conclusions

The use of word embeddings introduces a new approach to the field of sentiment analysis in the social sciences that offers potential to improve on current bag-of-words approaches. The major advantage of using word embeddings is their potential to detect and classify unseen or out-of-context words that are not included in the training data. Drawing on vector representations of text that allocate similar words closer to each other, such approaches are able to supplement training data, which may improve the results of machine learning tasks. Social scientists increasingly turn to machine learning for sentiment analysis (Van Atteveldt, Kleinnijenhuis et al., 2008a; Burscher et al., 2014; Ceron et al., 2016; Hopkins & King, 2010). As training data for these applications is typically scarce, word embeddings have the potential to facilitate applications of machine learning in the discipline.

Our validation on previously unseen training examples shows that word embeddings may improve results obtained from bag-of-words classifiers. For a difficult "three classes of negativity"

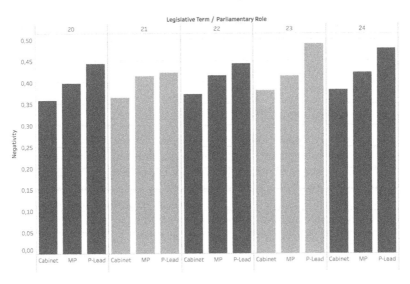

Figure 5. Negativity distinction per legislative term and parliamentary role: Average scores of cabinet members, MPs, and parliamentary party group leaders.

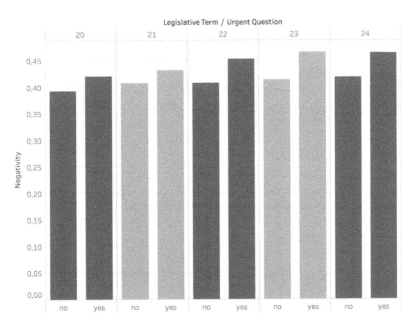

Figure 6. Negativity distinction per legislative term and type of debate: Average scores of Urgent Question Debates and all other types of debates.

prediction task, word embeddings have a higher accuracy level than traditional bag-of-words approaches. The results also indicate that word embeddings seem to learn a more realistic class distribution than bag-of-words classifiers. Comparing the two classifiers shows the potential of word embeddings and neural networks for text classification.

An empirical application measures negative sentiment in parliamentary debates. Using non-controversial hypotheses on patterns of negativity, our findings provide external validity for the word embeddings approach. In line with our expectations, we find that (1) opposition parties exhibit higher levels of negativity than government parties, (2) the negativity levels of speakers in parliamentary debates are consistent with their political roles, and (3) Urgent Question Debates exhibit higher levels of negativity than other parliamentary debates.

We identify some technical limitations and avenues for future improvements.

Preprocessing of German

Tools available for natural language processing of German language texts are less developed than tools available for the English language. Compound words which are a characteristic of the German language are more difficult to handle with word embedding corpora that offer a limited amount of embeddings. There is a method for splitting compound words into their single components by translating them into another language and the resulting single words back into German (Fritzinger & Fraser, 2010). The preprocessing unit of our pipeline could be extended with such an application to achieve a higher coverage of word embeddings per sentence.

Word and sentence embeddings and classification

The introduction of distributed word embeddings (Mikolov et al., 2013, 2013) had a major impact on the field of natural language processing. Several approaches (Le & Mikolov, 2014; Parikh, Täckström, Das, & Uszkoreit, 2016) build on the concept of distributed word embeddings but use more sophisticated modeling techniques than a simple averaging of "standard" word embeddings. Future work could integrate advanced embedding approaches for modeling text documents or test word embeddings that focus on the representation of sentiment-specific features (Tang et al., 2014). Similarly, using context specific word embeddings, for example from annotated parliamentary speeches (Rauh, De Wilde, & Schwalbach, 2017), could further enhance the performance of our approach. The same applies to other neural network types like convolutional neural networks that can make use of the spatial structure of words within a sentence.

Visualization

The last part of our pipeline covers the aggregation and visualization of sentiment scores according to additional structured information extending the application data (such as date, time, topic, politician, party, gender, or age). We plan to implement more sophisticated text visualizations for a deeper exploration of the Austrian parliamentary debates in the future. There are multiple tools that show advanced text visualization techniques with a focus on sentiment (Diakopoulos, Naaman, & Kivran-Swaine, 2010; Gold, Rohrdantz, & El-Assady, 2015; Gregory et al., 2006).

Web interface

A web application that will offer end user access to the implementation of our sentiment procedure is currently under development. It will provide a graphical user interface for our pipeline. With a focus on user interaction and active learning it will support users without deeper technical background in performing machine learning on textual data. Our goal is to enable communication researchers and practitioners to apply a word embedding based sentiment analysis to their own data sets more easily.

Notes

1. The Austrian parliament carefully revises the transcripts of speeches which then are very similar to written text.
2. We present a translated version of the coding instructions in Appendix A.

3. Most existing labeled data sets are in English and not in the domain of political communication. Examples include Kotzias et al. (2015): https://archive.ics.uci.edu/ml/datasets/Sentiment±Labelled±Sentences, Socher et al. (2013): https://nlp.stanford.edu/sentiment/code.html, Maas et al. (2011): http://www.cs.jhu.edu/~mdredze/datasets/sentiment/or the "classic" Pang et al. (2002) dataset: http://www.cs.cornell.edu/people/pabo/movie-review-data/.
4. Some cases require language-dependent preprocessing prior to sentence tokenization. In our case, without custom preprocessing Polyglot would have wrongly identified academic titles which are unique to Austria.

Acknowledgments

We thank Elisabeth Graf, Lisa Hirsch, Christoph Kralj, Michael Oppermann and Johanna Schlereth for their research assistance.

Funding

This work was supported by the Österreichische Forschungsförderungsgesellschaft FFG [845898]; Hochschuljubiliäumsstiftung der Stadt Wien [H-304565/2015].

ORCID

Elena Rudkowsky http://orcid.org/0000-0003-3193-6242
Martin Haselmayer http://orcid.org/0000-0002-7765-5158
Marcelo Jenny http://orcid.org/0000-0003-1535-9094

References

Aaldering, L., & Vliegenthart, R. (2016). Political leaders and the media. Can we measure political leadership images in newspapers using computer-assisted content analysis? *Quality and Quantity*, 50(5), 1871–1905.

Al-Rfou, R., Perozzi, B., & Skiena, S. (2013, August). *Polyglot: Distributed word representations for multilingual NLP*. Proceedings of the seventeenth conference on computational natural language learning (pp. 183–192). Sofia, Bulgaria. Association for Computational Linguistics. Retrieved from http://www.aclweb.org/anthology/W13-3520

Baumeister, R. A., Bratlavsky, E., & Finkenauer, C. (2001). Bad Is Stronger Than Good. *Review of General Psychology*, 5(4), 323–370. doi:10.1037/1089-2680.5.4.323

Benoit, K., Conway, D., Lauderdale, B., Laver, M., & Mikhaylov, S. (2016). Crowd-sourced text analysis: Reproducible and agile production of political data. *American Political Science Review*, 110(2), 278–295. doi:10.1017/S0003055416000058

Boumans, J. W., & Trilling, D. (2016). Taking stock of the toolkit: An overview of relevant automated content analysis approaches and techniques for digital journalism scholars. *Digital Journalism*, 4(1), 8–23. doi:10.1080/21670811.2015.1096598

Burscher, B., Odijk, D., Vliegenthart, R., De Rijke, M., & De Vreese, C. H. (2014). Teaching the computer to code frames in news: Comparing two supervised machine learning approaches to frame analysis. *Communication Methods and Measures*, 8(3), 190–206. doi:10.1080/19312458.2014.937527

Ceron, A., Curini, L., & Iacus, S. M. (2015). Using sentiment analysis to monitor electoral campaigns: Method matters-evidence from the United States and Italy. *Social Science Computer Review*, 33(1), 3–20. doi:10.1177/0894439314521983

Ceron, A., Curini, L., & Iacus, S. M. (2016). First-and second-level agenda setting in the twittersphere: An application to the Italian political debate. *Journal of Information Technology and Politics*, 13(2), 159–174.

Ceron, A., Curini, L., & Iacus, S. M. (2017). *Politics and big data: Nowcasting and forecasting elections with social media*. London, UK: Routledge.

Chollet, F. (2015). *Keras*. Retrieved from https://github.com/fchollet/keras

Diakopoulos, N., Naaman, M., & Kivran-Swaine, F. (2010). *Diamonds in the rough: Social media visual analytics for journalistic inquiry*. 2010 IEEE symposium on Visual Analytics Science and Technology (VAST) (pp. 115–122), Salt Lake City, UT.

Fayyad, U., Piatetsky-Shapiro, G., & Smyth, P. (1996). From data mining to knowledge discovery in databases. *AI Magazine*, 17(3), 37.

Fritzinger, F., & Fraser, A. (2010). *How to avoid burning ducks: Combining linguistic analysis and corpus statistics for german compound processing*. Proceedings of the Joint Fifth Workshop on Statistical Machine Translation and Metrics MATR (pp. 224–234), Uppsala, Sweden.

Gold, V., Rohrdantz, C., & El-Assady, M. (2015). Exploratory text analysis using lexical episode plots. In E. Bertini, J. Kennedy, & E. Puppo (Eds.), *Eurographics Conference on Visualization (EuroVis) - short papers*, Cagliaria, Italy. The Eurographics Association. doi:10.2312/eurovisshort.20151130

Goldberg, Y. (2016). A primer on neural network models for natural language processing. *Journal of Artificial Intelligence Research, 57*, 345–420.

Greene, Z., Ceron, A., Schumacher, G., & Fazekas, Z. (2016). *The nuts and bolts of automated text analysis.* Comparing Different Document Pre-Processing Techniques in Four Countries. Retrieved from osf.io/ghxj8

Gregory, M. L., Chinchor, N., Whitney, P., Carter, R., Hetzler, E., & Turner, A. (2006). *User-directed sentiment analysis: Visualizing the affective content of documents*. In Proceedings of the workshop on sentiment and subjectivity in text (pp. 23–30), Sydney, Australia.

Grimmer, J., & Stewart, B. M. (2013). Text as data: The promise and pitfalls of automatic content analysis methods for political texts. *Political Analysis, 21*(3), 267–297. doi:10.1093/pan/mps028

Harris, Z. S. (1954). Distributional Structure. *Word, 10*(2–3), 146–162. doi:10.1080/00437956.1954.11659520

Haselmayer, M., Hirsch, L., & Jenny, M. (2017). Love is blind. Partisan bias in the perception of positive and negative campaign messages. Paper prepared for presentation at the 7th Annual Conference of the European Political Science Association (EPSA), June 22–24, Milan, Italy.

Haselmayer, M., & Jenny, M. (2017). Sentiment analysis of political communication: Combining a dictionary approach with crowdcoding. *Quality and Quantity, 51*(6), 2623–2646. doi:10.1007/s11135-016-0412-4

Helms, L. (2008). Studying parliamentary opposition in old and new democracies: Issues and perspectives. *The Journal of Legislative Studies, 14*(1–2), 6–19. doi:10.1080/13572330801920788

Hopkins, D. J., & King, G. (2010). A method of automated nonparametric content analysis for social science. *American Journal of Political Science, 54*(1), 229–247. doi:10.1111/ajps.2010.54.issue-1

Kandel, S., Heer, J., Plaisant, C., Kennedy, J., Van Ham, F., Riche, N. H., ... Buono, P. (2011). Research directions in data wrangling: Visualizations and transformations for usable and credible data. *Information Visualization, 10*(4), 271–288. doi:10.1177/1473871611415994

Kingma, D., & Ba, J. (2014). Adam: A method for stochastic optimization. *arXiv preprint arXiv:1412.6980*.

Kleinnijenhuis, J., Schultz, F., Oegema, D., & Van Atteveldt, W. (2013). Financial news and market panics in the age of high-frequency sentiment trading algorithms. *Journalism, 14*(2), 271–291. doi:10.1177/1464884912468375

Kotzias, D., Denil, M., De Freitas, N., & Smyth, P. (2015, August). *From group to individual labels using deep features*. Proceedings of the 21th ACM SIGKDD International Conference on Knowledge Discovery and Data Mining (pp. 597–606), Sydney, Australia.

Krippendorff, K. (2013). *Content Analysis. An Introduction to its methodology* (3rd ed.). Los Angeles, CA: Sage.

Le, Q., & Mikolov, T. (2014). *Distributed representations of sentences and documents*. International Conference on Machine Learning (ICML)(pp. 1188–1196), Beijing, China.

Lind, F., Gruber, M., & Boomgaarden, H. G. (2017). Content analysis by the crowd: Assessing the usability of crowdsourcing for coding latent constructs. *Communication Methods and Measures, 11*(3), 191–209. doi:10.1080/19312458.2017.1317338

Loper, E., & Bird, S. (2002). *NLTK: The natural language toolkit*. ACL workshop on effective tools and methodologies for teaching natural language processing and computational linguistics, Philadelphia, PA.

Lowe, W., & Benoit, K. (2013). Validating estimates of latent traits from textual data using human judgment as a benchmark. *Political Analysis, 21*(3), 298–313. doi:10.1093/pan/mpt002

Lucas, C., Nielsen, R. A., Roberts, M. E., Stewart, B. M., Storer, A., & Tingley, D. (2015). Computer-assisted text analysis for comparative politics. *Political Analysis, 23*(2), 254–277. doi:10.1093/pan/mpu019

Maas, A. L., Daly, R. E., Pham, P. T., Huang, D., Ng, A. Y., & Potts, C. (2011). *Learning word vectors for sentiment analysis*. In Proceedings of the 49th Annual Meeting of the Association for Computational Linguistics: Human language technologies (ACL 2011) (pp. 142–150), Portland, OR.

Mikolov, T., Chen, K., Corrado, G., & Dean, J. (2013). Efficient estimation of word representations in vector space. *CoRR*. Retrieved from http://arxiv.org/abs/1301.3781

Mikolov, T., Sutskever, I., Chen, K., Corrado, G. S., & Dean, J. (2013, December). Distributed representations of words and phrases and their compositionality. In Proceedings of the 26th International Conference on Neural Information Processing Systems (pp. 3111–3119), Lake Tahoe, CA.

Moraes, R., Valiati, J. F., & Neto, W. P. G. (2013). Document-level sentiment classification: An empirical comparison between SVM and ANN. *Expert Systems with Applications, 40*(2), 621–633. doi:10.1016/j.eswa.2012.07.059

Mozetič, I., Grčar, M., & Smailović, J. (2016). Multilingual twitter sentiment classification: The role of human annotators. *PloS One, 11*(5), e0155036. doi:10.1371/journal.pone.0155036

Müller, W. C. (1993). Executive–Legislative relations in Austria: 1945– 1992. *Legislative Studies Quarterly, 18*(4), 467–494. doi:10.2307/439851

Müller, W. C., Jenny, M., Dolezal, M., Steininger, B., Philipp, W., & Westphal, S. (2001). *Die österreichischen Abgeordneten: Individuelle Präferenzen und politisches Verhalten*. Wien, Austria: WUV Universitätsverlag.

Nasukawa, T., & Yi, J. (2003). *Sentiment analysis: Capturing favorability using natural language processing*. Proceedings of the 2nd international conference on knowledge capture (pp. 70–77), Sanibel Island, FL.

Nobata, C., Tetreault, J., Thomas, A., Mehdad, Y., & Chang, Y. (2016). *Abusive language detection in online user content*. Proceedings of the 25th international conference on world wide web (pp. 145-153), Montréal, Canada.

Pang, B., Lee, L., & Vaithyanathan, S. (2002). Thumbs up? sentiment classification using machine learning techniques. Proceedings of the Conference on Empirical Methods in Natural Language Processing (EMNLP-2002) (pp. 79-86), Philadelphia, PA.

Parikh, A. P., Täckström, O., Das, D., & Uszkoreit, J. (2016). A decomposable attention model for natural language inference. Proceedings of the 2016 Conference on Empirical Methods in Natural Language Processing (pp. 2249-2255), Austin, Texas.

Parliament Austria. (2013). *Parliamentary speeches from the Austrian National Parliament*. Retrieved from https://www.parlament.gv.at/PERK/NRBRBV/NR/STENO/

Pennington, J., Socher, R., & Manning, C. D. (2014). *Glove: Global vectors for word representation*. Proceedings of the Empirical Methods in Natural Language Processing (EMNLP 2014) (Vol. 14, pp. 1532-1543). Retrieved from https://nlp.stanford.edu/projects/glove/

Raschka, S. (2014). *Naive Bayes and text classification I - Introduction and theory*. arXiv preprint arXiv:1410.5329.

Rauh, C., De Wilde, P., & Schwalbach, J. (2017). *The ParlSpeech data set: Annotated full-text vectors of 3.9 million plenary speeches in the key legislative chambers of seven European states*. Harvard Dataverse, V1. doi:10.7910/DVN/E4RSP9

Rheault, L., Beelen, K., Cochrane, C., & Hirst, G. (2016). Measuring emotion in parliamentary debates with automated textual analysis. *PLoS One, 11*(12), e0168843. doi:10.1371/journal.pone.0168843

Rozin, P., & Royzman, E. B. (2001). Negativity bias, negativity dominance, and contagion. *Personality and Social Psychology Review, 5*(4), 296-320. doi:10.1207/S15327957PSPR0504_2

Russell, M., & Gover, D. (2017). *Legislation at westminster: Parliamentary actors and influence in the making of British law*. Oxford, UK: Oxford University Press.

Salton, G., & McGill, M. J. (1986). *Introduction to modern information retrieval*. New York, NY: McGraw-Hill, Inc.

Slapin, J. B., & Proksch, O. (2014). Words as data: Content analysis in legislative studies. In S. Martin, K. Strom, & T. Saalfeld (Eds.), *The Oxford handbook of legislative studies*. Oxford, UK: Oxford University Press.

Socher, R., Perelygin, A., Wu, J. Y., Chuang, J., Manning, C. D., Ng, A. Y., & Potts, C. (2013). *Recursive deep models for semantic compositionality over a sentiment treebank*. Proceedings of the Conference on Empirical Methods in Natural Language Processing (EMNLP) (Vol. 1631, p. 1642), Seattle, WA.

Soroka, S., & McAdams, S. (2015). News, politics, and negativity. *Political Communication, 32*(1), 1-22. doi:10.1080/10584609.2014.881942

Soroka, S., Young, L., & Balmas, M. (2015). Bad news or mad news? Sentiment scoring of negativity, fear, and anger in news content. *The Annals of the American Academy of Political and Social Science, 659*(1), 108-121. doi:10.1177/0002716215569217

Stolte, C., Tang, D., & Hanrahan, P. (2002). Polaris: A system for query, analysis, and visualization of multidimensional relational databases. *IEEE Transactions on Visualization and Computer Graphics, 8*(1), 52-65. doi:10.1109/2945.981851

Tang, D., Wei, F., Yang, N., Zhou, M., Liu, T., & Qin, B. (2014). *Learning sentiment-specific word embedding for Twitter sentiment classification*. ACL (Vol. 1, pp. 1555-1565), Baltimore, MD.

Turney, P. D., & Pantel, P. (2010). From frequency to meaning: Vector space models of semantics. *Journal of Artificial Intelligence Research, 37*, 141-188.

Van Atteveldt, W., Kleinnijenhuis, J., & Ruigrok, N. (2008b). Parsing, semantic networks, and political authority using syntactic analysis to extract semantic relations from dutch newspaper articles. *Political Analysis, 16*(4), 428-446. doi:10.1093/pan/mpn006

Van Atteveldt, W., Kleinnijenhuis, J., Ruigrok, N., & Schlobach, S. (2008a). Good news or bad news? Conducting sentiment analysis on dutch text to distinguish between positive and negative relations. *Journal of Information Technology and Politics, 5*(1), 73-94. doi:10.1080/19331680802154145

Van Atteveldt, W., Sheafer, T., Shenhav, S. R., & Fogel-Dror, Y. (2017). Clause analysis: Using syntactic information to automatically extract source, subject, and predicate from texts with an application to the 2008-2009 gaza war. *Political Analysis, 25*(2), 207-222. doi:10.1017/pan.2016.12

Wilkerson, J., & Casas, A. (2017). Large-scale computerized text analysis in political science: Opportunities and challenges. *Annual Review of Political Science, 20*(1), 529-544. doi:10.1146/annurev-polisci-052615-025542

Wang, H., Can, D., Kazemzadeh, A., Bar, F., & Narayanan, S. (2012). A system for real-time Twitter sentiment analysis of 2012 U.S. presidential election cycle. Paper presented at theProceedings of the ACL 2012 System Demonstrations, Jeju Island, Korea, 115-120.

Wueest, B., Clematide, S., Bünzli, A., Laupper, D., & Frey, T. (2011). Electoral campaigns and relation mining: Extracting semantic network data from newspaper articles. *Journal of Information Technology and Politics, 8*(4), 444-463. doi:10.1080/19331681.2011.567387

Wulczyn, E., Thain, N., & Dixon, L. (2016). Ex machina: Personal attacks seen at scale. *CoRR, abs/1610.08914*. Retrieved from http://arxiv.org/abs/1610.08914

Young, L., & Soroka, S. (2012). Affective news: The automated coding of sentiment in political texts. *Political Communication, 29*(2), 205-231. doi:10.1080/10584609.2012.671234

Appendix A. CrowdFlower coding instructions (translation)

These coding instructions were pretested by colleagues, student assistants and a few online coders.

How negative are these statements?

What is this about?

We present you sentences from political and media texts. Many, although not all, of these sentences include direct or indirect criticism, allegations or attacks.

Task

Please read each sentence carefully and decide, whether it includes a positive, neutral or negative statement. In a second step, we ask you to rate the intensity of the statement using the following scale:

- Not negative (neutral or positive)
- Very weakly negative
- Weakly negative
- Strongly negative
- Very strongly negative
- Not codable

What should you consider?

Only rate the actual content of the text! Stay impartial, your personal preferences towards persons or organizations should not influence your coding decisions.

Not negative

A sentence should be coded as "not negative" if it contains a neutral or positive statement.

Example "not negative":

"I serve the Austrian citizens with passion and commitment."

Not codable

A sentence is "not codable" if it is incomprehensible or if it does not make any sense to you. Some sentences may be incomplete, as they have been processed automatically. As long as you are able to purposefully decide, whether they are positive, neutral or negative, we ask you to rate them anyhow.

Example "not codable":

"Ic$%$#* we retain%, that &%§"

Negative

Negative sentences contain direct or indirect criticism, allegations or attacks in varying intensity.

Examples with increasing negativity:

"We demand that the government finally delivers a better job!"

"These are bad actions, which come at the expense of the population."

"This minister promotes corruption and consciously dupes the people."

"This is a scam on all of us: The dishonesty of these politicians stinks to high heavens."

Special case: sentences containing specific coding instructions

Some sentences may contain instructions, asking you to choose a specific category. In such cases, you should ignore all other textual information and directly follow the instructions.

Example:

*"The government has failed to address these issues in the past legislative term. **Please ignore the previous part of the text and code this unit as "not codable".***

In case of any question regarding the coding process or if you would like to provide us with feedback, please send us an E-Mail: crowdsourcing@autnes.at

Thank you for your contribution!

Appendix B

Table B1 shows the average confusion matrix for unseen test data of our classifier trained on bag-of-words representations. There is an obvious tendency of this classifier to choose the middle class whereas the word embedding variant shows a clear diagonal in its confusion matrix (Table B2). The bias of the bag-of-words classifier explains its higher accuracy for middle class examples compared to the word embedding approach. The bag-of-words variant nevertheless shows lower accuracies for the two outer classes. Class 2 (very negative) is slightly lower while class 0 (not/slightly negative) is significantly lower compared to our proposed word embedding approach.

Table B1 Average confusion matrix for unseen test data: Bag-of-words

		Predicted		
		not/slightly negative	Negative	very negative
Actual	not/slightly negative	170.6	284.6	69.1
	negative	27.3	569.7	208.7
	very negative	7.7	334.4	387.9

Table B2. Average confusion matrix for unseen test data: word embeddings.

		Predicted		
		not/slightly negative	Negative	very negative
Actual	not/slightly negative	337.2	120.3	64.9
	negative	146.5	412.7	240.0
	very negative	91.3	238.6	409.5

Scaling up Content Analysis

Damian Trilling and Jeroen G. F. Jonkman

ABSTRACT
Employing a number of different standalone programs is a prevalent approach among communication scholars who use computational methods to analyze media content. For instance, a researcher might use a specific program or a paid service to scrape some content from the Web, then use another program to process the resulting data, and finally conduct statistical analysis or produce some visualizations in yet another program. This makes it hard to build reproducible workflows, and even harder to build on the work of earlier studies. To improve this situation, we propose and discuss four criteria that a framework for automated content analysis should fulfill: scalability, free and open source, adaptability, and accessibility via multiple interfaces. We also describe how to put these considerations into practice, discuss their feasibility, and point toward future developments.

Introduction

Manual content analysis is still one of the core methods used in Communication Science (e.g., Lacy, Watson, Riffe, & Lovejoy, 2015). But in our digitized media environment, datasets grow larger and larger, which is why automated content analysis (ACA) has gained importance and popularity (Boumans & Trilling, 2016; Grimmer & Stewart, 2013; Günther & Quandt, 2016; Jacobi, Van Atteveldt, & Welbers, 2016; Scharkow, 2011). It has been used in, for instance, studies about sources and topics in news (e.g., Burscher, Vliegenthart, & De Vreese, 2015; Scharkow, 2011; Sjøvaag & Stavelin, 2012) or agenda setting and framing (e.g., Burscher, Odijk, Vliegenthart, de Rijke, & de Vreese, 2014; Russell Neuman, Guggenheim, Mo Jang, & Bae, 2014; Tsur, Calacci, & Lazer, 2015). In this article, rather than introducing a new technique or tool, we reflect on the current state of scaling up content analysis and present a set of guidelines to further advance the field.

From time to time, a discipline needs to pause for a moment and reflect on its own theories and methods. For instance, in a 1983 special issue of the *Journal of Communication* on the "Ferment in the field",[1] Gerbner (1983) argued that the discipline of communication science "requires an intellectual domain, a body of theories and approaches that fit its subject matter [...]" (p. 355). Given the enormous changes in the possibilities of one of the most central methods of our field, it is worth to pause again for a moment and reflect on how approaches and best practices could look like. While we are somewhat reluctant to use the often abused buzzword Big Data, the emerging field of *Computational Social Science* (Cioffi-Revilla, 2014; Lazer et al., 2009)—or, in the words of Shah, Cappella, and Neuman (2015), *Computational Communication Science*—deals with research questions and data sets that require re-thinking traditional approaches to content analysis.

---

[1] Comparable special issues were published in 1993, 2008, and 2018.

Recently, several scholars have published thoughtful pieces on this development. For instance, Kitchin (2014a) has written on the epistemological and paradigm shifts that come along with the use of Big Data in the social sciences, and Freelon (2014b) has reflected on how the analysis of digital trace data can be fruitfully incorporated into the discipline of communication science. In a special issue on "Toward Computational Social Science: Big Data in Digital Environments" of *The ANNALS* of the American Academy of Political and Social Science, several authors give specific advice on how to incorporate recent methodological and computational developments into our discipline. For example, Hindman (2015) discusses how machine learning-related approaches can be used within communication science, and Zamith and Lewis (2015) discuss the possibility of hybrid forms of content analysis. Furthermore, in the afterword of a special issue of the *Journal of Communication* on "Big Data in Communication Research", Parks (2014) concludes that we face "significant challenges [...] as we move into the era of Big Data" (p. 360).

With this article, we want to contribute to this discussion of where the field is heading. Our field is at crossroads: As computational methods are gaining ground, there is a pressing need to establish standards of *how* these techniques should be employed and implemented. Going beyond suggestions for specific standards, programs, or environments, we set out to develop a series of criteria that a framework for scaled-up ACA needs to fulfill. By framework, we mean a coherent combination of research practices, software packages, and hardware solutions, which together allow to conduct scaled-up ACA. We explicitly do not want to come up with "yet another standard",[2] but rather want to present criteria that may be worth considering when our discipline is working on scaling up content analysis.

While also manual content analyses nowadays make use of computers (for instance, to facilitate data entry; e.g., Lewis, Zamith, & Hermida, 2013), we only consider those forms of content analysis "automated" where the coding itself is not performed manually; vice versa, also automated content analyses need human insight and human decisions. A very basic form of ACA entails the coding the occurance of some terms in a dataset, which can be accomplished in standard and easy-to-use software like Stata, SPSS, or Excel (Boumans & Trilling, 2016; Krippendorff, 2004). As the actual counting is not performed by hand and the texts themselves are not read by the researchers, even such simple approaches can be classified as ACA. Nevertheless, they are not "scaled up": When applied to only a couple of thousands of items, such an analysis does not require the researcher to think about the necessary infrastructure. Neither hardware nor software requirements exceed what any standard laptop offers. But this changes drastically once datasets grow larger—or when datasets do not consist of plain text, but include images, video, or other types of data.

The prevalent approach among many communication scholars who use computational methods to analyze large collections of texts has for a long time been to employ a number of different standalone programs—and this is also how common content analysis textbooks present computer-aided methods (e.g., Krippendorff, 2004).[3] While this is somewhat understandable, as it is easier to get financing for a project with a clearly defined scope than for the development and the maintenance of a more general framework, in the long run, doing the latter will save resources, allow to answer new research questions, and facilitate collaboration. Such a framework can and probably should include the use of environments like R or Python, which already include many libaries and therefore allow for unifying the workflow (see, e.g., Freelon, 2014a), but goes beyond this. For instance, it would need to also include other components such as a database backend.

Recently, the use and development of more sustainable systems gained momentum within communication science. Examples that are clearly aiming at providing a framework that is not tied to a single project include the AmCAT framework developed at Vrije Universiteit Amsterdam

---

[2]We would like to thank an anonymous reviewer for pointing us to the comic strip available at https://xkcd.com/927/, which claims that an attempt to unify 14 competing standards will result in 15 competing standards.

[3]This situation has improved, though, since more and more social scientists use environments like R or Python that allow for integrated workflows. Nevertheless, the large market for commercial tools like Provalis Wordstat or standalone-tools developed by individual scientists (e.g., http://leydesdorff.net/) illustrate that the use of standalone programs is still considerable.

(Van Atteveldt, 2008) and used at several other departments as well; the xTAS framework, which is geared more towards computer science (De Rooij, Vishneuski, & De Rijke, 2012); or the Leipzig Corpus Miner (Niekler, Wiedemann, & Heyer, 2014). In this paper, we want to go beyond discussing the merits and shortcomings of individual frameworks, but aim at bringing this discussion to a higher level, on which we conceptualize guidelines for designing such frameworks.

Unfortunately, such frameworks are not in widespread use across the discipline yet. What is particularly problematic is that—without such a framework—a lot of work is unnecessarily repeated, which happens too often. For example, if texts from a certain source have already been collected, or if such texts have already been pre-processed or coded (annotated) in some way or another, it should be avoided to do this tedious work again in a similar project. This should be easy with digitally available data, but the use of different, partly proprietary programs, makes it difficult to cooperate and replicate or enhance existing research. While it is a well-known problem that researchers often are too reluctant to share data; making it easier to actually share data by integrating data sharing facilities into a framework of ACA might help alleviate the problem.

Although automated content analysis techniques have been employed decades ago (as an illustration, see, e.g., a study analyzing word co-occurrences by Leydesdorff & Zaal, 1988), they only recently became widely adapted in communication science (see, e.g., Boumans & Trilling, 2016). However, also today, many of automated content analyses still follow the same approach of such early studies, in that they rely on standalone tools to solve a problem at hand. For example, a wide range of programs exist to handle tasks like processing text files, counting word frequencies, or visualizing co-occurrences (see, e.g, the large amount of different tools suggested Krippendorff, 2004). Similarly, the Digital Methods Initiative developed a set of excellent tools[4] for conducting some very specific analyses tailored to online content. However, using a number of different standalone programs and services that cannot be chained together without manual interventions, is neither transparent nor scalable.

Partly, these problems can be solved by using a framework like R, which is very extensible and therefore allows researchers to do many of these steps within one environment. But even though this is a very good step toward more reproducible research, having standalone R installations on researchers' computers does not completely solve the problem. In particular, one would at least need some common database backend to share the data.

We therefore started thinking about implementing a framework that can be used across research projects and allows re-running models, extending them, and avoid redundant work in data collection and preprocessing. We argue that such a framework should incorporate state-of-the art libraries (e.g., scikit-learn, Pedregosa et al., 2011; or gensim, Řehůřek & Sojka, 2010) and allow people who do have some programming knowledge to extend it, but at the same time be usable for others as well. While thinking about the design of such a system, we quickly realized that the scale of the system goes beyond what communication researchers usually can handle on their laptop or desktop computer. But, more importantly, even if it is technically possible to run the analysis on a local computer, it makes sense to move to a larger scale, in order to make better long-term use of the data.

In this article, we therefore (1) ask what the criteria are that a framework for scaled-up content analysis has to fulfill, (2) describe how to put these considerations into practice, and (3) point toward future developments.

Scaling up content analysis

The decision for scaling up content analysis is a decision that frequently arises from the need to keep pace with the "data revolution" (Kitchin, 2014b). We have more data and different data at our disposal, and these data are available in digital formats. From a technical point of view, this can lead to three bottlenecks. We will first discuss the relevance of these points before moving on toward developing a more encompassing and broader set of criteria for scaled-up content analysis.

---

[4]They are available at https://wiki.digitalmethods.net/Dmi/ToolDatabase.

(1) A lack of storage capacity, i.e., the dataset is too large to store on the own harddrive.
(2) A lack of memory, i.e., the part of the dataset needed for some calculation is too large to be loaded.
(3) A lack of computing power, i.e., the calculation would take prohibitively long.

First, the lack of storage capacity usually is a minor issue: It is inconvenient if a dataset is too large to store on the researcher's laptop, but in an age where external hard drives of several terabytes are affordable and offer more space than even several decades of newspaper data (or, e.g., comprehensive sets of press releases, parlamentary speeches, etc.) require, this would not prevent us from conducting a content analysis. However, there are cases where storage is a problem. For example, Yahoo has released a Yahoo News dataset, which, although it only contains four months of data, has an uncompressed size of 13.5 TB, which is larger than the size of external hard drives available on the consumer market.

Second, the lack of memory can be a much more important limiting factor. For a lot of analyses, it is necessary to construct a matrix of, for instance, word frequencies. Such a matrix can easily outgrow the computer's memory, effectively limiting the number of documents or the number of words that can be taken into account. But problems can start much earlier: A data set of 8 GB size (which is not too uncommon) cannot even be loaded into the 8 GB memory that a laptop might have, so we have to let go of the idea of "opening" a file and instead have to somehow process it in parts.

Third, the lack of computing power deserves attention: It might be acceptable to wait even some days for the result of an analysis. But it is usually not acceptable to block the researcher's own computer for such a long time, especially if additional requirements like permanent high-speed internet connection, have to be fulfilled. And also if a dedicated computer is available, even longer calculation times might not be acceptable. To illustrate the scope of the problem, let us consider a study that aims at comparing different texts. For example, a researcher might want to find out whether different articles are based on the same original material (e.g., Boumans, 2016; Welbers, van Atteveldt, Kleinnijenhuis, & Ruigrok, 2016). However, the number of neccessary comparisons increases exponentially. If the dataset comprises 100 articles, $100 \cdot 100 = 10,000$ comparisons have to be made; with a still not too high number of 10, 000 articles, this increases to 100, 000, 000 comparisons, and quickly, we arrive in regions that become problematic both in terms of memory and computing time.

As the examples described above illustrate, a naïve approach (i.e., load all data into memory, compare everything with everything) is perfectly fine with small datasets, but once we scale up, problems arise. Thus, we need to carefully think about how to build a framework that deals with such tasks in a smarter way.

One might object that the advent of cloud-computing services has turned these challenges from unsurmountable ones to ones that can be tackled. This is indeed the case, but in fact it actually highlights the need for the systematic planning of a research infrastructure. After all, using such services come with certain requirements—like, in general, some programming knowledge, and the selection of tools and approaches that can be efficiently run on such a cloud-computing platform. In addition, as a framework for scaled-up content analysis should also be sustainable (for instance, reusable for later projects), the task of scaling up content analysis is not one of mere availability of storage, memory, and computational power.

Using our own research practice and that of our colleagues to inform our choices, we see four essential requirements.

(1) The framework should be usable on a laptop, but should be designed in a way that it can be run on a powerful server or even a cluster of servers to analyze millions of documents (*scalability*).

(2) The framework should not depend on any commercial software and run on all major operating systems, which, in fact, is also necessary to satisfy the first criterion. In practice, that means that it needs to be *free and open source*.
(3) The framework should be flexible and programmed in a way that facilitates users in adopting it to their own needs and to use it for collaboration on a wide range of projects (*adaptability*). The second criterion is a precondition for this.
(4) The framework should have a powerful database engine on the background which gives the advanced user full control; but at the same time, there must be a easy-to-use interface for the inexperienced user (*multiple interfaces*).

We discuss these four criteria one by one in the following subsections.

Scalability

Traditional content analyses typically deal with a number of cases in the order of magnitude of thousands. In some rare exceptions, tens of thousands are reached. But even in a massive study of news coverage of the 2009 EP elections in all 27 EU member states (Schuck, Xezonakis, Elenbaas, Banducci, & De Vreese, 2011), "only" $N = 52,009$ news items were (manually) analyzed. However, larger and larger collections of texts become digitally available and, as computing is cheap while human coders are expensive, it does not make sense to draw a sample of texts to be analyzed. This has been famously dubbed as the $N =$ all approach of Big Data analysis (Mayer-Schönberger & Cukier, 2013). In the words of Kitchin (2014a), "Big Data is characterized by being generated continuously, seeking to be exhaustive and fine-grained in scope, and flexible and scalable in its production" (p. 2).[5] Consequently, this means that methods for analyzing such data have to be scalable as well.

Scalability and the efficiency of the implementation of an analysis could be neglected when the amount of data was limited. But this has changed, and it is argued that "[s]ocial research has to embrace more efficient and scalable methods if it is to use online data to improve current models and theories" (Gonzalez-Bailon & Paltoglou, 2015, p. 106). In fact, one does not need to analyze really big Big Data to run into scalability problems.

For example, in a study in which $N = 6,142$ agency releases articles had to be linked to $N = 22,928$ news articles, Boumans (2016) used a specific custom-written program to do so. However, when he wanted to conduct a similar analysis on sets of about $N = 100,000$ and $N = 250,000$ items, he found that re-using the software from the smaller study was unfeasible, both in terms of memory and computing time needed. While on a small dataset, the difference between the old program and the new, more efficient program was irrelevant (it does not really matter whether it takes a few minutes or some hours to arrive at the result), this difference in efficiency translated to few hours vs. several weeks on the larger dataset. Such analyses that focus on research questions asking about the overlap between collections of texts are a prime example that can only be answered in a scaled-up framework: human coding is inherently impossible, as remembering the content of so many articles to find it back in other articles exceeds the capacity of the human brain; and small-scale standalone programs to link similar strings (e.g., Schnell, Bachteler, & Reiher, 2005) are designed for other purposes and simply cannot deal with such large datasets.

To ensure scalability, one thus has to consider the efficiency of the algorithms used. For example, communication scholars conducting large-scale automated content analysis are often interested in co-occurrences of words in texts, such as media articles, internet posts, and institutional communication (e.g., Hellsten, Dawson, & Leydesdorff, 2010; Jonkman & Verhoeven, 2013; Leydesdorff &

---

[5] While we have argued above that *Big Data* is not the most appropriate term for the type of data most social scientists work with, the general argument here remains true for smaller, but still very large datasets: There is little reason to draw a sample if enough computing power is available.

Welbers, 2011; Van der Meer, Verhoeven, Beentjes, & Vliegenthart, 2014). When comparing words in hundreds of thousands of texts, most words do actually *not* occur in a given text, and most texts actually are *not* linked to other texts (e.g., Jonkman & Verhoeven, 2013).

Consequently, a matrix of such data structures contains a lot of zeros. A much more efficient way of doing calculations based on these data is therefore to use a so-called sparse matrix, in which only the non-zero values are stored. Somewhat related, packages achieve scalability by using streaming techniques that do not load all data into memory before estimating a model, but update the model continuously while reading the data, as for example the topic modeling package by Řehůřek and Sojka (2010) does. More generally, whether a given algorithm is efficient or not does not matter in small datasets, but becomes increasingly important once we scale up content analysis.

A second consideration is the need for a modular architecture. By this, we mean that in a framework for scaled-up content analysis, it must be possible to have different parts of the framework located at different systems. For instance, the actual analysis does not necessarily need to be conducted on the same computer as where the data is stored. For example, to run the analyses in his dissertation, Van Atteveldt (2008) ran the AmCAT (Amsterdam Content Analysis Toolkit) infrastructure, which he developed, on two servers: a dedicated database server and a dedicated script server. Of course, one could also opt to install both on the same physical machine. Similarly, the xtas (eXtensible Text Analysis Suite) infrastructure (De Rooij et al., 2012) as well as the Leipzig Corpus Miner (Niekler et al., 2014) distinguish between workers, a web frontend, and a database. While all of this can be run locally on one computer, the framework is scalable in that it also allows of distributing tasks between a number of machines. Similarly, toolkits for analyzing social media messages rely on SQL database servers (e.g., DMI-TCAT, Borra & Rieder, 2014) or NoSQL database servers (e.g., smappPy, Social Media and Political Participation Lab at New York University, 2016), which may or may not be run on the same machine as where the analyses are conducted. Extending this line of reasoning, one could also argue that using MapReduce-frameworks like Hadoop can be of added value here. However, most datasets used in our discipline do not reach a size that would require this.[6]

Open source

From the above, it follows that we need to be able to run our framework on (multiple) real or virtual machines. Already from a purely financial and practical standpoint, it becomes clear that it is impractical to acquire and administer multiple licenses for each and every machine. But there are more reasons to strive for independence from closed-source and proprietary software.

Without a doubt, the scientific community has profited from the rise of open software and a culture of sharing source code free of charge (e.g., Günther & Quandt, 2016). This is not only true in financial terms, but also because it allows re-combining and improving existing code without having to reinvent the wheel all the time. In particular, Python and R, two languages used extensively in the data science community, but also in communication science research, are continuously extended by additional modules that users share with the community, which leads to a virtuous circle of increasing popularity and improvement of the software. This popularity also means that many cutting-edge techniques are first implemented in such open-source frameworks, before they are used in proprietary packages. For instance, Günther and Quandt (2016) note that:

> "with open-source toolsets like Voyant Tools (voyant-tools.org) and vivid user communities for R and Python, there are many resources available for social scientists who aim to include automated text analysis methods into their projects. Using sophisticated tools and resources from disciplines such as computer science and computational linguistics, journalism scholars can gain insight into the constant information flow and make big data a regular feature in the scientific debate" (p. 86).

---

[6] For an example of an exception, see Lansdall-Welfare et al. (2017).

Examples for such open-source components that can be included in a content-analysis framework include highly popular modules like the Natural Language Toolkit NLTK (Bird, Loper, & Klein, 2009) or the Stanford Natural Language Processing tools (Manning et al., 2014), but also general-purpose libraries for efficient computation of, e.g., machine-learning problems (e.g., Pedregosa et al., 2011; Řehůřek & Sojka, 2010).

It is also important to consider the use of proprietary closed-source software from the perspective of research standards. First of all, if the source code is not open, the software is essentially a black box. For instance, if one uses a proprietary package to do a sentiment analysis, but the underlying algorithm is not public, this does not contribute much to scientific knowledge and errors might not be discovered (Broussard, 2016; Busch, 2014). In line with this argument, Heiberger and Riebling (2016) identify one big problem of contemporary social science research, namely "using a patchwork of different, specialized programs most of which are proprietary, thereby making it almost impossible to know their exact inner workings or definitions and resulting in an inflexible workflow" (p. 6).

In addition, it is impossible to reproduce the results when the software is not available any more. An open-source algorithm, on the other hand, can be re-implemented again, even for systems that do not even exist yet. In such a long-term perspective, the reliance on open-source solutions also mitigates the risk of vendor lock-in, i.e., the problem that once one has chosen for a specific (proprietary) system, it is hard or even impossible to switch to another one. For example, if a system would not store or at least is able to export its data in a widely recognized open format (e.g., CSV, XML, JSON), it might be hard or even impossible to transfer it to another system.

Moreover, if all parts of a content analysis framework are kept open source, results can be replicated by any researcher, regardless of their financial means.

Adaptability

The two aforementioned criteria (scalability and open-source) are related to a third criterion, which we refer to as adaptability. By this, we mean that the framework should be flexible enough to be adapted with a reasonable effort. For example, it should be possible to extend the framework by including new functions for analyses or new input filters for new types of content. Users with some technical knowledge should be able to make such changes, which—in general—is achieved by using open-source components and popular programming environments. In addition, also less technically savvy users should be able to tailor the analyses to their needs. For example, rather than just offering an option to remove stopwords, it should be possible to modify the stopword list. This also means that such options should not be hard-wired in the program itself, but rather be provided in the form of configuration files that can be easily changed by the users themselves. This makes it also possible to use tailored configuration files for each research project one runs. Communication scholars are increasingly interested in communication data entailing multiple character encodings. For instance, social media data (e.g., Twitter and Facebook) standardly includes characters such as emoticons, hashtags, and mixed languages. Adaptability therefore also means that there should not be any inherent barriers that prevent analyzing context from different languages and scripts. While the unicode standard, for example, has been in place for decades, there are still some tools in use that operate only on the basis of the limited set of 256 ASCII-characters. This means that each emoticon in a social media message, and each quotation in Hebrew or Arabic, cannot be handled. Even though most natural language processing techniques are only implemented for a few languages up until now, there should be the possibility to integrate support once such a resource becomes available.

Another important aspect of adaptability concerns the ability to integrate (by-)products of own research projects to use them for later projects. In practice, we often see that once a (Ph.D.-) project is finished, models and other resources that have been build disappear. For instance, a researcher might have trained some machine learning models, or created an extensive list of regular expressions, or any other asset. Losing information and knowledge is not only costly and inefficient in the long run, it may also pose severe problems in the case of longitudinal projects where several consecutive studies may build on each other. Hence, a flexible framework should make it easy to add resources, in order to enable others to re-use them.

Simple interface for beginners, but no limits for power users

At this point, one of the obstacles for wide-spread use of ACA is the lack of easy-to-use tools. While a lot of techniques are known, especially in fields like computer science, there are comparably few communication scientists who can apply these methods (for a discussion on this see Boumans & Trilling, 2016). This is actually a dilemma: While having an easy-to-use tool would enable more people to apply ACA methods, this is potentially at odds with the adaptability criterion the scalability criterion formulated above. Consequently, even though it may be tempting in the short term, ease-of-use must not be achieved at the expense of other crucial conditions for being able to scale up content analysis.

To solve this dilemma, we suggest that a framework for scaled-up content analysis should provide multiple ways of accessing it. This makes it accessible for different groups of researchers with different needs. For instance, one can think of a combination of the following elements:

- a web interface that provides point-and-click access to the most common analyses and allows exporting subsets of the data;
- a web interface that allows the use of a flexible query language;
- a command-line interface to allow scripting and batch processing of (complicated or time-consuming) analyses;
- an API to link the system to statistical packages like R; and
- direct access to the underlying database, bypassing the whole toolkit itself.

Such a design makes the infrastructure usable for research groups with diverse needs and different levels of technical understanding.

Scaling up in practice

Having established the criteria for scaling up content analysis, we would like to emphasize that the journey towards scaled-up content analysis is a continuum rather than a binary either/or question. We tried to systematize different dimensions of scalability in Figure 1.

One dimension of scaling up is scaling up the scope of the project – moving from one-off studies (P1 in the figure) via re-using data (P2) to a permanent, flexible framework for cross-project data collection and analysis (P3), as indicated by the upper x-axis. For instance, a number of projects at the University of Amsterdam joined forces to build an infrastructure as we will present in this chapter to create synergies and answer research questions reaching from an investigation of differences between online and offline news (Burggraaff & Trilling, 2017), via the predictors of news sharing (Trilling, Tolochko, & Burscher, 2017) to the characteristics of company news coverage (Jonkman, Trilling, Verhoeven, & Vliegenthart, 2016) and the influence of such coverage on stock rates (Strycharz, Strauss, & Trilling, 2018). All of these studies were conducted using a Python-based framework with a NoSQL database backend, making use of techniques ranging from regular-expression based keyword searches to supervised and unsupervised machine learning, and further analyzing the aquired data using regression models and time series analysis.

Collecting data not for a single project, but for re-use in various projects, goes hand in hand with scaling up the size of the dataset, as the lower x-axis in Figure 1 indicates. Let us illustrate the scale of such analyses with some more—admittedly rather arbitrary—examples. Manual content analyses (M1) usually comprise a couple of hundreds of items. An upper bound may be given by an example of a massive project with an exceptionally high number of more than 50,000 news items (Schuck et al., 2011), which involved dozens of annotators.

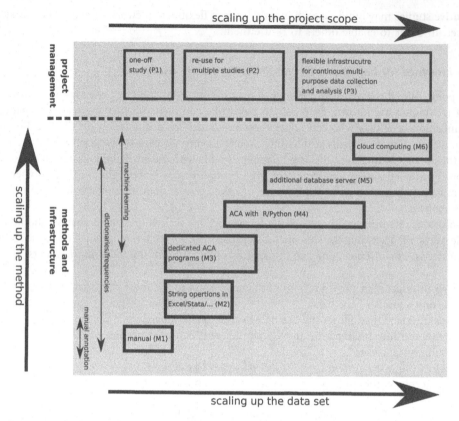

Figure 1. Dimensions of scaling up content analysis.

In contrast, in a study that used simple SPSS string operations (M2) to count the occurrence of actors, but also words indicating concepts like "conflict" or "negativity", Vliegenthart, Boomgaarden, and Boumans (2011) were able to automatically code more than 400,000 articles without needing any human annotator, allowing them to study the prevalence of personalization, presidentialization, conflict, and negativity over time.

An example for ACAs using dedicated programs (M3) could be a large agenda-setting study by Zoizner, Sheafer, and Walgrave (2017), involving almost half a million news articles and speeches, and allowing them to answer the question how media coverage sets the agenda of politicians. For this, they used a proprietary program called Lexicoder. A limitation of such approaches is their inflexibility: Even though the list of indicators for specific concepts supplied by the program might have worked very well in their case, it can be problematic to adapt the methodology. For instance, if one wanted to use only slightly more complicated rules (e.g., X must be mentioned, but Y not), then it becomes hard or impossible to adapt such a program—but such an adjustment would be trivial if a language like R or Python is used. This is illustrated in a study by Kroon (2017): In a very similar fashion, she was interested in measuring frames in communication about older employees. However, she did not use fixed lists of words in a standalone program, but implemented the same functionality using regular expressions and AND-, OR-, as well as NOT-conditions.

Even though dedicated programs for ACA exist, Jacobi et al. (2016), who analyzed more than 50,000 news articles, note: "The easiest way to get started with LDA [a popular ACA technique; DT & JJ] is through the open-source statistical package R. Although specialized software for topic models is available [...], an advantage of using R is that it is a statistical package that many social scientists already use for other analyses." (p. 95). Indeed, using an environment like R or

Python (M4) becomes increasingly popular among communication scientists. Another example might be a topic model of 77 million tweets processed by Guo, Vargo, Pan, Ding, and Ishwar (2016).

Many studies take scalability a step further an use a dedicated database in combination with R (e.g., Driscoll & Walker, 2014; Kleinnijenhuis, Schultz, & Oegema, 2015) or Python (e.g., Jonkman et al., 2016; Strycharz et al., 2018), which frequently is not run locally, but on a dedicated server (M5). These can be dedicated, physical servers, but also virtual machines on a cloud computing platform. The studies of Kleinnijenhuis et al. (2015) and Strycharz et al. (2018) both dealt with similar research questions: They were interested in the relationship between news and stock exchange rates. In such cases, the availability of a large-scale database, in which complicated searches can be done, and in which subsequent analyses can be executed in languages such as R (as in Kleinnijenhuis et al., 2015) or Python (as in Strycharz et al., 2018), pays off. A final example would be a study by Lansdall-Welfare, Sudhahar, Thompson, Lewis, and Cristianini (2017), who used distributed computing (M6) to analyze 150 years of British periodicals, which amounts to millions of articles, using Hadoop.

Moving from projects of a limited scope (P1) to larger projects (P3) also implies that different methods and different technical infrastructures come into play. As we can see, scaling up the size of the dataset (depicted on the lower x-axis) is related to scaling up the method (M1–M6, as denoted on the y-axis). The manually collected and annotated dataset (M1) is clearly not scalable. While dictionary and frequency-based methods can be used already with simple software (M2), the use of more advanced methods like machine learning requires more skills (usually M4) and shows its power mostly in larger datasets. While a dedicated content analysis software (M3) might already have some machine learning functions integrated, their capabilities are usually not scalable enough, for instance due to their inflexibility or limitations on the amount of documents they can process.

In other words: For a limited study (P1), a manual method (M1) may still be feasible. Once the scope of the projects grows, we move from the non-scalable manual approach (M1), via a slightly better scalable approach using common software packages (M2 and M3) and programming languages (M4) to the use of dedicated database servers (M5) and possibly cloud computing (M6).[7]

Proposing a scheme like the one in Figure 1 inherently loses nuance (e.g., supervised machine learning might require some manual annotation); however, it can provide a rough guide on what to take into account when planning to scale-up content analysis. Let us outline how a scaled-up content analysis that could be placed in the upper-right corner of Figure 1 might look like.

As an example, Figure 2 shows the general design for a system that can be used to conduct content analyses like the examples discussed above. It comprises of three steps: (1) retrieving, structuring, and storing the data; (2) cleaning the data; and (3) analyzing the data.

Structuring and storing the data

The researcher first has to decide on a format in which to store the data. To meet the criteria of scalability, independence, and adaptability, we choose an open format that allows us to store all kind of data—for example tweets, news items, and Facebook comments. We decide to use a JSON-based approach: an open standard to store key-value pairs in a human-readable way. It is flexible, supports nested data structures, and allows us to store full texts (in fact, any kind of data) in a database, along with other fields that provide some meta-information (e.g., date of

---

[7]We do not discuss specific frameworks like Hadoop in detail, because they are for even large-scale content analysis not (yet) neccessary (for an exception, see Lansdall-Welfare et al., 2017). This may change, however, once it becomes more common to analyze non-textual data. For a comparison between MongoDB and Hadoop for social media research, we refer to Murthy and Bowman (2014).

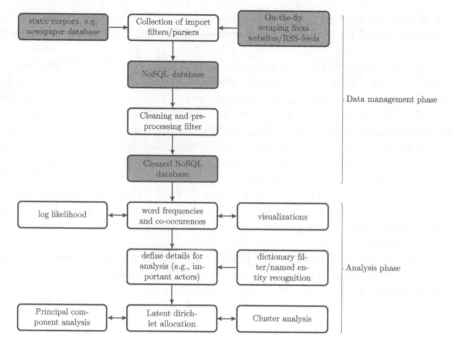

Figure 2. An example of different phases in a scaled-up automated content analysis.

publication, source, length, language, etc.). We use an open-source database (like MongoDB or ElasticSearch) as backend to comply with our criteria (see Günther, Trilling, and Van de Velde (2018) for a discussion on the use of these databases in the social sciences).

Cleaning the data

In content analysis, it is crucial to avoid missing mentions of the core concepts regarding the topic of study. We address this issue in two ways. First, we use a preprocessing step in which possible variations of core concepts (e.g., Wal-Mart or Wal Mart) are replaced by a uniform code (e.g., Walmart). To do so, we propose using a priori listings of case-specific actors and concepts (see, e.g., Jonkman et al. (2016) for an implementation of this). These can be words, but also patterns. Also, things like part-of-speech tagging (POS) or named entity recognition (NER) can be performed at this stage. Because the results are fed back into the database, even operations that take a long time to run (maybe prohibitively long on an individual computer) can be used more efficiently, as it only has to be executed once. This is an important consideration for developing a truly scalable system, that at the same time avoids doing the same tasks over and over again. Because of its widespread use within the community, a good choice could be to implement these functions using Python (e.g., Freelon, 2014a; Günther & Quandt, 2016).

Analyzing the data

Communication researchers often use methods that are based on word frequencies—e.g., assessment of Log-Likelihood scores; Principal Component Analyses (PCA); co-occurrence or semantic networks, and cluster analyses (see, e.g., Van der Meer, 2016). Recently, a new tool has extended this collection: topic models like Latent Dirichlet Allocation (LDA) (for examples of LDA in communication research, see Günther & Quandt, 2016; Jacobi et al., 2016; Strycharz et al., 2018; Tsur et al.,

2015) and its extensions author-topic models and structured topic models. All these methods have their owns merits, and they are often used together to reach a deeper understanding. In particular, all of the analysis functions can be conducted using popluar open-source modules like the Python packages NLTK (Bird et al., 2009), scikit-learn (Pedregosa et al., 2011), and gensim (Řehůřek & Sojka, 2010), which makes the complete workflow transparent and reproducible. But while the analysis of texts if the prevalent use case in today's communication science, there is no inherent reason not to also use such methods to analyze pictures or other type of data, which could as well be stored within the system.

As this example shows, using only open-source components and components that as far as possible are suitable for later scaling up and that are integrated into a consistent workflow, we can build a system that conforms with the criteria we developed and falls in the right-upper corner of the scalability-scheme we presented in Figure 1.

A note on feasibility

Some might object that we sketched an "ideal world scenario" that proposes standards and guidelines that cannot be adhered to by colleagues and teams with limited means. However, we argue that the hurdles are surmountable.

Regarding our first point, scalability and the ability to run the infrastructure on a server, the resources needed are limited. Many universities or regional or national scientific platforms offer server infrastructure for free, and the event of commercial cloud computing platforms like Amazon Web Services allow renting the necessary resources for a couple of hundreds of euros per year—a negligible cost compared to the costs for human annotators in manual content analyses. What usually is necessary, though, is some knowledge of the Linux operating system—a skill that is not exactly rocket science.

Our second point, that all components should be free open source software (FOSS), obviously does not involve any financial investment. Regarding the third point, adaptability, the main investment lies in actually *doing* all these adoptions. For instance, looking at the steps outlined in Figure 2, probably one of the most time-consuming steps is the adoption of the import filters and parsers, as these need to be tailored to the specific types of data at hand. The necessary time for this, though, can be massively reduced by providing standard templates that people with limited training can adapt. While it is difficult to give an accurate estimate of the level of training that is needed, an indication might be provided that we regularly hire graduate students, which had no prior programming knowledge but followed an eight-week course on automated content analysis, to work on and enhance a framework like the one we presented.

Regarding the fourth point, the availability of multiple interfaces, is probably the most demanding one, while at the same time, one of the most important ones: fter all, ease-of-use is crucial to encourage the adoption of the system. While there are systems that feature easy-to-use web interfaces that allow untrained users to interact with the system (e.g., Borra & Rieder, 2014; Niekler & Wiedemann, 2015; Niekler et al., 2014; Van Atteveldt, 2008), developing such an interface takes a lot of time and asks for specific skills. What can help is a step-by-step approach, in which first ready-to-use components are used (like, e.g., the Kibana dashboard for the ElasticSearch database) as a temporal solution, before developing a custom web interface that unlocks the full potential also for users with less technical knowledge.

To sumamrize, it is probably safe to say that setting up a basic infrastructure that conforms to our guidelines—even if its done for the first time—can be done in a few days with limited effort and financial means, provided that one makes use of the available building blocks and systems out there (e.g., Van Atteveldt, 2008). Getting everything "right" and optimally adapted to the own needs and purposes, however, might take some months, and in particular hiring some research assistants.

Conclusion

In this article, we set out to present a framework for scaling up content analysis. In particular, we proposed four criteria: scalability, open source, adaptability, and multiple interfaces.

We demonstrated that these criteria can be fulfilled by setting up a framework relying on a NoSQL database (like MongoDB or ElasticSearch) as backend and a set of tools around it to effectively implement all functions needed for data collection, structuring, preprocessing, and analysis. Because of the wide availability of packages for text analysis and machine learning, implementing such a system in the Python programming language could be a good choice. However, we would like to stress that our argument is language-agnostic: others might choose for other backends and languages.

In doing so, we reflected on the state of the art and aimed at providing a road map for the field. While there is an increasing interest in automated content analysis techniques, many current approaches lack scalability. While standalone packages offer ease-of-use, this limitation leads to automated content analysis falling short of its possibilities. Given the growing role of large-scale data analysis in social science research (see for an extensive discussion Kitchin, 2014a), it is of crucial importance to have the necessary infrastructure and one's disposal. And here, communication scientists should be at the forefront: as Big Data analysis requires not only technical skills, but also thorough knowledge of the field (Kitchin, 2014a, p. 162), the design of a framework for content analysis is not merely an engineering problem that could be outsourced or bought in.

Numerous subfields in communication science can benefit from using a framework as we described in Figure 2. For instance, continuously accumulating texts from different sources, like news media, social media, or press releases, would allow to conduct analyses that are difficult or impossible to conduct with smaller samples, such as answering questions about framing or agenda-setting effects on a fine-grained level. Most actors are actually *not* in the news on most days, so studying them requires enormous amounts of data. Being able to use ACA techniques to identify topics in such a corpus and to study their development over time allows us to answer exciting questions around news hypes and dynamics of news dissemination.

The relevance of having a flexible and scalable framework is even more apparent when analyzing user-generated comment like product reviews, comments on articles, and so on. This kind of data, which is increasingly of interest to researchers from various fields, has numerous properties which call for a framework as we described. In particular, their nested structure (reviews belonging to a product, comments belonging to an article), their highly diverse structure, and their ever-growing volume make it infeasible to use off-the-shelf software. Moreover, to study personalized content (i.e., different users getting a different version of an article, an advertisement, and so on) it is necessary to have a technological framework that allows storing the different versions and comparing their similarities and differences.

To do all this, however, communication scientists have to break with several habits. First of all, they must shift the project management focus toward more long-term data collection and re-usability of data and infrastructure across projects. In manual content analysis, the cost associated with data collection and analysis is roughly proportional to the amount of data. Apart from relatively low startup costs for things like coder training, it essentially is twice as expensive to code twice as many articles. In contrast to this, automated content analysis can have a rather high startup cost, but doubling the amount of data does not cost much. This is why it should be avoided to invest in project-specific solutions, and why an extensible, flexible, and open framework geared towards re-usability should be preferred. Second, communication scientists have to let go of the idea of analyzing a dataset represented by *one* file. Instead, as illustrated in our figures, they should switch to using databases, which can be updated with new data, re-used for multiple projects, and also store intermediate results (like preprocessed text). Third, they should define the scope of their needs according to a scheme like the one we presented in Figure 1. While they might not end up in the upper right corner, which is the most heavily scaled-up approach, they should make an informed decision of how much scaling up is feasible and necessary for them.

Our notion of scaling up content analysis therefore should be seen as a guiding principle and aid for researchers that are in the adopting automated content analysis techniques. The principle of scaling up implies that already at the design phase one should think about how to re-use data and analysis, thereby focusing on the scalability of the approach. Scalability does not only refer to storage size of computational power, but also to things like making it scriptable, and to the avoidance of manual interventions. Manually copy-pasting something might be fine for one file, but what if you have hundreds of them?

For future work, the line of reasoning to behind our criteria for a framework for scaled-up content analysis can be extended. For instance, one can think of making sure that each module in such a framework (input filters, text-processing facilities, analyses) is implemented in a standardized way, to make sure that people with minimal programming knowledge can add or modify these elements (think of student assistants who followed a methods course). This would also make it easier to increase the number of modules to make it more useful for more colleagues to create synergy effects.

An additional way to extend an implemention as discribed in Figure 2 is to follow the example of frameworks which offer the possibility for human *coders* or *annotators* (in communication science lingo and computer science lingo, respectively) to manually code or annotate content (e.g., Niekler & Wiedemann, 2015; Van Atteveldt, 2008). This can be either useful in itself (if the automated part of the analysis is only meant to reduce the number of relevant articles), or it can be used as input to train a machine learning algorithm, which then classifies the rest of the material automatically.

Strycharz et al. (2018) used such a function: They used a regular expression-based search query to identify potentially relevant articles in their database backend, but the retrieved articles where then presented to human annotators who could tag the articles as either relevant or not. While this approach, obviously, does not scale well, it nevertheless could be interesting as an additional component in a scalable framework: Because the annotators' tags where stored in the database itself, one could try to train a supervised machine learning algorithm on it to improve future search results, which, in fact, would add to the system's scalability.

Seeing the increased use of automated content analysis in communication science, we hope to see more implementations of systems that allow scaling up content analysis—but even more, we hope to spark a discussion on best practices for scaling up content analysis. After all, the journey has just begun.

Funding

This work was carried out on the Dutch national e-infrastructure with the support of SURF Foundation.

ORCID

Damian Trilling http://orcid.org/0000-0002-2586-0352

References

Bird, S., Loper, E., & Klein, E. (2009). *Natural language processing with Python*. Sebastopol, CA: O'Reilly.
Borra, E., & Rieder, B. (2014). Programmed method: Developing a toolset for capturing and analyzing tweets. *Aslib Journal of Information Management*, 66(3), 262–278. doi:10.1108/AJIM-09-2013-0094
Boumans, J. W. (2016). *Outsourcing the news? An empirical assessment of the role of sources and news agencies in the contemporary news landscape* (Ph.D. dissertation, University of Amsterdam). Retrieved from http://hdl.handle.net/11245/1.532941

Boumans, J. W., & Trilling, D. (2016). Taking stock of the toolkit: An overview of relevant autmated content analysis approaches and techniques for digital journalism scholars. *Digital Journalism*, 4(1), 8–23. doi:10.1080/21670811.2015.1096598

Broussard, M. (2016). Big data in practice. *Digital Journalism*, 4, 266–279. doi:10.1080/21670811.2015.1074863

Burggraaff, C., & Trilling, D. (2017). Through a different gate: An automated content analysis of how online news and print news differ. *Journalism*. doi:10.1177/1464884917716699

Burscher, B., Odijk, D., Vliegenthart, R., de Rijke, M., & de Vreese, C. H. (2014). Teaching the computer to code frames in news: Comparing two supervised machine learning approaches to frame analysis. *Communication Methods and Measures*, 8(3), 190–206. doi:10.1080/19312458.2014.937527

Burscher, B., Vliegenthart, R., & De Vreese, C. H. (2015). Using supervised machine learning to code policy issues: Can classifiers generalize across contexts? *The ANNALS of the American Academy of Political and Social Science*, 659(1), 122–131. doi:10.1177/0002716215569441

Busch, L. (2014). A dozen ways to get lost in translation: Inherent challenges in large-scale data sets. *International Journal of Communication*, 8, 1727–1744.

Cioffi-Revilla, C. (2014). *Introduction to computational social science: Principles and applications*. London, UK: Springer.

De Rooij, O., Vishneuski, A., & De Rijke, M. (2012). xTAS: Text analysis in a timely manner. *Proceedings of the 12th Dutch-Belgian Information Retrieval Workshop (DIR 2012)*, 89–90.

Driscoll, K., & Walker, S. (2014). Working within a black box: Transparency in the collection and production of big twitter data. *International Journal of Communication*, 8, 1745–1764.

Freelon, D. (2014a). On the cutting edge of big data: Digital politics research in the social computing literature. In S. Coleman, & D. Freelon (Eds.), *Handbook of digital politics*. Northampton, MA: Edward Elgar.

Freelon, D. (2014b). On the interpretation of digital trace data in communication and social computing research. *Journal of Broadcasting & Electronic Media*, 58(1), 59–75. doi:10.1080/08838151.2013.875018

Gerbner, G. (1983). The importance of being critical—In one's own fashion. *Journal of Communication*, 33(3), 355–362. doi:10.1111/j.1460-2466.1983.tb02435.x

Gonzalez-Bailon, S., & Paltoglou, G. (2015). Signals of public opinion in online communication: A comparison of methods and data sources. *The ANNALS of the American Academy of Political and Social Science*, 659(1), 95–107. doi:10.1177/0002716215569192

Grimmer, J., & Stewart, B. M. (2013). Text as data: The promise and pitfalls of automatic content analysis methods for political texts. *Political Analysis*, 21(3), 267–297. doi:10.1093/pan/mps028

Günther, E., & Quandt, T. (2016). Word counts and topic models. *Digital Journalism*, 4(1), 75–88. doi:10.1080/21670811.2015.1093270

Günther, E., Trilling, D., & Van de Velde, B. (2018). But how do we store it? data architecture in the social-scientific research process. In C. M. Stuetzer, M. Welker, & M. Egger (Eds.), *Computational social science in the age of big data. Concepts, methodologies, tools, and applications* (pp. 161–187). Cologne, Germany: Herbert von Halem.

Guo, L., Vargo, C. J., Pan, Z., Ding, W., & Ishwar, P. (2016). Big social data analytics in journalism and mass communication: Comparing dictionary-based text analysis and unsupervised topic modeling. *Journalism & Mass Communication Quarterly*, 93, 332–359. doi:10.1177/1077699016639231

Heiberger, R. H., & Riebling, J. R. (2016). Installing computational social science: Facing the challenges of new information and communication technologies in social science. *Methodological Innovations*, 9, 1–11. doi:10.1177/2059799115622763

Hellsten, I., Dawson, J., & Leydesdorff, L. (2010). Implicit media frames: Automated analysis of public debate on artificial sweeteners. *Public Understanding of Science*, 19(5), 590–608. doi:10.1177/0963662509343136

Hindman, M. (2015). Building better models: Prediction, replication, and machine learning in the social sciences. *The ANNALS of the American Academy of Political and Social Science*, 659(1), 48–62. doi:10.1177/0002716215570279

Jacobi, C., Van Atteveldt, W., & Welbers, K. (2016). Quantitative analysis of large amounts of journalistic texts using topic modelling. *Digital Journalism*, 4(1), 89–106. doi:10.1080/21670811.2015.1093271

Jonkman, J. G. F., Trilling, D., Verhoeven, P., & Vliegenthart, R. (2016). More or less diverse: An assessment of the effect of attention to media salient company types on media agenda diversity in Dutch newspaper coverage between 2007 and 2013. *Journalism, Online First*. doi:10.1177/1464884916680371

Jonkman, J. G. F., & Verhoeven, P. (2013). From risk to safety: Implicit frames of third-party airport risk in Dutch quality newspapers between 1992 and 2009. *Safety Science*, 58, 1–10. doi:10.1016/j.ssci.2013.03.012

Kitchin, R. (2014a). Big Data, new epistemologies and paradigm shifts. *Big Data & Society*, 1(1), 1–12. doi:10.1177/2053951714528481

Kitchin, R. (2014b). *The data revolution: Big data, open data, data infrastructures and their consequences*. London, UK: Sage.

Kleinnijenhuis, J., Schultz, F., & Oegema, D. (2015). Frame complexity and the financial crisis: A comparison of the United States, the United Kingdom, and Germany in the period 2007–2012. *Journal of Communication*, 65(1), 1–23. doi:10.1111/jcom.12141

Krippendorff, K. (2004). *Content analysis: An introduction to its methodology* (2nd ed.). Thousand Oaks, CA: Sage.

Kroon, A. C. (2017). *Images of older workers: Content, causes, and consequences* (PhD dissertation, University of Amsterdam). Retrieved from http://hdl.handle.net/11245.1/0980ab70-3251-498a-b5a3-9bc288023062

Lacy, S., Watson, B. R., Riffe, D., & Lovejoy, J. (2015). Issues and best practices in content analysis. *Journalism & Mass Communication Quarterly*, 1–21. doi:10.1177/1077699015607338

Lansdall-Welfare, T., Sudhahar, S., Thompson, J., Lewis, J., & Cristianini, N. (2017). Content analysis of 150 years of British periodicals. *Proceedings of the National Academy of Sciences, 114*(4), E457–E465. doi:10.1073/pnas.1606380114

Lazer, D., Pentland, A., Adamic, L., Aral, S., Barabási, A.-L., Brewer, D., ... Van Alstyne, M. (2009). Computational social science. *Science, 323*, 721–723. doi:10.1126/science.1167742

Lewis, S. C., Zamith, R., & Hermida, A. (2013). Content analysis in an era of big data: A hybrid approach to computational and manual methods. *Journal of Broadcasting & Electronic Media, 57*(1), 34–52. doi:10.1080/08838151.2012.761702

Leydesdorff, L., & Welbers, K. (2011). The semantic mapping of words and co-words in contexts. *Journal of Infometrics, 5*(3), 469–475. doi:10.1016/j.joi.2011.01.008

Leydesdorff, L., & Zaal, R. (1988). Co-words and citations relations between document sets and environments. In *Informetrics* (pp. 105–119). Elsevier.

Manning, C. D., Surdeanu, M., Bauer, J., Finkel, J., Bethard, S. J., & McClosky, D. (2014). The Stanford CoreNLP natural language processing toolkit. In *Association for Computational Linguistics (ACL) system demonstrations* (pp. 55–60). Retrieved from http://www.aclweb.org/anthology/P/P14/P14-5010

Mayer-Schönberger, V., & Cukier, K. (2013). *Big Data: A revolution that will transform how we live, work, and think*. Boston, MA: Houghton Mifflin Harcourt.

Murthy, D., & Bowman, S. A. (2014). Big Data solutions on a small scale: Evaluating accessible high-performance computing for social research. *Big Data & Society, 1*(2), 1–12. doi:10.1177/2053951714559105

Niekler, A., & Wiedemann, G. (2015). Semi-automatic content analysis for the identification of neo-liberal justifications in large newspaper corpora. In *GESIS Computational Social Science Winter Symposium*. doi: 10.13140/RG.2.1.2283.1128

Niekler, A., Wiedemann, G., & Heyer, G. (2014). Leipzig Corpus Miner – A text mining infrastructure for qualitative data analysis. In *Terminology and knowledge engineering 2014 (TKE 2014)*. Berlin.

Parks, M. R. (2014). Big Data in communication research: Its contents and discontents. *Journal of Communication, 64*(2), 355–360. doi:10.1111/jcom.12090

Pedregosa, F., Varoquaux, G., Gramfort, A., Michel, V., Thirion, B., Grisel, O., ... Duchesnay, E. (2011). Scikit-learn: Machine learning in Python. *Journal of Machine Learning Research, 12*, 2825–2830.

Řehůřek, R., & Sojka, P. (2010). Software framework for topic modelling with large corpora. In *Proceedings of the LREC 2010 Workshop on New Challenges for NLP Frameworks* (pp. 45–50). Valletta, Malta: ELRA. http://is.muni.cz/publication/884893/en

Russell Neuman, W., Guggenheim, L., Mo Jang, S., & Bae, S. Y. (2014). The dynamics of public attention: Agenda-setting theory meets Big Data. *Journal of Communication, 64*(2), 193–214. doi:10.1111/jcom.12088

Scharkow, M. (2011). Thematic content analysis using supervised machine learning: An empirical evaluation using German online news. *Quality & Quantity, 47*(2), 761–773. doi:10.1007/s11135-011-9545-7

Schnell, R., Bachteler, T., & Reiher, J. (2005). MTB: Ein Record-Linkage-Programm für die empirische Sozialforschung. *ZA-Information, 56*, 93–103.

Schuck, A. R., Xezonakis, G., Elenbaas, M., Banducci, S. A., & De Vreese, C. H. (2011). Party contestation and Europe on the news agenda: The 2009 European parliamentary elections. *Electoral Studies, 30*(1), 41–52. doi:10.1016/j.electstud.2010.09.021

Shah, D. V., Cappella, J. N., & Neuman, W. R. (2015). Big Data, digital media, and computational social science: Possibilities and perils. *The ANNALS of the American Academy of Political and Social Science, 659*(1), 6–13. doi:10.1177/0002716215572084

Sjøvaag, H., & Stavelin, E. (2012). Web media and the quantitative content analysis: Methodological challenges in measuring online news content. *Convergence: the International Journal of Research into New Media Technologies, 18*(2), 215–229. doi:10.1177/1354856511429641

Social Media and Political Participation Lab at New York University. (2016). *smapPy*. Retrieved from https://github.com/SMAPPNYU/smappPy

Strycharz, J., Strauss, N., & Trilling, D. (2018). The role of media coverage in explaining stock market fluctuations: Insights for strategic financial communication. *International Journal of Strategic Communication, 12*(1), 67–85. doi:10.1080/1553118X.2017.1378220

Trilling, D., Tolochko, P., & Burscher, B. (2017). From newsworthiness to shareworthiness. *Journalism & Mass Communication Quarterly, 94*(1), 38–60. doi:10.1177/1077699016654682

Tsur, O., Calacci, D., & Lazer, D. (2015). A frame of mind: Using statistical models for detection of framing and agenda setting campaigns. In *Proceedings of the 53rd annual meeting of the association for computational linguistics and the 7th international joint conference on natural language processing* (pp. 1629–1638). ACL.

Van Atteveldt, W. (2008). *Semantic network analysis: Techniques for extracting, representing, and querying media content*. Charleston, SC: BookSurge.

Van der Meer, G. L. A. (2016). *Communication in times of crisis: The interplay between the organization, news media, and the public* (PhD thesis, University of Amsterdam). Retrieved from http://hdl.handle.net/11245/1.532222

Van der Meer, G. L. A., Verhoeven, P., Beentjes, H., & Vliegenthart, R. (2014). When frames align: The interplay between PR, news media, and the public in times of crisis. *Public Relations Review, 40*(5), 751–761. doi:10.1016/j.pubrev.2014.07.008

Vliegenthart, R., Boomgaarden, H. G., & Boumans, J. (2011). Changes in political news coverage: Personalisation, conflict and negativity in British and Dutch newspapers. In K. Brants, & K. Voltmer (Eds.), *Political communication in postmodern democracy: Challenging the primacy of politics* (pp. 92–110). London, UK: Palgrave Macmillan.

Welbers, K., van Atteveldt, W., Kleinnijenhuis, J., & Ruigrok, N. (2016). A gatekeeper among gatekeepers. *Journalism Studies, Online First*. doi:10.1080/1461670X.2016.1190663

Zamith, R., & Lewis, S. C. (2015). Content analysis and the algorithmic coder: What computational social science means for traditional modes of media analysis. *The ANNALS of the American Academy of Political and Social Science, 659*(1), 307–318. doi:10.1177/0002716215570576

Zoizner, A., Sheafer, T., & Walgrave, S. (October 2017). How politicians' attitudes and goals moderate political agenda setting by the media. *The International Journal of Press/Politics, 22*(4), 431–449. doi:10.1177/1940161217723149

How Team Interlock Ecosystems Shape the Assembly of Scientific Teams: A Hypergraph Approach

Alina Lungeanu, Dorothy R. Carter, Leslie A. DeChurch, and Noshir S. Contractor

ABSTRACT
Today's most pressing scientific problems necessitate scientific teamwork; the increasing complexity and specialization of knowledge render "lone geniuses" ill-equipped to make high-impact scientific breakthroughs. Social network research has begun to explore the factors that promote the *assembly* of scientific teams. However, this work has been limited by network approaches centered conceptually and analytically on "nodes as people," or "nodes as teams." In this article, we develop a *"team-interlock ecosystem"* conceptualization of collaborative environments within which new scientific teams, or other creative team-based enterprises, assemble. Team interlock ecosystems comprise teams linked to one another through overlapping memberships and/or overlapping knowledge domains. They depict teams, people, *and* knowledge sets as nodes, and thus, present both conceptual advantages as well as methodological challenges. Conceptually, team interlock ecosystems invite novel questions about how the structural characteristics of embedding ecosystems serve as the primordial soup from which new teams assemble. Methodologically, however, studying ecosystems requires the use of more advanced analytics that correspond to the inherently multilevel phenomenon of scientists nested within multiple teams. To address these methodological challenges, we advance the use of *hypergraph methodologies* combined with bibliometric data and simulation-based approaches to test hypotheses related to the ecosystem drivers of team assembly.

Introduction

The idea that high-impact scientific breakthroughs are the work of "lone geniuses" has long lost its appeal. Narrative (e.g., Charney, 2003) as well quantitative accounts (Uzzi & Spiro, 2005) reveal that today's most pressing scientific problems—those within domains ranging from translational medicine to environmental sustainability, from cyber learning to disaster response—present a degree of complexity that necessitates scientific *teamwork* (Barabási, 2005; Wuchty, Jones, & Uzzi, 2007).

For the most part, studies of scientific teamwork have focused on the factors related to team effectiveness occurring *after* a team has assembled (e.g., National Research Council, 2015). However, studies of team functioning post-assembly miss important dynamics occurring *prior* to team assembly that impinge on scientists' decisions to join teams in the first place. Scientific organizations, such as universities or research institutes, afford individuals substantial autonomy and flexibility on forming or join new teams. Given that science is a human endeavor, scientists are susceptible to natural human social preferences (e.g., McPherson, Smith-Lovin, & Cook, 2001) and cognitive limitations (e.g., De Solla Price, 1965; Dunbar, 1992) when making decisions related to team assembly. These natural human proclivities often lead individuals to assemble into teams that are suboptimal in their effectiveness. In fact, effectively assembling scientific teams can be a daunting task, both logistically as well as technically, and many scientific teams suffer from the consequences of suboptimal team assembly (Cummings & Kiesler, 2008).

To address these challenges, researchers have begun to investigate the mechanisms that promote the assembly of new scientific teams. Research on scientific team assembly often relies on *bibliometric* approaches, which leverage publically available information on publication, co-authorship, and/or citation activity. These approaches are used to understand how prior patterns of collaborative activities influence future team assembly. For the most part, research investigating drivers of scientific collaboration has depicted collaborations as ties between *pairs* of researchers (e.g., Cummings & Kiesler, 2007; Lungeanu, Huang, & Contractor, 2014). These "person-to-person" approaches focus on the likelihood of a collaboration tie between a pair of researchers in a team. Lost in these approaches, however, is the ability to distinguish a network of (1) three researchers linked pairwise because all three collaborated on one publication from (2) three researchers linked pairwise because pairs of them collaborated on three separate publications. Thus, the representation used by current network approaches that model collaboration as dyads are unable to discriminate between these two substantially different collaboration scenarios.

Scientists often work in teams including more than two individuals. Thus, representations of collaboration should explicitly characterize multiple individuals in teams. Furthermore, most scientists work on *multiple* teams, concurrently, and across time, as they engage with new and old collaborators to address research problems requiring unique and overlapping knowledge domains. Thus, representations of collaboration should explicitly characterize teams that overlap or "interlock" with other teams based on common members (i.e., *member interlocks*) and/or common research topics (i.e., *knowledge interlocks*). Poole and Contractor (2011) argue that, for the aforementioned reasons, we should examine how scientific teams nucleate within complex *multilevel ecosystems*. The structures of interlocking *teams* within scientific ecosystems are relevant to understanding team assembly because social phenomena, such as social bonding, knowledge generation, and learning, are team experiences that are likely to shape the assembly of future teams.

Research on scientific team assembly needs to move beyond a dyadic person-to-person framework that characterizes collaboration as a collection of pairs of researchers and explore the ways in which characteristics of the interlocking team structures, in which scientists are embedded, influence team assembly. This article leverages an extension to graph theory, *hypergraphs*, to address methodological limitations of current network approaches and better account for the nesting of individuals in teams and the patterns of interlocks among teams. We begin by describing key aspects of scientific team ecosystems, and operationalize these concepts using a hypergraph framework. Then, we provide exemplar hypotheses suggesting that there are certain characteristics of scientific ecosystems that enhance the likelihood that certain scientific teams will assemble. Finally, we demonstrate the combined use of hypergraph methodologies with an advanced computational technique to test these hypotheses. The hypergraph methodological approach enables researchers to operationalize the patterns of team interlock structures characterizing scientific ecosystems. The computational technique, *ecosystem simulations*, tests ecosystem-based hypotheses by comparing observed characteristics of scientific ecosystems with the ecosystem characteristics from a distribution of randomly generated ecosystems.

Team interlock ecosystems

Research on scientific team assembly has significantly advanced our understanding of scientific teamwork by demonstrating that there are certain fundamental human tendencies that give rise to new teams. This research uncovered three categories of fundamental characteristics that predict future collaboration between any given *pair* of scientists: individual attributes of the scientists, prior collaboration relations between them, and characteristics associated with the broader structure in which the scientists' dyad is embedded.

Collaboration dyads are more likely to form when scientists have complementary skills (Lee & Bozeman, 2005), are geographically proximate (Cummings & Kiesler, 2007), and when both members have longer tenure, are affiliated with lower tier institutions, or have lower H-index scores (Lungeanu et al., 2014). Research also shows that prior collaboration reduces uncertainty about the likelihood that the pair will engage in a future collaboration (Cummings & Kiesler, 2008; Gruenfeld, Mannix, Williams, & Neale, 1996; Guimera, Uzzi, Spiro, & Amaral, 2005; Hinds, Carley, Krackhardt, & Wholey, 2000; Lungeanu & Contractor, 2015; Lungeanu et al., 2014). Finally, the patterns of relationships within the broader collaboration networks also affect the likelihood of collaboration between pairs of scientists. For example, Newman (2001, p. 408) showed that "friend-of-a-friend" mechanism (Heider, 1958) predicts future collaboration, with researchers having a "30% or greater probability of collaborating if both have collaborated with a third scientist."

Whereas prior work has built on the notion that collaboration occurs at the level of a *dyad*, in reality, collaboration takes place within *multilevel* social structures, with individuals engaged in *multiple teams* that each often have many more than two members (Bordons & Gómez, 2000). In fact, evidence suggests 65–90% of knowledge workers are members of multiple teams at any given time (O'Leary, Mortensen, & Woolley, 2011). Figure 1 provides an illustration of this "multiple team membership" phenomenon. This figure depicts ten individual scientists (labeled m1–m10 in orange) who are organized into six teams (labeled T1–T6 with lines indicating their boundary).

In Figure 1, let us assume two researchers (m5 and m6) have assembled into a newly formed team (Team 1), with boundaries indicated by the dotted red line. The figure indicates that in addition to Team 1, Member 5 also belongs to Team 2, and Member 6 belongs to both Teams 4 and 6. Thus, Team 1 is *directly* interlocked with Teams 2, 4, and 6 based on common members (i.e., a *member interlock*). In turn, the three teams in Team 1's *proximal* ecosystem (i.e., the team's with which it has direct member interlocks) include additional members who belong to other teams, and so on. Thus, as Figure 1 depicts, more distally, Team 1 is *indirectly* linked to Teams 3 and 5 through interlocks with teams that are directly interlocked with Team 1. In scientific ecosystems organized into teams,

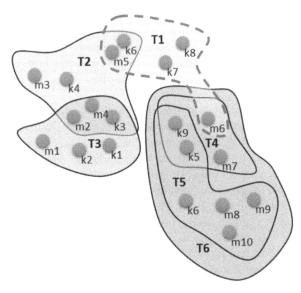

Figure 1. Sample representation of a scientific ecosystem characterized by interlocking teams. Note. The red dotted line represents the external boundary of a newly assembled scientific team; the solid black lines represent the boundaries of other scientific teams in the proximal and more distal surrounding ecosystem; A letter T represents a scientific team; A letter m represents a member of one or more scientific team; A letter k represents the knowledge domain considered within a scientific team.

knowledge "flows through network ties via the individuals that connect different teams by virtue of co-memberships on teams" (Zaheer & Soda, 2009, p. 3). Thus, the structures of team interlocks surrounding scientists are likely to be relevant to understanding the situations that give rise to new teams.

Figure 1 also depicts the knowledge domains (e.g., topics, areas of inquiry) relevant to each team (labeled k1–k9 in green), and the ways in which the teams are interlocked based on overlapping knowledge. Within the context of Team 1, Members 5 and 6 pursue research related to Knowledge Domains 6, 7, and 8. However, both scientists have also worked as members of teams that have considered other knowledge domains. As a member of Team 2, Member 5 investigates Knowledge Domains 3, 4, and 6. Thus, Team 1 is not only interlocked with Team 2 based on overlapping membership, the teams are joined through a *knowledge interlock* based on the overlapping engagement with Knowledge Domain 6. In fact, Member 5 might be bringing her prior experiences investigating Knowledge Domain 6 to bear within the context of Team 1. In contrast to Member 5, the teams that Member 6 has contributed to previously did not investigate any of the topics that are considered within Team 1. However, this scientist has had experience working within other knowledge domains that might be relevant to the topics of investigation within Team 1. Thus, the ways in which teams are interlocked through knowledge are relevant to understanding team assembly.

A hypergraph approach to characterizing team interlock ecosystems

The team interlock view of scientific ecosystems, illustrated in Figure 1, depicts more accurately and richly the embedded social and intellectual milieu within which scientific collaboration occurs. However, the structure of team interlock ecosystems can be challenging to identify and describe. In fact, one reason for the paucity of studies examining overlapping teams is that such ecosystem-focused investigations entail multiple levels of analysis (e.g., individuals nested in multiple interlocking teams), which, in turn, requires the use of more complex statistical analyses and tools (Lungeanu, Sullivan, Wilensky, & Contractor, 2015). Network researchers interested in collectives have typically employed one of two analytic approaches to capture relational properties unfolding at multiple levels (e.g., person-to-person; person-to-team) of social systems. The first is to capture actor-to-actor relationships and represent their structure in a one-mode network; the second is to capture the linkages of actors-to-collectives in a two-mode or bipartite network linking individuals to teams. The former fails to represent the entitativity of the collective; put simply, three links between three nodes could imply one entity (or team) of three researchers or three entities (or teams) of three separate pairs of researchers. The latter, bimodal network approach, links individuals to collectives, but fails to capture individuals' relations with one another or other relations (e.g., overlap in knowledge domains) among teams.

In our conceptualization of collaboration, scientific teamwork constitutes more than a collection of dyadic person-to-person or person-to-team connections. Collaboration draws together a team of authors, publishing articles involving multiple knowledge areas. This collaboration cannot be accurately represented by projecting onto a one-mode network (researcher-to-researcher or person-to-person) or a two-mode network (researcher-to-article or person-to-team). Instead, the collaboration is better formalized as a **hypergraph**, in which authors, keywords, and/or journals are combined in (possibly overlapping) sets (Shi, Foster, & Evans, 2015). Hypergraphs have been well established in the area of mathematics, as an extension to graph theory, beginning with foundational work by Berge (1973). Just as edges represent links between pairs of nodes within a network (or, what graph theorists call, a graph), **hyperedges** represent "links" connecting multiple (not necessarily a pair of) nodes that represent a single entity within a "hypergraph." For instance, in the case of a publication, a single hyperedge connects all of the authors on the team as well as all of the keywords for the article. A collection of hyperedges (with possible overlaps) constitutes a hypergraph, or what we refer to as a *team interlock ecosystem*. Recently, researchers have begun to recognize the value of hypergraphs as a means of representing and analyzing more complex data about teams, with promising results (Ghasemian, Zamanifar, & Ghasem-Aghaee,

2017; Ghasemian, Zamanifar, Ghasem-Aqaee, & Contractor, 2016; Sharma, Srivastava, & Chandra, 2014; Shi et al., 2015; Taramasco, Cointet, & Roth, 2010).

Key components of hypergraphs

Hypergraph approaches are beneficial for characterizing the structures of team-based enterprises like scientific research. Here, we review key hypergraph components that can be used to characterize team interlock ecosystem structures.

First, in the context of scientific collaboration, a *hyperedge* represents the boundary of a scientific team such as those indicated by lines in Figure 1. Hyperedges are comprised of multiple *nodes* of one or more "type." For example, nodes could be researchers participating in a collaboration and the knowledge domains associated with that collaboration). Nodes can have connections to other nodes (as in one-mode person-to-person networks) as well as to hyperedges (as in bipartite person-to-team networks).

As a whole, a *hypergraph* constitutes a set of hyperedges which can be connected to one another based on node overlaps (i.e., member or knowledge interlocks). For example, Figure 1 depicts a hypergraph based on the publications involving members of a focal team. Mathematically, a hypergraph is represented as $H = (V, E)$. V is a set of *nodes* (or vertices), $V = \{v_1, v_2, \ldots, v_n\}$, that can be authors, keywords, methods, etc. E is a set of *hyperedges*, $E = \{e_1, e_2, \ldots, e_m\}$, that include as many or as few as zero nodes. This is an important departure from one-mode social networks in which edges are required to have exactly *two* nodes.

The interlocks between hyperedges based on overlapping nodes constitute *hyperties*. A hypertie indexes the set of nodes shared by two or more hyperedges, which can include any arbitrary number of nodes in theory. Mathematically, we have: $T = e_1 \cap e_2 \cap \ldots \cap e_i$, for any i number of hyperedges e_1 through e_i, where $i \geq 2$.

The *local neighborhood* $L(e)$ of a hyperedge e is defined as $L(e) = \{h \in E : \exists v, s.t.\ v \subset \{e, h\}\}$, that is the set of all hyperedges h (i.e., other teams) such that there is at least one node v shared by both e and h. In the case of scientific collaboration, the local neighborhood of a team is composed of the set of other teams that are directly connected to the focal team through at least one member or knowledge interlock.

Key hypergraph characteristics

The core components of hypergraphs—nodes, ties, hyperedges, hyperties, and local neighborhoods—give rise to structural characteristics at multiple levels (e.g., node, hyperedge, hypergraph levels) (Sullivan, Zhu, Lungeanu, & Contractor, 2012). Thus, hypergraph approaches are particularly useful for characterizing the multilevel ecosystems with connections among people, knowledge, and/or other types of nodes organized into teams. Below we present a short description of these metrics. The full description of these metrics, together with the mathematical equations and the graphical representation, is available in the *Supplemental Material* Appendix.

Node metrics

At the nodal (i.e., person, keyword) level, we compute a *node's degree* and a *node's hyperdegree*. *Node degree* refers to the number of distinct nodes with which a focal node is connected (Ghoshal, Zlatic, Caldarelli, & Newman, 2009; Wang, Rong, Deng, & Zhang, 2010), a *node's hyperdegree* is the number of hyperedges (e.g., teams) in which the node participates (Estrada & Rodríguez-Velázquez, 2006; Wang et al., 2010; Zlatic, Ghoshal, & Caldarelli, 2009).

Hyperedge metrics

At the level of a single team (i.e., a hyperedge), *hyperedge degree* reflects to the number of other hyperedges (teams) with the focal hyperedge (team) is interlocked via overlapping members

(Wang et al., 2010; Zlatic et al., 2009). Next, a *hyperedge clustering coefficient* reflects the degree to which the set of teams that are directly connected to the focal team—the team's "local" neighborhood—exhibit the network property of *triadic closure* among teams through interlock connections. A hyperedge clustering coefficient for a focal team represents the degree to which the set of teams that are directly interlocked with the focal team are, themselves, interlocked with one another.

Hypergraph metrics

Hypergraph metrics move beyond characterizing patterns of connections surrounding individual nodes or individual teams to characterize the patterns of team interlocks for an entire scientific ecosystem (i.e., the hypergraph level). We consider three hypergraph metrics in particular: First, *hypergraph density* represents the proportion of interlocks among teams out of the total possible number of team interlocks (e.g., through overlapping membership; through overlapping knowledge). Second, a "*hypergraph clustering coefficient*" which indicates the degree to which *all* possible triads of teams in a hypergraph exhibit the property of closure. A final hypergraph metric, *hypergraph centralization* indicates the degree of variance in the distribution of hyperedge degree centrality scores across a hypergraph.

Illustrative hypotheses linking characteristics of team interlock ecosystems to scientific team assembly

Adopting a team-interlock perspective to conceptualize scientific collaboration and a hypergraph methodological approach to characterize structures of scientific ecosystems enables researchers to more accurately understand the ecosystem factors influencing team assembly. Research on teams has shown that important phenomena related to social bonding (e.g., cohesion, trust), knowledge generation, and learning emerge at the *level of the team* as a whole, and that teams often differ from one another substantially in terms of their team-level properties (Edmondson, 1999; Kozlowski & Klein, 2000). Thus, we propose that in addition to person-to-person connections among researchers, the patterns of interlock connections between teams are relevant to team assembly. The overarching question addressed by this research is: *What structural characteristics of scientific ecosystems affect the likelihood that sets of researchers will assemble into a new team?*

To demonstrate how this research question might be addressed, we provide illustrative hypotheses considering the extent to which team assembly is influenced by three of the key structural characteristics of scientific ecosystems: (1) *hypergraph clustering coefficient;* (2) *hyperedge clustering coefficient;* and (3) *hypergraph centralization.* These three characteristics are similar to three characteristics of person-to-person social networks (e.g., Oh, Chung, & Labianca, 2004; Oh, Labianca, & Chung, 2006) that have been shown to have important implications for individual and collective outcomes (i.e., "social network clustering", "individual brokerage," and "social network centralization," respectively). We extend work on person-to-person social networks to explore three research questions considering the degree to which the presence of these properties within scientific ecosystems influences team assembly.

Research Question 1: Are researchers more likely to assemble into a team in ecosystems characterized by greater "coherence" (i.e., higher hypergraph clustering coefficient scores)?

Substantively, a hypergraph clustering coefficient characterizes the extent to which teams tend to be organized into **coherent** intellectual communities, whose membership and knowledge overlap. Ecosystem coherence has the potential of impacting the assembly of new scientific teams because the creation of new knowledge is a result of a social process in which individual researchers share expertise and gain legitimacy by working across overlapping teams (Acedo, Barroso, Casanueva, & Galán, 2006; Moody, 2004; Wuchty et al., 2007).

The process of sharing and learning diverse knowledge, however, can be complicated by the loss of meaning during the transfer process (Grant, 1996). As a result, scholars argue that the transfer and combination of knowledge needs to be facilitated by the development of a common language and exchange norms (Grant, 1996; West & Anderson, 1996). A more coherent ecosystem structure—one with higher levels of clustering—reflects the presence of a community of scientists who have built common socio-cognitive models that allow them to adopt a common language for the knowledge that they exchange. Such cognitive models are necessary in order to recognize the knowledge held by others, understand current knowledge sharing practices, and understand the rules to identify new and useful knowledge and recombine prior knowledge in order to generate new ideas (Murray & O'Mahony, 2007; Uzzi & Spiro, 2005). For example, Murray and O'Mahony (2007) argue that in order for innovation to occur, existing knowledge must be shared within intellectual communities, but, in addition, knowledge must be reused, recombined, and accumulated. Higher levels of ecosystem coherence offer opportunities for scientists to share, search for, access, and apply knowledge. Accordingly, we hypothesize that scientific teams are more likely to assemble in ecosystems that are coherent by virtue of having triadic closure among teams based on overlapping members, overlapping knowledge domains or both (the intersection of the team and knowledge interlocks).

Hypothesis 1: Scientific teams are more likely to assemble in ecosystems that are coherent by virtue of having triadic closure among teams based on overlapping members.

Hypothesis 2: Scientific teams are more likely to assemble in ecosystems that are coherent by virtue of having triadic closure among teams based on overlapping knowledge domains.

Hypothesis 3: Scientific teams are more likely to assemble in ecosystems that are coherent by virtue of having triadic closure among teams based on having both overlapping members and overlapping knowledge domains.

In summary, we have proposed three hypotheses linking scientific ecosystems to the assembly of teams. The first specified the effect of ecosystem coherence in team member interlocks, whereas the second specified the effect of ecosystem coherence in knowledge interlocks. Understanding the joint effects of ecosystem coherence captured by the intersection of member and knowledge interlocks (Hypothesis 3) is important because it prompts us to further inquire: Which of these structural properties is more important for team assembly: ecosystem coherence with regard to: (a) team member interlocks, (b) team knowledge interlocks, or (c) intersection of team member and knowledge interlocks?

Next, we turn to the second of our three research questions exploring how ecosystems influence team assembly.

Research Question 2: Are researchers more likely to assemble into a team when their local neighborhoods exhibit greater "local brokerage" (i.e., lower hyperedge clustering coefficient scores)?

Although our first three hypotheses posit that closure across the *broader* ecosystem (i.e., ecosystem coherence) support team assembly, scholars have also pointed out that excessive closure might hurt creativity. In fact, research suggests that having a sufficient level of diversity in knowledge and social connections is a critical factor underpinning creative and/or innovate ideas (Fleming, Mingo, & Chen, 2007; Guimera et al., 2005; Reagans, Zuckerman, & McEvily, 2004; Uzzi & Spiro, 2005). Substantively, a hyperedge clustering coefficient metric represents the degree of diversity (or lack thereof) in team memberships and expertise in a team's local community. When there are no interlocks between the set of teams that are interlocked with a focal team, the hyperedge clustering coefficient for that focal team would be zero. In this case, the members of the focal team are uniquely positioned to draw upon and combine *different* resources from other teams of which they are also members. Thus, a lower hyperedge clustering coefficient is an indicator that the team is a broker between other teams.

In person-to-person networks, research suggests individuals who occupy positions of brokerage —those with connections to people who themselves are unconnected—can reap career benefits, in part, because they have greater access to diverse ideas (Burt, 1992). Likewise, we expect that a team of scientists whose local ecosystem communities exhibit *lower* levels of closure (i.e., higher brokerage at the team-level) are more likely to have access to diverse ideas that lead to new research projects. Hence, our next set of hypotheses posit teams will be more likely to assemble when there is sufficient opportunity for potential team members to broker ideas from other teams they belong to, but which do not have overlapping members (besides them) or overlapping knowledge domains. Accordingly:

Hypothesis 4: Scientific teams are more likely to assemble when they are brokering ties within the local neighborhood of their team member interlock ecosystem.

Hypothesis 5: Scientific teams are more likely to assemble when they are brokering ties within the local neighborhood of their team knowledge interlock ecosystem.

Hypothesis 6: Scientific teams are more likely to assemble when they are brokering ties within the local neighborhood of their team member and knowledge interlock ecosystem.

Whereas these hypotheses test specific predictions rooted in prior research on network brokerage, we also explore the question of which structural properties are more important to team assembly: *local brokerage with regard to: (a) team member interlocks, (b) team knowledge interlocks, or (c) team member and knowledge interlocks?*

Finally, we turn to the last of our three research questions exploring how ecosystems influence team assembly.

Research Question 3: Are researchers more likely to assemble into a team in ecosystems characterized by greater "ecosystem decentralization" (i.e., lower hypergraph centralization scores)?

A final consideration when sets of scientists decide to assemble into a new team is whether there are sufficient opportunities to impact the broader scientific community through the generation of scientific output. As Murray and O'Mahony (2007) note, expectation of reward is a key consideration when engaging in creative work. One ecosystem characteristic that may impact whether a set of scientists expect rewards for assembling into a new team is the degree to which the ecosystem is **centralized** around one or a few teams that are interlocked with many other teams (i.e., hypergraph centralization).

On the one hand, well-developed theories and concepts are beneficial for the advancement of scientific fields because they provide a sense of direction for knowledge development and enable understanding of key research topics (Kuhn, 1996). High ecosystem centralization indicates that a few teams of productive individuals have successfully achieved the development of conceptual frameworks and have disseminated those ideas by collaborating with many other teams. As such, higher ecosystem centralization signify ecosystems with less opportunity for impact. Thus, scientists operating in highly centralized ecosystems may not have the motivation to assembly into a new team, unless the new team does contains members of a highly central team. Thus, we posit that when ecosystems are more **de-centralized** (i.e., less centralized), scientific teams are more likely to assemble.

Hypothesis 7: Scientific teams are more likely to be assembled when the ecosystem formed by team member interlock is highly decentralized.

Hypothesis 8: Scientific teams are more likely to be assembled when the ecosystem formed by team knowledge interlock is highly decentralized.

Hypothesis 9: Scientific teams are more likely to be assembled when the ecosystem formed by team member and knowledge interlock is highly decentralized.

Here, again, we explore the question of which of these effects is more important: *Decentralization in a (a) team member interlock, (b) team knowledge interlock, or (c) team member and knowledge interlock ecosystem?*

Method

We deploy a novel hypergraph methodology to test our hypotheses using bibliographic data about teams submitting research proposals to a Clinical and Translational Science Award (CTSA) competition hosted at a large Midwestern University and funded by the National Institutes of Health (NIH). A total of 101 research teams, consisting of 147 participants, submitted proposals in two rounds of the grant competition. Given that we are examining the team assembly process, we excluded 47 proposals that were solo-authored. Additionally, eight proposals were excluded because either the exact same proposal team submitted proposals in both rounds of the competition (three teams) or because of data collection issues (five teams). The final dataset contains 46 proposals co-authored by 98 scientists, out of which only four proposals were awarded.

For each proposal team, we extracted team members' collaborators and the collaboration (co-authorship) relations among those collaborators. First, we used the *Web of Science (WoS)* database provided by Thomson Reuters to extract each team member's publication history. Author name disambiguation is a recognized issue when constructing bibliometric measures (Torvik, Weeber, Swanson, & Smalheiser, 2005). This is the problem of ensuring that we only consider, for instance, the publications by John Smith who submitted a research proposal and not others with the same name. To overcome this limitation, we manually verified each publication against researchers' resumes available on the institution website. Second, we identified all co-authors listed on the above publications and disambiguated their names. For example, "Smith, J" and "Smith, JH" were considered same person. This is because the probability that one researcher will collaborate with two different researchers named "Smith, J" and "Smith, JH" is very low. Third, we extracted all publications of the extended list of co-authors from the WoS database. We considered only those publications that were co-authored by at least two researchers from our dataset to be valid.

Based on this information, we created 46 unique team interlock ecosystems (i.e., one for each proposal team). Each interlock ecosystem included the focal proposal team, all of the focal team's interlocking teams (all publications co-authored by members of the focal team), and all of the second-order interlocking teams connected to those initial interlocking teams (all publications co-authored by co-authors of the focal team). Additionally, for each publication included in the ecosystem, we extracted both the "author keywords" (i.e., keywords provided by the original authors) and the "keywords plus" (i.e., keywords extracted from the titles of the cited references by Thomson Reuters) available in the WoS database. Therefore, each team ecosystem is formed from teams (i.e., hyperedges) that contain two type of nodes: scientists and keywords. The teams are linked together through a team membership interlock, team knowledge (keywords) interlock, or the intersection of the team membership and knowledge interlock. It is important to note that this depiction of the scientific ecosystem begins with interlocks based on overlapping team membership and then measures the degree to which teams with interlocking membership also have overlap on the topics studied by the focal team.

Figures 2a–2c present the visual representation of one of the 46 team interlock ecosystems from our dataset. As shown in this figure, the team interlocks (i.e., hyperties between teams) differ when we consider a network based on member interlock, knowledge interlock, or the intersection of the member and knowledge interlock.

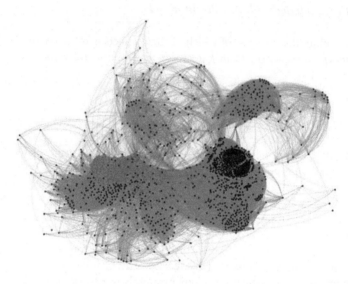

Figure 2a. A random sample team ecosystem from our dataset (ecosystem with 1612 teams, 246 scientists, and 5,462 keywords). The green diamond node represents the focal team (team that was assembled). The red dots represent teams in the local ecosystem (with which they had direct overlapping members). The black dots represent the remaining teams in the ecosystem (with which they had indirect overlapping members via the teams represented by the red dots). The links are based on team member interlock.

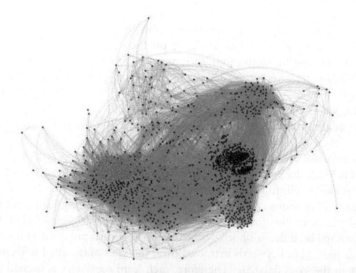

Figure 2b. A random sample team ecosystem from our dataset (ecosystem with 1612 teams, 246 scientists, and 5,462 keywords). The green diamond node represents the focal team (team that was assembled). The red dots represent teams in the local ecosystem (with which they had direct overlapping members). The black dots represent the remaining teams in the ecosystem (with which they had indirect overlapping members via the teams represented by the red dots). The links are based on team knowledge interlock.

Figure 2c. A random sample team ecosystem from our dataset (ecosystem with 1612 teams, 246 scientists, and 5,462 keywords). The green diamond node represents the focal team (team that was assembled). The red dots represent teams in the local ecosystem (with which they had direct overlapping members). The black dots represent the remaining teams in the ecosystem (with which they had indirect overlapping members via the teams represented by the red dots). The links are based on team member and knowledge interlock both being present.

Hypergraph indices representing team interlock ecosystem characteristics

In order to characterize properties of coherence, brokerage, and centralization for each of the 46 team interlock ecosystems, we computed a set of hypergraph-based descriptive metrics corresponding to each concept. Ecosystem coherence was computed using the *hypergraph clustering coefficient* measure. As mentioned previously, hypergraph clustering coefficient indicates the degree to which all possible triads of teams exhibit closure across a hypergraph. A high hypergraph clustering coefficient indicates that there is a high amount of overlap or "coherence" across the ecosystem, based on teams that share common members (team member interlock), common knowledge (team knowledge interlock), or the combination of members and knowledge (team member and knowledge interlock).

Local brokerage was computed using the *hyperedge clustering coefficient* metric. The hyperedge clustering coefficient is defined as the amount of overlap that exists among the teams that share common members with the focal team (team member interlock), or amount of overlap that exists among the teams that share the same keywords (team knowledge interlock) or both (the intersection of the team member and knowledge interlock). It is computed as the density of ties among the alters of the focal team. For instance, when there is no overlapping team membership among the teams with which the focal team members co-authored, the hyperedge clustering coefficient would be zero. In other words, high clustering (or low brokerage) means that researchers tend to collaborate with the collaborators of their collaborators.

Ecosystem decentralization was computed using the *hypergraph centralization* measure. Hypergraph centralization indicates the degree of variance in the distribution of teams' degree centrality scores across the ecosystem. In other words, a high ecosystem centralization implies that one or a few teams have a disproportionate number of team interlock connections with other teams based on overlapping membership and/or overlapping knowledge domain.

Ecosystem simulation analytic approach

The aforementioned descriptive metrics were computed for each of the 46 ecosystems in which each of the 46 focal (proposal) teams were embedded. However, by themselves these descriptive measures do not tell us if the relevant metric is high or low—as compared to chance, captured by a null model. Therefore, to test our hypotheses, we developed a computational technique to compare the observed team ecosystems with simulated *null models*. For each team ecosystem, which is a network of teams, we began by generating 200 simulated synthetic networks which served as the null models. The output of the simulation included means, δ_{sim}, and standard deviations, $\sigma(\delta_{sim})$, for the following measures: hypergraph clustering coefficient, hyperedge clustering coefficient of the focal team, and hypergraph centralization. Second, we tested whether the frequency distribution of these measures in the null models were normally distributed. Third, we tested our hypotheses by comparing the ecosystem metrics generated from the simulated networks with the observed ecosystem. Specifically, we computed the z-scores of the observed measures relative to the random measures: $z(\delta_{obs}) = (\delta_{obs} - \delta_{sim})/\sigma(\delta_{sim})$.

Null model simulation

For each of the 46 focal team interlock ecosystems, we created a null model reflecting a set of random synthetic networks that incorporate realistic aspects of the observed data and its network structure. In particular, the null model for each ecosystem was based on generating synthetic networks that shared the following empirical facts with the observed ecosystems: the number of teams, the number of authors per team, and the number of keywords per team. Therefore, the null model preserves for each ecosystem the same number of teams, authors, and keywords as our observed ecosystems.

In order to test the team member interlock hypotheses (H1, H4, and H7), we started from the observed network and generated 200 random samples, while holding constant the number of authors, the number of publications, the distribution number of authors per publication, and the distribution of number of publications per author. In order to test the team knowledge interlock hypotheses (H2, H5, and H8), we generated 200 random samples, fixing the number of keywords, the number of publications, the distribution number of keywords per publication, and the distribution of number of publications per keyword. Finally, in order to test the team member and knowledge interlock hypotheses (H3, H6, and H9), we generated 200 random samples, fixing the number of authors and keywords, the number of publications, the distribution number of authors and keywords per publication, and the distribution of number of publications per author and per keyword.

For each of the 200 simulated ecosystems, we computed the same hypergraph metrics we obtained for the observed ecosystem. We then computed a z-score comparing each of the observed hypergraph metrics with the distribution of that corresponding metric in the 200 simulated ecosystems. A positive z-score indicates a score that is higher than expected by chance. A negative z-score indicates a score that is less than expected by chance. The larger the z-score, the greater the difference between the observed score and the mean score obtained from simulations. Since utilizing the z-score assumes that the data is a normally distributed, we tested the distribution of each of the hypergraph metrics for each ecosystem. We computed Skewness/Kurtosis values for each metric obtained from the simulation of the 46 team ecosystems. Using Bulmer's (1979) rule of thumb, we assessed if each of the distributions were approximately symmetric (i.e., skewness is between –½ and +½,) or moderately skewed (i.e., skewness is between –1 and –½ or between +½ and +1) for all ecosystems. Furthermore, we also conducted the Kolmogorov-Smirnov test for normality which yields a p-value for each metric for each ecosystem. A p-value higher than 0.05 implies that the distribution is normal. When a distribution is deemed not to be normal, we do not report the z-score results.

Results

Descriptive statistics

Table 1 and Figures 3–5 provide descriptive information about our team ecosystems. We examine traditional descriptive statistics such as the number of observed teams, authors, and keywords, and features of team interlocks. We also examine whether the team interlock structures follow a power law distribution.

Table 1. Descriptive statistics.

Variable	Metric	Mean	SD	MIN	MAX
Proposal team: Team size		2.39	0.61	2	4
Ecosystem - general measures	**Hypergraph - general measures**				
Ecosystem: Number of teams in the ecosystem	Number of hyperedges in the hypergraph	2441.93	2572.52	47	8576
Ecosystem: Number of authors in the ecosystem	Number of nodes (node type = scientist) in the hypergraph	242.67	205.02	14	925
Ecosystem: Number of keywords in the ecosystem	Number of nodes (node type = keyword) in the hypergraph	5420.13	4720.11	238	15589
Local ecosystem: Number of teams (direct links) to the focal team	Local neighborhood: number of hyperedges with direct hyperties to the focal hyperedge	143.78	122.81	12.00	615.00
Local ecosystem: Number of unique teams (direct links) to the focal team	Local neighborhood: number of unique hyperedges with direct hyperties to the focal hyperedge	140.28	119.96	12.00	596.00
Team member interlock					
Density	Hypergraph Density	0.15	0.11	0.02	0.44
Centralization	Hypergraph Centralization	0.26	0.09	0.11	0.43
Ecosystem coherence	Hypergraph Clustering coefficient	0.85	0.05	0.74	0.95
Local closure	Hyperedge (local) clustering coefficient	0.61	0.15	0.32	0.93
Team knowledge interlock					
Density	Hypergraph Density	0.05	0.07	0.01	0.35
Centralization	Hypergraph Centralization	0.15	0.07	0.07	0.33
Ecosystem coherence	Hypergraph Clustering coefficient	0.57	0.05	0.50	0.75
Local closure	Hyperedge (local) clustering coefficient	0.16	0.15	0.02	0.72
Team member & knowledge interlock					
Density	Hypergraph Density	0.02	0.04	0.00	0.18
Centralization	Hypergraph Centralization	0.09	0.07	0.01	0.28
Ecosystem coherence	Hypergraph Clustering coefficient	0.60	0.07	0.40	0.76
Local closure	Hyperedge (local) clustering coefficient	0.11	0.11	0.01	0.50

N = 46 team ecosystems

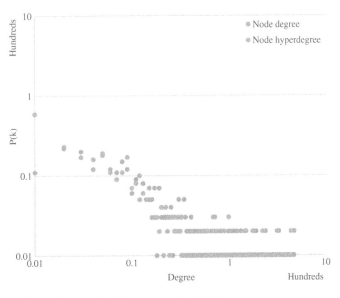

Figure 3. Degree distribution for node type scientist (team ecosystem T024).

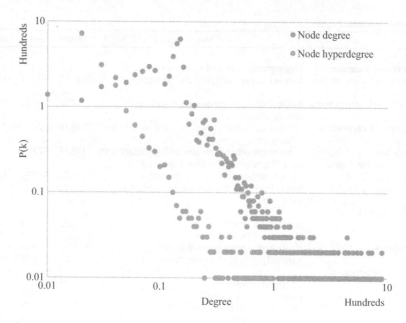

Figure 4. Degree distribution for node type keyword (team ecosystem T024).

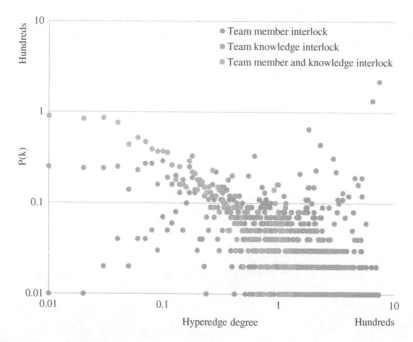

Figure 5. Hyperedge degree distribution (team ecosystem T024).

Team descriptive statistics

The team ecosystems ranged from being comprised of between 47 and 8,576 teams (M = 2,441.93, SD = 572.52), each with between 14 and 925 unique authors (M = 242.67, SD = 205.02), and between 238 and 15,589 unique keywords (M = 5,420.13, SD = 4,720.11). Table 1 presents the overall descriptive statistics for the observed team ecosystems we created around each focal proposal.

Generally, all hypergraph metrics decrease as we move from team member interlocks to team knowledge interlocks to the combined team member and knowledge interlocks. The ecosystems have low density, and, as expected, the density is lowest for the combined team member and knowledge interlocks, because there are fewer hyperties between teams when the ecosystems are based on the presence of both, that is the intersection of, member *and* knowledge interlocks. Furthermore, the ecosystems have an average clustering coefficient of 0.85 (team member interlocks), 0.57 (team knowledge interlocks), and, respectively, 0.60 (combination of team member and knowledge interlocks).

As discussed previously, a hypergraph approach enables us to compute different degree metrics: node degree, node hyperdegree, and hyperedge degree. To illustrate the differences between node degree and node hyperdegree we use one randomly selected team ecosystem from our dataset. A quick examination of these measures provides interesting insights. For example, in the ecosystem for team T024, a scientist can be linked to a maximum of 466 scientist (i.e., maximum node degree for node type scientist in ecosystem T024) and to a maximum of 433 teams (i.e., maximum node hyperdegree for node type scientist in ecosystem T024). See Figure 3 for a presentation of the degree distribution for node type scientist. However, a keyword can be linked to maximum of 998 other keywords (i.e., maximum node degree) but only to a maximum 100 teams (i.e., maximum node hyperdegree). Figure 4 presents the degree distribution for node type keywords. This is an important distinction when we discuss member or knowledge overlap and how far knowledge can spread. This property of knowledge spread relative to team member spread raises an interesting feature of ecosystems. Whereas members have fewer other members to reach out to, they have far more knowledge domains with which they can connect.

Power law distribution

Next, we examined how team interlocks are distributed in the ecosystem. Specifically, we explored whether the team interlock structures exhibit a specific pattern, such as a power law distribution (Barabási & Albert, 1999), i.e., $P(k) \sim k^{-\gamma}$, where k is the degree and $P(k)$ is the fraction of hyperedges that have the degree k. A power law distribution will show that the most hyperedges (i.e., teams) have a low degree and a few hyperedges have a very high degree. This situation will indicate a hierarchy in the ecosystem. Figure 5 presents the hyperedge degree distribution. None of the team interlock ecosystems in our sample followed a power law distribution. This could have been an artifact of the way we constructed the teams' ecosystems: We started from the focal team and considered only those teams (i.e., scientific articles), authors and keywords, that are linked to the focal team directly in one step or indirectly in two steps. Therefore, we excluded the collaborating teams for those teams that are more than two-steps away from the focal team and hence do not belong to the team ecosystem.

Inferential statistics: Hypothesis testing

Before interpreting the results of our hypotheses, it is important to acknowledge that our analysis examines the ecosystem structures of those teams that successfully assembled and submitted grant proposals. Therefore, our analysis does not include those researchers who intended to collaborate and submit proposals, but never submitted the proposals. However, given that we include teams that submitted proposals in two rounds of the grant competition, we are cautiously confident that researchers who had the intention to submit a proposal and had started to collaborate on writing the proposal, had the opportunity to submit the grant proposal in the specified time frame. Furthermore, as discussed above, to partially address this limitation, our analysis compares the observed ecosystem of the assembled team with a set of random simulated ecosystems that match basic characteristics of the observed ecosystem in terms of members, teams, and knowledge areas.

Ecosystem coherence

Our first set of analyses examine the level of coherence in the scientific ecosystem, and the overarching Research Question 1: Are scientists more likely to assemble into a team in ecosystems characterized by higher levels of clustering (i.e., greater ecosystem coherence)? Table 2 presents the hypergraph clustering coefficient for the observed ecosystems and their z-scores based on 200 simulations. A positive z-score indicates a score that is higher than expected by chance. A negative z-score indicates a score that is less than expected by chance. The larger the z-score, the greater difference there is between the score and the mean score obtained from simulations.

Hypothesis 1 posited that scientific teams are more likely to assemble within team ecosystems characterized by greater coherence in team member interlocks. The simulation results showed that the observed hypergraph clustering coefficient in the team member interlock network is higher than expected by chance for all 46 team ecosystems. The results support Hypothesis 1: team ecosystem coherence increases the likelihood for a team to assemble.

Hypothesis 2 posited that scientific teams are more likely to assemble within team ecosystems characterized by greater coherence in team knowledge interlocks. The simulation results showed that the observed hypergraph clustering coefficient in the team knowledge interlock network is higher than expected by chance for 21 team ecosystems and lower than expected by chance for 25 team ecosystems. Interestingly, our hypothesis is supported only for small size team ecosystems. For large ecosystems, ecosystem coherence in team knowledge interlocks does not predict team assembly. This result is explained by the fact that large ecosystems contain interdisciplinary teams that are composed of researchers from different disciplines that publish both single discipline and interdisciplinary articles. The interdisciplinary articles are linked to multiple single discipline articles by virtue of using the same keywords, but the single discipline articles are not interlocked. Therefore, the coherence based on knowledge interlock is lower than expected by chance in such large ecosystems.

Hypothesis 3 posited that scientific teams are more likely to assemble within team ecosystems characterized by greater coherence in the intersection of the team member *and* knowledge interlocks. The simulation results showed that the observed hypergraph clustering coefficient in the member and knowledge interlock network is higher than expected by chance for all 46 team ecosystems. The results support our hypothesis: team ecosystem coherence, where the interlock represents the intersection of the member and knowledge interlock network increases the likelihood for a team to assemble.

We concluded our investigation of the effect of ecosystem coherence on team assembly with the exploratory research question: Which interlock type is more important? To address this question, we conducted paired sample t-tests to compare each pair of ecosystem clustering coefficient scores: team member interlocks, team knowledge interlocks, and the intersection of member and knowledge interlocks. Examining the results of these t-tests shows the hypergraph clustering coefficient for team member interlock networks (M = 0.85, SD = 0.01) is significantly higher than the hypergraph clustering coefficient effect for team knowledge interlock networks (M = 0.57, SD = 0.01); t(45) = 31.92, p = 0.000, and significantly higher than the hypergraph clustering coefficient for the intersection of the team member and knowledge interlock networks (M = 0.60, SD = 0.01); t(45) = 30.17, p = 0.000. Furthermore, paired t-test results show that the hypergraph clustering coefficient for team knowledge interlock networks (M = 0.57, SD = 0.01) is significantly lower than the hypergraph clustering coefficient for the intersection of the team member and knowledge interlock networks (M = 0.60, SD = 0.01); t(45) = −2.99, p = 0.002. These results suggest that high levels of ecosystem coherence with regard to team member interlock networks is most important to team assembly, and relatively more so than high levels of ecosystem coherence for the intersection of the member and knowledge interlock networks or for team knowledge interlock networks alone.

Table 2. Hypergraph clustering coefficient.

Team Id	Team member interlock		Team knowledge interlock		Team member & knowledge interlock	
	Observed value	Z-score	Observed value	Z-score	Observed value	Z-score
T001	0.86	121.16***	0.75	32.38***	0.61	27.36***
T002	0.93	228.69***	0.68	7.05***	0.76	105.56***
T003	0.88	194.66***	0.59	44.67***	0.65	83.02***
T004	0.85	280.19***	0.64	53.88***	0.73	157.05***
T005	0.89	284.23***	0.65	75.99***	0.68	129.04***
T006	0.91	223.14***	0.64	71.70***	0.67	72.02***
T007	0.95	291.49***	0.69	139.24***	0.74	163.99***
T008	0.93	812.33***	0.55	40.98***	0.56	125.09***
T009	0.93	600.68***	0.64	29.04***	0.64	104.34***
T010	0.88	352.07***	0.56	43.90***	0.61	192.64***
T011	0.87	759.84***	0.58	−9.90***	0.63	242.25***
T012	0.80	423.79***	0.55	55.97***	0.61	233.71***
T013	0.85	839.32***	0.59	−50.24***	0.61	258.03***
T014	0.93	1284.03***	0.50	41.77***	0.64	426.10***
T015	0.86	830.83***	0.50	−61.17***	0.57	202.08***
T016	0.81	142.83***	0.60	30.23***	0.60	156.36***
T017	0.89	354.23***	0.58	149.31***	0.66	318.89***
T018	0.88	777.47***	0.52	−10.65***	0.63	336.57***
T019	0.85	709.02***	0.57	90.24***	0.62	314.02***
T020	0.94	1124.12***	0.62	−92.02***	0.69	315.51***
T021	0.88	551.96***	0.51	−34.63***	0.54	209.73***
T022	0.81	507.98***	0.55	175.28***	0.43	140.96***
T023	0.82	1013.03***	0.60	−133.95***	0.59	252.39***
T024	0.86	556.24***	0.60	206.00***	0.64	417.94***
T025	0.89	630.19***	0.60	43.81***	0.67	312.78***
T026	0.77	684.44***	0.55	120.19***	0.61	396.07***
T027	0.83	947.78***	0.54	−58.12***	0.55	312.86***
T028	0.82	821.08***	0.60	−49.84***	0.61	304.41***
T029	0.88	713.93***	0.52	−261.31***	0.55	228.93***
T030	0.88	1317.14***	0.58	−69.06***	0.66	409.78***
T031	0.84	930.66***	0.54	−24.71***	0.61	377.31***
T032	0.86	876.08***	0.51	−326.27***	0.56	234.78***
T033	0.83	1197.30***	0.57	−102.37***	0.59	555.33***
T034	0.87	1325.66***	0.53	−38.17***	0.63	491.63***
T035	0.86	1565.94***	0.58	−289.57***	0.65	517.23***
T036	0.78	785.48***	0.55	25.58***	0.57	466.46***
T037	0.86	1665.84***	0.55	−298.17***	0.60	499.70***
T038	0.79	483.72***	0.56	87.82***	0.53	506.50***
T039	0.82	980.39***	0.56	−201.52***	0.56	462.03***
T040	0.78	1578.92***	0.54	−449.68***	0.54	578.55***
T041	0.79	1923.84***	0.57	−165.54***	0.43	279.81***
T042	0.82	1848.76***	0.54	−409.16***	0.62	853.42***
T043	0.79	2045.62***	0.57	−476.72***	0.58	675.79***
T044	0.74	1956.96***	0.55	−900.15***	0.53	544.91***
T045	0.78	2031.74***	0.55	−645.67***	0.40	233.40***
T046	0.79	2090.51***	0.52	−579.41***	0.56	702.76***

Notes:
1. Teams are sorted based on hypergraph size (from small to large).
2. Z-score is based on 200 simulations. Z-score is presented only for normal distribution frequencies. + 0.10 * 0.05 ** 0.01 *** 0.001.

Local brokerage

Our second set of analyses examined the level of local brokerage and the overarching Research Question 2: Are scientists more likely to assemble into a team when their local ecosystems are characterized by lower levels of clustering (i.e., greater local brokerage)? For these analyses, we compared the local clustering coefficient of the focal team with the overall or global ecosystem clustering coefficient. Therefore, we conducted a paired sample t-test to compare the local and global clustering coefficient.

Hypothesis 4 posited that scientific teams are more likely to be assembled when they are brokering ties within the local neighborhood of their team member interlock ecosystem. The paired t-test showed that the focal team's hyperedge clustering coefficient (M = 0.61, SD = 0.15) was significantly lower than the overall hypergraph clustering coefficient (M = 0.85, SD = 0.01); t (45) = −9.86, p = 0.000. The results support Hypothesis 4: Scientific teams are more likely to assemble when there is more brokerage in the local neighborhood of their team member interlock ecosystem than the global neighborhood.

Hypothesis 5 posited that scientific teams are more likely to be assembled when they are brokering ties within the local neighborhood of their team knowledge interlock ecosystem. The paired t-test showed that the focal team's hyperedge clustering coefficient (M = 0.16, SD = 0.02) is significantly lower than the hypergraph clustering coefficient (M = 0.57, SD = 0.01); t(45) = −23.77, p = 0.000. The results support Hypothesis 5: Scientific teams are more likely to assemble when there is more brokerage in the local neighborhood of their team knowledge interlock ecosystem than the global neighborhood.

Hypothesis 6 posited that scientific teams are more likely to be assembled when they are brokering ties within the local neighborhood of their team member and knowledge interlock ecosystem. The paired t-test showed that the focal team's hyperedge clustering coefficient (M = 0.10, SD = 0.01) is significantly smaller than hypergraph clustering coefficient (M = 0.60, SD = 0.01); t(45) = −35.03, p = 0.000. The results support Hypothesis 6: Scientific teams are more likely to assemble when there is more brokerage in the local neighborhood of their team member and knowledge interlock ecosystem than the global neighborhood.

We concluded our investigation of the effects of local brokerage on team assembly with the exploratory research question: Which interlock type is more important? We conducted paired sample t-tests to compare each pair of local clustering coefficient scores: team member interlocks, team knowledge interlocks, and the intersection of member and knowledge interlocks. Examining the results of these t-tests shows that the hyperedge clustering coefficient for team member interlock networks (M = 0.61, SD = 0.02) is significantly higher than the hyperedge clustering coefficient for team knowledge interlock networks (M = 0.16, SD = 0.02); t(45) = 14.02, p = 0.000 and significantly higher than the hyperedge clustering coefficient for the intersection of the team member and knowledge interlock networks (M = 0.11, SD = 0.01); t(45) = 18.95, p = 0.000. Furthermore, paired t-test showed that the hyperedge clustering coefficient for team knowledge interlock networks (M = 0.16, SD = 0.02) tends to be significantly higher than the hyperedge clustering coefficient for team member and knowledge interlock networks (M = 0.11, SD = 0.01); t(45) = 7.122, p = 0.000.

These results suggest that high local brokerage (i.e., low hyperedge clustering coefficient) in the intersection of the team member and knowledge interlock networks has a stronger effect on team assembly than local brokerage in knowledge or team member interlock networks alone.

Ecosystem decentralization

Our last set of analyses examined the level of hypergraph centralization across the scientific ecosystem, and the Research Question 3: Are scientists more likely to assemble into a team in ecosystems characterized by lower levels of centralization (i.e., greater ecosystem decentralization)? Table 3 presents the hypergraph centralization for the observed ecosystems and their z-scores based on 200 simulations. A positive z-score indicates a score that is higher than expected by chance. A negative z-score indicates a score that is less than expected by chance. The larger the z-score, the greater difference there is between the score and the mean.

Hypothesis 7 posited that scientific teams are more likely to assemble within team ecosystems characterized by decentralization in team member interlocks. The simulation results showed that the observed hypergraph centralization in the member interlock network is lower than expected by chance for 44 out of the 46 team ecosystems. We further analyzed the two team ecosystems with high hypergraph centralization. Our analyses showed that the members of the focal teams were also

Table 3. Hypergraph centralization.

	Team member interlock		Team knowledge interlock		Team member & knowledge interlock	
Team Id	Observed value	Z-score	Observed value	Z-score	Observed value	Z-score
T001	0.22	−26.15***	0.33	−2.72**	0.21	−22.35***
T002	0.28	−43.12***	0.33	−15.17***	0.28	−14.93***
T003	0.32	−43.14***	0.23		0.25	
T004	0.27	−35.31***	0.30	−2.25*	0.20	−5.43***
T005	0.43	10.83***	0.33	4.51***	0.22	2.36*
T006	0.39	−26.37***	0.11		0.09	
T007	0.36	23.83***	0.23	−22.12***	0.20	−22.26***
T008	0.24	−94.49***	0.21	−23.11***	0.16	−11.52***
T009	0.36	−49.94***	0.13		0.12	7.44***
T010	0.29	−47.70***	0.28	4.28***	0.18	2.02+
T011	0.22	−63.85***	0.16	−20.19***	0.12	45.53***
T012	0.15	−66.19***	0.22	12.81***	0.10	
T013	0.29	−57.87***	0.20	−36.06***	0.07	−23.49***
T014	0.37	−39.08***	0.16	−25.42***	0.09	14.41***
T015	0.31	−73.27***	0.07	−22.71***	0.06	37.68***
T016	0.32	−55.22***	0.17		0.16	
T017	0.36	−52.26***	0.14		0.08	−11.57***
T018	0.25	−59.04***	0.17	13.32***	0.07	11.22***
T019	0.21	−33.74***	0.23		0.11	
T020	0.13	−119.98***	0.12	−37.63***	0.11	33.22***
T021	0.37	−82.26***	0.11	1.41	0.06	
T022	0.33	−45.04***	0.09	−7.11***	0.03	−9.18***
T023	0.39	−76.80***	0.15	−16.30***	0.08	27.58***
T024	0.22	−74.26***	0.15	−8.15***	0.07	6.90***
T025	0.28	−85.82***	0.10	−30.85***	0.10	77.60***
T026	0.18	−53.61***	0.12	−13.34***	0.03	
T027	0.37	−83.60***	0.09		0.05	19.87***
T028	0.20	−78.71***	0.10	−31.49***	0.11	80.59***
T029	0.30	−223.40***	0.11		0.06	−12.80***
T030	0.18	−63.69***	0.10	−31.76***	0.07	
T031	0.19	−54.94***	0.08	−28.18***	0.06	65.88***
T032	0.30	−85.36***	0.09	−22.64***	0.03	−20.48***
T033	0.33	−49.72***	0.18		0.06	−13.46***
T034	0.14	−65.29***	0.08	−19.13***	0.03	
T035	0.17	−66.85***	0.09	−27.46***	0.04	41.57***
T036	0.21	−89.40***	0.07	−21.21***	0.04	26.21***
T037	0.19	−84.23***	0.15	12.70***	0.06	41.44***
T038	0.42	−29.00***	0.08		0.04	
T039	0.25	−132.80***	0.12	−18.66***	0.04	−0.88
T040	0.17	−68.91***	0.11	−18.23***	0.03	25.74***
T041	0.13	−92.15***	0.08	−23.58***	0.01	
T042	0.14	−62.07***	0.15	−6.47***	0.03	−1.88+
T043	0.17	−62.53***	0.15	−1.43	0.02	−3.35**
T044	0.17	−68.71***	0.14		0.04	11.60***
T045	0.11	−71.89***	0.15	11.42***	0.02	
T046	0.15	−68.88***	0.12		0.02	

Notes:
1. Teams are sorted based on hypergraph size (from small to large).
2. Z-score is based on 200 simulations. Z-score is presented only for normal distribution frequencies. + 0.10 * 0.05 ** 0.01 *** 0.001.

members of the highly central teams. So, the results support Hypothesis 7: Greater decentralization in team member interlocks across a scientific ecosystem tends to increase the likelihood of team assembly, unless the ecosystem is dominated by the members of the focal team.

Hypothesis 8 posited that scientific teams are more likely to assemble within team ecosystems characterized by greater decentralization in team knowledge interlocks. The simulation results showed that the observed hypergraph centralization in the team knowledge interlock network is lower than expected by chance for 26 out of 46 teams. For the remaining 20 teams, the frequency distribution in the null models did not follow a normal distribution, or the results showed that team knowledge interlock network is higher than expected by chance. These partial results might be explained by the fact that few teams publish interdisciplinary articles that connect to a high number of single discipline articles, thus having a high degree of centrality, which in turn generate ecosystems with high centralization.

Hypothesis 9 posited that scientific teams are more likely to assemble within team ecosystems characterized by decentralization in the intersection of the team member and knowledge interlocks. The simulation results showed that the observed hypergraph centralization in the intersection of the team member and knowledge interlock network is lower than expected by chance in only for 14 out of 46 teams. For the remaining 32 teams, the frequency distribution in the null models did not follow a normal distribution or the results showed that team member and knowledge interlock network is higher than expected by chance. Therefore Hypothesis 9 is not supported.

The results reveal the answer to our final exploratory question: *Which is most important: decentralization in a (a) team member interlock, (b) team knowledge interlock, or (c) intersection of team member and knowledge interlock ecosystem?* Given that only Hypothesis 7 was fully supported, there was no reason to proceed with paired sample t-tests comparing the effects of each pair of ecosystem centralization scores. Our results suggest that decentralization in the team member interlock network is more important to team assembly as compared to decentralization in the knowledge interlock network or the intersection of the team member and knowledge interlock network.

Discussion

Today's most pressing problems necessitate that individuals work in teams. Social network approaches have proved valuable in providing theoretical lenses and methodological approaches to advance key questions about the assembly of teams. However, the network lens as it has been previously applied, using one and two mode networks with scientists or teams as nodes, misses important structural forces at the ecosystem level that shape the assembly of teams. Whereas some prior research has recognized this shortcoming, this article advances conceptual thinking by introducing a novel set of metrics and methods to systematically explore the multilevel forces affecting team assembly. By doing so, it makes two primary contributions.

Contribution #1: The effects of ecosystems on teams

This article elucidates the significance of team interlock ecosystems, arguing that their characteristics determine the availability of unique knowledge teams use to solve complex issues, and the degree to which knowledge is shared and new ideas are generated. Therefore, understanding the drivers of team assembly requires modelling the ecosystem characteristics from which teams nucleate. There is a well-worn adage in networks research that first people make networks, but then, networks make the people (Padgett & Powell, 2012). The same can be extended to teams. First teams help us make ecosystems, but then ecosystems make the team.

We examined two components of the collaboration ecosystems that we believe are especially relevant to team assembly: team and knowledge interlocks. Our results demonstrated the potential of the larger social (member interlocks) and cognitive (knowledge network interlocks) environment in which scientists work to influence team assembly. Additionally, our depiction of scientific team interlock ecosystems incorporates the distinct effects of proximal (i.e., local) neighborhood and as well as distal (i.e., global) neighborhood effects on team assembly. We argue that this more nuanced view is necessary in order to accurately capture the various features of scientific ecosystems that play a role in team assembly.

Our findings make several substantive, albeit preliminary, contributions to the impact of ecosystems on assembly of scientific teams. First, we find that scientific teams are more likely to assemble when the *global* ecosystem formed by team member, team knowledge, and the confluence (or intersection) between membership and knowledge interlocks form a *coherent* (i.e., cohesive) intellectual ecosystem. Interestingly, we find that, as posited in Hypothesis 1, the extent to which the ecosystem exhibits teams with higher overlapping membership (as compared to overlapping knowledge or the confluence or intersection of the two) is the most important motivator for teams to assemble.

We also find that scientific teams are more likely to assemble when the *local* ecosystem exhibits higher brokerage (i.e., low hyperedge clustering coefficient) for team member and knowledge interlocks (the confluence or intersection between the two). Interestingly, the team member interlocks and team knowledge interlocks each taken by themselves were less powerful motivators for teams to assemble. We interpret these results as evidence that individuals are especially motivated to come together as a team when they feel challenged to come up with new ideas that break norms and when they perceive that their scientific endeavors will benefit from bringing diverse individuals and the accompanying resources from other teams that do not have substantial member or knowledge overlap.

Finally, when examining global ecosystem decentralization, we only found support for our hypothesis regarding team member interlocks (H7). Our findings show that the global ecosystem decentralization in team member interlocks increases the likelihood for a team to assemble. A decentralized ecosystem essentially means there is not one or a few dominant teams that have member and/or knowledge overlap with a high number of other teams. Importantly, whereas decentralization in interlocks among team members positively influenced team assembly, decentralization in knowledge interlocks, or in the confluence (or intersection) of the team member and knowledge interlock network did not motivate team assembly. Thus, the interlocks among *people* were a stronger force than the interlocks among ideas. These insights about team assembly could not be discerned using traditional network methods. And so our second primary contribution is the advancement of a relatively new approach to the study of teams (and other collectives) using network analysis based on hypergraphs.

Contribution #2: Development of hypergraph methodology for describing and testing hypotheses about team ecosystems

We advanced the use of a *hypergraph* methodological approach, which better accounts for the nested structure of individuals in teams and the interlocks among teams with regard to knowledge and shared membership. Specifically, we model how characteristics of ecosystem coherence, local brokerage, and ecosystem decentralization affect team-based assembly. We conceptualized collaboration ecosystems as comprised of interlocking teams that overlap by virtue of shared members and shared knowledge or research topics.

Specifically, we introduced *hypergraph* measures, which better characterize the nested structure of multiple individuals and knowledge domains in multiple teams and the interlocks among them. Hypergraph approaches take sets of nodes, or hyperedges, and examine hyperties of overlapping members or knowledge domains existing between hyperedges. In our study, scientific articles (i.e., hyperedges) represent the members of a team and the knowledge areas they represent—the outcome of assembly processes in which different types of nodes (scientists and knowledge topics) are combined within an ecosystem of prior relations (i.e., hypergraph). We used the notion of local hyperedge clustering coefficient to examine the effect of brokerage within the proximal (i.e., local) neighborhood of focal team on team assembly. We used the notion of hypergraph clustering coefficient to account for the cohesion in the team's global ecosystem. And, finally, we used the notion of hypergraph centralization to describe whether the team's ecosystem is dominated by central teams.

In addition to contributing to the development of new hypergraph metrics to describe ecosystems, we also contribute new methods to test hypotheses about the impact of these metrics on team assembly. Specifically, we proposed a methodology to test hypotheses by comparing the hypergraph metrics in the observed ecosystem to those that were computed in randomly generated ecosystems that matched the observed ecosystem in terms of number of teams, number of members in teams, and number of knowledge areas in teams.

Limitations and future directions

Our study advances a hypergraph approach to understanding scientific teams, and presents initial evidence documenting substantively significant effects of the local and global ecosystem on team assembly. However, there are a number of important limitations that need to be acknowledged. First, it is important to recognize that we examined the factors influencing team assembly considering only teams that had successfully assembled. We did not have access to the "invisible" collection of individuals who considered submitting a proposal but did not get around to doing so. To partially address this limitation, we compared the observed ecosystem of the assembled team with a set of randomly simulated ecosystems. Future research should explore the development of an analytic approach that compares the ecosystem of an assembled team with the observed ecosystem of a random group of researchers, matched on some key characteristics, who never assembled into a team.

Second, the ecosystem of teams used in this study was created based on a set of focal teams who submitted research proposals to a specific grant competition. There are likely to be specifics of the domain and competition that affect the nature of the ecosystem. Thus, it is important for future work to continue to explore other types of collaborative ecosystem contexts. For example, it would be valuable for future research to explore the effects of policy interventions like the creation of centers or calls for learning communities or research coordination networks as discontinuities in how teams assemble. Furthermore, future research should examine whether the results are supported in other contexts. Our study examined the influence of team ecosystem structures on team assembly in the area of clinical and translational science. It would be important to identify the ecosystem structures influencing the assembly of teams and their subsequent team interactions within other areas of research—and indeed beyond scientific collaboration to other contexts where teams are increasingly being self-assembled to engage in critical tasks.

A third limitation concerns the creation of our knowledge network. We built our database of keywords by identifying those keywords contained in the proposal of at least one team. However, the entirety of available knowledge circulating within the ecosystems surrounding a focal team would likely contain keywords that were in articles not written by these proposal teams. Future work on knowledge interlocks should consider alternative methods of building knowledge networks.

A fourth limitation of this study is that we did not examine the *consequences* of team assembly. The scope of this article was to develop the methodology to examine ecosystem forces driving the assembly of teams. An interesting next question is, which team assembly mechanisms are beneficial or detrimental in terms of the ultimate creativity and innovation produced by a new team. At the ecosystem level, comparing the characteristics of multiple ecosystems could allow researchers to explore questions of which ecosystem characteristics are more or less functional to spawning the assembly of innovative teams. Although these cross-ecosystem comparisons were beyond the scope of this article, the methodology developed here can easily be adapted to answer questions such as: Which ecosystem factors are likely to explain why most teams form? And, are there different ecosystem factors that explain why only some of those teams perform effectively?

A final limitation is the context of studying assembly in response to a call for funding proposals. First, in some areas, funding does not play a major role in scientific advancement and the insights from this study may not generalize to those areas. In the area examined here—clinical and translational science—there is a very strong reliance on funding. But even in this case, the call for proposals was for a relatively small amount of seed funding. It is possible that the ecosystem included people who were already well funded and in established teams who would not be motivated to submit a proposal even if the domain of their research is well aligned with the call for proposals. It is noteworthy that we found significant ecosystem effects on team assembly despite the aforementioned reasons why some might not be motivated to assemble into teams to submit a proposal.

Conclusion

Given the increasing importance of teams for innovation, research is needed to uncover the factors that shape the assembly of teams in domains like scientific knowledge production. This article advances this area by introducing new hypergraph metrics and simulation-methodologies for inferentially testing hypotheses about the impact of team and knowledge interlocks on team assembly. These efforts will pave the way for conceptual advances that have been called for by practitioners as well as researchers studying teams, but heretofore, have remained largely unexplored theoretically and empirically.

Funding

The preparation of this manuscript was supported by funding from the Army Research Office [ARO W911NF-14-10686] and the National Institutes of Health [R01GM112938, U01GM112623, UL1RR025741].

ORCID

Alina Lungeanu http://orcid.org/0000-0003-3368-6339

References

Acedo, F. J., Barroso, C., Casanueva, C., & Galán, J. L. (2006). Co authorship in management and organizational studies: An empirical and network analysis. *Journal of Management Studies*, *43*(5), 957–983. doi:10.1111/j.1467-6486.2006.00625.x

Barabási, A.-L. (2005). Network theory–The emergence of the creative enterprise. *Science*, *308*(5722), 639–641. doi:10.1126/science.1112554

Barabási, A.-L., & Albert, R. (1999). Emergence of scaling in random networks. *Science*, *286*(5439), 509–512. doi:10.1126/science.286.5439.509

Berge, C. (1973). *Graphs and hypergraphs*. Amsterdam, The Netherlands: North-Holland.

Bordons, M., & Gómez, I. (2000). Collaboration networks in science. *The web of knowledge: A festschrift in honor of Eugene Garfield*. Medford, NJ: Information Today, 197–213.

Bulmer, M. G. (1979). *Principles of statistics*. New York, NY: Dover Publications, Inc.

Burt, R. S. (1992). *Structural holes: The social structure of competition*. Cambridge, MA: Harvard University Press.

Charney, D. (2003). Lone geniuses in popular science: The devaluation of scientific consensus. *Written Communication*, *20*(3), 215–241. doi:10.1177/0741088303257505

Cummings, J. N., & Kiesler, S. (2007). Coordination costs and project outcomes in multi-university collaborations. *Research Policy*, *36*(10), 1620–1634. doi:10.1016/j.respol.2007.09.001

Cummings, J. N., & Kiesler, S. (2008). *Who collaborates successfully?: Prior experience reduces collaboration barriers in distributed interdisciplinary research*. Paper presented at the Proceedings of the 2008 ACM conference on Computer supported cooperative work, San Diego, CA, USA.

De Solla Price, D. J. (1965). Networks of scientific papers. *Science*, *149*(3683), 510–515. doi:10.1126/science.149.3683.510

Dunbar, R. I. (1992). Neocortex size as a constraint on group size in primates. *Journal of Human Evolution*, *22*(6), 469–493. doi:10.1016/0047-2484(92)90081-J

Edmondson, A. (1999). Psychological safety and learning behavior in work teams. *Administrative Science Quarterly*, *44*(2), 350–383. doi:10.2307/2666999

Estrada, E., & Rodríguez-Velázquez, J. A. (2006). Subgraph centrality and clustering in complex hyper-networks. *Physica A: Statistical Mechanics and its Applications*, *364*, 581–594. doi:10.1016/j.physa.2005.12.002

Fleming, L., Mingo, S., & Chen, D. (2007). Collaborative brokerage, generative creativity, and creative success. *Administrative Science Quarterly*, *52*(3), 443–475. doi:10.2189/asqu.52.3.443

Ghasemian, F., Zamanifar, K., & Ghasem-Aghaee, N. (2017). Composing scientific collaborations based on scholars' rank in hypergraph. *Information Systems Frontiers*, 1–16.

Ghasemian, F., Zamanifar, K., Ghasem-Aqaee, N., & Contractor, N. (2016). Toward a better scientific collaboration success prediction model through the feature space expansion. *Scientometrics*, *108*(2), 777–801. doi:10.1007/s11192-016-1999-x

Ghoshal, G., Zlatic, V., Caldarelli, G., & Newman, M. E. J. (2009). Random hypergraphs and their applications. *Physical Review E, 79*(6), 066118. doi:10.1103/PhysRevE.79.066118

Grant, R. M. (1996). Toward a knowledge-based theory of the firm. *Strategic Management Journal, 17,* 109–122. doi:10.1002/smj.4250171110

Gruenfeld, D. H., Mannix, E. A., Williams, K. Y., & Neale, M. A. (1996). Group composition and decision making: How member familiarity and information distribution affect process and performance. *Organizational Behavior and Human Decision Processes, 67,* 1–15. doi:10.1006/obhd.1996.0061

Guimera, R., Uzzi, B., Spiro, J., & Amaral, L. A. N. (2005). Team assembly mechanisms determine collaboration network structure and team performance. *Science, 308*(5722), 697–702. doi:10.1126/science.1106340

Heider, F. (1958). *The psychology of interpersonal relations.* Hillsdale, NJ: Lawrence Erlbaum Associates.

Hinds, P. J., Carley, K. M., Krackhardt, D., & Wholey, D. (2000). Choosing work group members: Balancing similarity, competence, and familiarity. *Organizational Behavior and Human Decision Processes, 81*(2), 226–251. doi:10.1006/obhd.1999.2875

Kozlowski, S. W., & Klein, K. J. (2000). A multilevel approach to theory and research in organizations: Contextual, temporal, and emergent processes. In K. J. Klein & S. W. Kozlowski (Eds.), *Multilevel theory, research, and methods in organizations: Foundations, extensions, and new directions.* San Francisco, CA: Jossey-Bass.

Kuhn, T. S. (1996). *The structure of scientific revolutions* (3rd ed.). Chicago, IL: University of Chicago Press.

Lee, S., & Bozeman, B. (2005). The impact of research collaboration on scientific productivity. *Social Studies of Science, 35*(5), 673–702. doi:10.1177/0306312705052359

Lungeanu, A., & Contractor, N. S. (2015). The effects of diversity and network ties on innovations: The emergence of a new scientific field. *American Behavioral Scientist, 59*(5), 548–564. doi:10.1177/0002764214556804

Lungeanu, A., Huang, Y., & Contractor, N. S. (2014). Understanding the assembly of interdisciplinary teams and its impact on performance. *Journal of Informetrics, 8*(1), 59–70. doi:10.1016/j.joi.2013.10.006

Lungeanu, A., Sullivan, S., Wilensky, U., & Contractor, N. S. (2015). *A computational model of team assembly in emerging scientific fields.* Paper presented at the Winter Simulation Conference, Huntington Beach, California.

McPherson, M., Smith-Lovin, L., & Cook, J. M. (2001). Birds of a feather: Homophily in social networks. *Annual Review of Sociology, 27,* 415–444. doi:10.1146/annurev.soc.27.1.415

Moody, J. (2004). The structure of a social science collaboration network: Disciplinary cohesion from 1963 to 1999. *American Sociological Review, 69*(2), 213–238. doi:10.1177/000312240406900204

Murray, F., & O'Mahony, S. (2007). Exploring the foundations of cumulative innovation: Implications for organization science. *Organization Science, 18*(6), 1006–1021. doi:10.1287/orsc.1070.0325

National Research Council. (2015). *Enhancing the effectiveness of team science.* Washington, DC: National Academies Press.

Newman, M. E. J. (2001). Clustering and preferential attachment in growing networks. *Physical Review E, 64*(2), 025102. doi:10.1103/PhysRevE.64.025102

O'Leary, M. B., Mortensen, M., & Woolley, A. W. (2011). Multiple team membership: A theoretical model of its effects on productivity and learning for individuals and teams. *Academy of Management Review, 36*(3), 461–478.

Oh, H., Chung, M.-H., & Labianca, G. (2004). Group social capital and group effectiveness: The role of informal socializing ties. *Academy of Management Journal, 47*(6), 860–875. doi:10.2307/20159627

Oh, H., Labianca, G., & Chung, M.-H. (2006). A multilevel model of group social capital. *Academy of Management Review, 31*(3), 569–582. doi:10.5465/AMR.2006.21318918

Padgett, J. F., & Powell, W. W. (2012). *The emergence of organizations and markets.* Princeton, NJ: Princeton University Press.

Poole, M. S., & Contractor, N. S. (2011). Conceptualizing the multiteam system as an ecosystem of networked groups. In S. J. Zaccaro, M. A. Marks, & L. A. DeChurch (Eds.), *Multiteam systems: An organizational form for dynamic and complex environments.* New York: Routledge Academic.

Reagans, R., Zuckerman, E., & McEvily, B. (2004). How to make the team: Social networks vs. demography as criteria for designing effective teams. *Administrative Science Quarterly, 49*(1), 101–133.

Sharma, A., Srivastava, J., & Chandra, A. (2014). *Predicting multi-actor collaborations using hypergraphs.* ArXiv eprints, 1401.6404.

Shi, F., Foster, J. G., & Evans, J. A. (2015). Weaving the fabric of science: Dynamic network models of science's unfolding structure. *Social Networks, 43,* 73–85. doi:10.1016/j.socnet.2015.02.006

Sullivan, S., Zhu, M., Lungeanu, A., & Contractor, N. S. (2012). *Hypergraph metrics.* Evanston, IL: Northwestern University.

Taramasco, C., Cointet, J. P., & Roth, C. (2010). Academic team formation as evolving hypergraphs. *Scientometrics, 85,* 721–740. doi:10.1007/s11192-010-0226-4

Torvik, V. I., Weeber, M., Swanson, D. R., & Smalheiser, N. R. (2005). A probabilistic similarity metric for Medline records: A model for author name disambiguation. *Journal of the Association for Information Science and Technology, 56*(2), 140–158. doi:10.1002/asi.20105

Uzzi, B., & Spiro, J. (2005). Collaboration and creativity: The small world problem. *American Journal of Sociology, 111*(2), 447–504. doi:10.1086/432782

Wang, J.-W., Rong, -L.-L., Deng, Q.-H., & Zhang, J.-Y. (2010). Evolving hypernetwork model. *The European Physical Journal B - Condensed Matter and Complex Systems, 77*(4), 493–498. doi:10.1140/epjb/e2010-00297-8

West, M. A., & Anderson, N. R. (1996). Innovation in top management teams. *Journal of Applied Psychology, 81*(6), 680–693. doi:10.1037/0021-9010.81.6.680

Wuchty, S., Jones, B. F., & Uzzi, B. (2007). The increasing dominance of teams in production of knowledge. *Science, 316*(5827), 1036–1039. doi:10.1126/science.1136099

Zaheer, A., & Soda, G. (2009). Network evolution: The origins of structural holes. *Administrative Science Quarterly, 54*(1), 1–31. doi:10.2189/asqu.2009.54.1.1

Zlatic, V., Ghoshal, G., & Caldarelli, G. (2009). Hypergraph topological quantities for tagged social networks. *Physical Review E, 80*(3), 036118. doi:10.1103/PhysRevE.80.036118

Methods and Approaches to Using Web Archives in Computational Communication Research

Matthew S. Weber

> **ABSTRACT**
> This article examines the role of web archives as a critical source of data for conducting computational communication research. Web archives are large-scale databases containing comprehensive records of websites showing how those websites have evolved over time. Recent communication scholarship using web archives is reviewed, demonstrating the breadth of research conducted in this space. Subsequently, a methodological framework is proposed for using web archives in computational communication research. As a source of data, web archives present a number of methodological challenges, particularly with regards to the accuracy and completeness of web archives. These problems are addressed in order to better inform future work in this area. The closing sections outline a forward-looking trajectory for computational communication research using web archives.

Shifts in technological capacity and increased access to data has enabled the emergence of new computational approaches to social science research (Lazer et al., 2009; Manovich, 2011; Ruths & Pfeffer, 2014). Simultaneously, the growth of computational social science can be traced in parallel to the growth of the World Wide Web and other Internet related platforms. The combined growth of the Internet and the World Wide Web revolutionized the way that humans communicate in modern times (Kraut et al., 2002; Newhagen & Rafaeli, 1996; Robinson et al., 2015). In particular, the World Wide Web, or the Web as it is known, emerged in the late 1980s and early 1990s (Brügger, 2016), and quickly gave rise to new modes of digital communication. By the mid 2010s, the Web reached its 25-year milestone, and has become a central tool for research in fields ranging from computer science to medicine to the social sciences and humanities (Meyer, Schroeder, & Cowls, 2016).

For those studying the Web, increased access in recent years to archived records of websites has become increasingly important for social scientists seeking to explore a wide range of phenomena. Moreover, in thinking about the utility of archival web data, there is clear evidence that simply using the live web provides an incomplete record of activity on the Web (Wouters, Hellsten, & Leydesdorff, 2004). As Bode, Hanna, Yang and Shah (2015) notes, however, work is needed to develop new schemas for assessing the reliability and validity of large-scale data, as well as methods for using these data. Thus, this article introduces web archives in the context of computational communication research. Subsequently, this article discusses recent research in this space and outlines key challenges associated with archived web data. A methodological approach for accessing archived web data is introduced. The concluding section points to a future research agenda leveraging the building blocks outlined in this article.

Color versions of one or more of the figures in the article can be found online at www.tandfonline.com/hcms.

Defining web archives

The Web is a tremendous record of social behavior, organizational activity, and human interaction. Nevertheless, the Web is problematic as a source of data for research. For instance, in a study of 10 million webpages, researchers found that the average webpage remains live for barely three years (Agata, Miyata, Ishita, Ikeuchi, & Ueda, 2014). Another contemporary report, looking at a smaller set of websites, found that the average duration of a webpage was 44 days (Cohen, 2005). Problems of permanence are not isolated to webpages; for example, a study of Twitter data focusing on major social events between 2009 and 2012 found that 11% of relevant tweets were not available after one year, and 27% of tweets were not available after two years (Salah Eldeen & Nelson, 2012). Another study found that approximately 65% of requested archived pages from user searches accessed webpages that no longer exist on the live web (AlNoamany, AlSum, Weigle, & Nelson, 2014). Moreover, webpage content is not well preserved; researchers studying a broad array of websites found that after 2 years, only 41% of the original content had actually been archived for future use (Salah Eldeen & Nelson, 2012).

Largely in response to the challenges of persistent access to web content, web archives were created to preserve the history of the Web, and to provide a permanent record for future access. Broadly, web archiving is defined as, "the process of gathering up data that has been recorded on the Web, storing it, ensuring the data is preserved in an archive, and making the collected data available for future research (Niu, 2012, p. 1)." The organization, storage, access, and use of a given web archive can vary from archive to archive. In general, web archives are created to collect and preserve pre-determined subsets of web content. the general process of web archiving begins with selection of the appropriate websites to archive, then proceeds to acquisition/harvest/capture of the relevant selected content, and final shifts to provision of access to potential users (Khannanov, 2003).

Web archives range from home-brewed collections to large-scale national archiving efforts. Libraries have also started building their own collections (Hockx-Yu, 2014). Local libraries are creating repositories and collecting relevant community web information in order to preserve local history. University libraries are actively creating repositories of webpages. For instance, Columbia University has built a vast repository of archived webpages focused on human rights (https://hrwa.cul.columbia.edu) (Kelleher, Sangwand, Wood, & Kamuronsi, 2010). National libraries often undertake archiving at a larger scale. The National Library of Iceland archives the Icelandic web domain; similarly the Portuguese Web Archive archives the full Portuguese domain (Gomes, Miranda, & Costa, 2011). The British Library has engaged in Web archiving activities since 2004, and regularly crawls and archives the .UK domain; similarly, the Bibliothéque nationale de France (the French National Library) has a legal mandate to crawl and archive the French web. Many of the national archiving efforts are dependent on national mandates. The United States, however, does not mandate a national web archiving program, but the Library of Congress has an active and growing web archiving program that works to provide research access to data where possible. The Library of Congress has created a number of niche web archives focused on specific events or topics, including material related to the September 11, 2001 terror attacks, as well as archives of election and .gov domain-related material (Niu, 2012). The Library of Congress further archives webpages within the .gov domain at regular intervals.

The Internet Archive is the world's largest repository of archived web content, and at present contains more than 280 billion webpages. Most archives are smaller in scale. Much of the early Web was archived by hobbyists who collected subsets of the Web (Stevens, 2004); some of that content was later donated to the Internet Archive. The Internet Archive is also one of the earliest organizations to engage in web archiving activity; the archive was founded by Brewster Kahle and Bruce Gilliat in 1996 in response to an early trend of websites and webpages rapidly disappearing from the live web (Rackley, 2000).

Web archives are created with the intent of providing content access to users via the Internet. Most archives provide users with an overview of the contents of the archive via metadata; these metadata are summary files that provide a brief description of what was crawled, over what time period, and how (e.g., from what seedlist, limited to what restrictions). Researcher access, such as the ability to download sets of webpages, varies widely from archive to archive; currently, many web archives are working to provide better mechanisms for researcher access (Niu, 2012). To that end, the Library of Congress recently launched labs.loc.gov as a way to provide researchers with access to data in order to learn about the type of research that can be conducted with web archives. To date, the focus of the lab's initiative has been on education about digital collections, but access is available to some initial datasets. In summary, however, much has been written regarding the way web archives are created (see Masanès, 2006; Niu, 2012; for an overview). Less work has been done to establish frameworks for engaging with web archives as a source for research.

Web archives and research

Communication on the web echoes many established patterns of social interaction, but new forms of communication and new patterns of interaction have arisen (Williams, 2000). Web archives are a key source of data for researchers, and in turn, new approaches are being developed for working with this type of data (Green et al., 2008). Scholars have turned to web archives as data source to address a host of communication questions. Communication researchers working with web archives are poised to address critical research questions. Theorizing points to computational communication research focused on network analysis, interpersonal and social influence, systems for developing recommendations, and intersecting work between interpersonal and mass communication domains (Cappella, 2017). Emerging work examining communication on the Web, social interactions, and politics has all started to take advantage of web archives.

Studies of the Web as a communication platform

Web archives provide a record of communicative action that occurred on a given website at a given moment in time. This occurs because the process of web archiving captures the structure of the website, but also captures the content, including any comments of social posting (Lomborg, 2012). For example, this means that user comments on a newspaper website in 2002 are likely still preserved on an archived webpage. Moreover, thematic analysis of the content of web archives provides a way for extracting the rich evolution of content and communication on websites (Foot, 2006). In an analysis of memorial websites created in the wake of the September 11, 2001 terror attacks, Foot, Warnick and Schneider (2005) showed how the website was used as a communicative platform to express grief and enable mourning. Archives of terrorist websites were used to study the way in which terrorists use websites as a communication platform for recruitment (Zhou, Reid, Qin, Chen, & Lai, 2005), as well as the degree to which terrorists interact and engage across websites (Qin, Zhou, Reid, Lai, & Chen, 2007). There are just a few examples of work using archives to study the Web as a communication platform.

Social interaction in web archives

Records of discourse (speeches, debates, etc.) and records of conversations on social media, among other sources, also allow linguistics scholars to examine the nature of conversation on a broad scale (Reyes, 2014). For example, using content extracted from popular review websites such as Yelp and TripAdvisor, linguistic analysis has been used to evaluate sentiment, and to develop new algorithms for textual analysis (Mi, Shan, Qiang, Stephanie, & Chen, 2014).

Web archive data has been useful from the perspective of organizational communication. Blending archived web data with theories of social movements, scholars have been able to examine the emergence of new types of movements. Argawal, Bennett, Johnson and Walker (2014) utilized a database of 60 million tweets in order to analyze the emergence of organizational structure out of Twitter interactions from the Occupy Wall Street Movement.[1] Their research demonstrates how large-scale distributed interactions can constitute organizations. Others have used web archive data to study how broad ecosystems reacted and adapted to the advent of online news (Weber & Nguyen, 2015, Weber & Monge, 2014; Weber 2012), developing new theories about macro-organizational change. In another vein, communication scholars are leveraging Internet data to examine the communication of knowledge across ecosystems. Scholars examined the use of web search and online video content to obtain health information, and found that individuals have a better comprehension of simplified broad data, as opposed to specified narrow data (Topps, Helmer, & Ellaway, 2013).

Archived web data and political communication

Web archives have enabled political scientists to examine ecosystems of political interactions, as well as large-scale patterns of political action. Foot and Schneider took a qualitative approach in using web archives; their work examined hundreds of U.S. campaign websites from elections in 2000, 2002, and 2004 in order to understand how campaigns changed the way they communicated with public audiences (Foot & Schneider, 2006). In another study, Bode and colleagues (2015) analyzed 9 million archived tweets from Twitter datasets in order to study interaction between candidates and citizens based on political affiliation. From a discourse perspective, political web archives have been used to understand how individuals talk about politics, and how different political spheres develop (Colleoni, Rozza, & Arvidsson, 2014). Historical data sources further enabled researchers to examine shifts in political discourse over longer periods of time (Zeng & Greenfield, 2015).

Tools and methods for improving access

Research using archived web content has lagged despite the vast amounts of data that are available, and most archives note low rates of researcher access (Lin, Gholami, & Rao, 2014). Scholars have worked to improve researcher access to web archives, recognizing early on that the data in web archives provided a vast treasure trove of data for social scientists (Arms, Huttenlocher, Kleinberg, Macy, & Strang, 2006).

Metadata as a method of access

The growth of metadata formats has proven critical for improving researcher access to web archives. In recent years, organizations including the Internet Archive, as well as the International Internet Preservation Consortium, have worked to establish metadata standards for improving access to web archives.

There are two primary standard web archive formats. Those formats are the ARChive file format (ARC) and the Web ARChive file format (WARC). The ARC format is the original web archiving format developed by the Internet Archive in 1996,[2] and the WARC was subsequently added as an update in 2009. The WARC envelope contains additional metadata that was not present in the original ARC format, including a record of outlinks from each archived webpage. WARC is a recognized International Organization for Standardization (ISO) standard file format.[3] A WARC/ARC file may contain information for multiple websites in a single record. The differences between the two formats are minimal, and the two formats are largely interoperable; WARC fields allow for a bit more flexibility in terms of fields specified.

In addition to ARC and WARC formats, the Internet Archive has produced a number of additional metadata standards that help researchers to access Web archive data. Web Archive Transformation (WAT) and Longitudinal Graph Analysis (LGA) formats are applicable in a number of cases. WAT files provide a summary of key metadata from an archived website. Key metadata include provenance, document size, content type (e.g., HTML, video, image) as well as information on links between websites. WATs are relatively small and require less than 20% of the storage space of a WARC. LGA files provide compressed resources that provide a listing of all outlinks from one archived domain to another. An LGA file is roughly one percent the size of a WARC file, and provides a format that allows for quick social network analysis. More broadly, the Internet Archive has launched a Researcher Services platform that provides resources for interested scholars and practitioners (https://webarchive.jira.com/wiki/spaces/ARS/overview).

In sum, metadata provide an easier way to access web archives beyond needing to make a significant investment in infrastructure. Many web archives already provide access to metadata, and the hope is this trend will continue in the future. Leveraging a combination of new tools and metadata formats, researchers have demonstrated that Web archive analysis can be conducted on machines as affordable as Rasberry Pi computers, which generally start at about $30 (Lin, 2015). When working with raw data, and larger collections, access to a distributed computing platforms continues to be important. More broadly, there are a number of research initiatives and programs focused on improving general research access; more information can be found via the RESAW (resaw.eu) initiative as well as via the International Internet Preservation Consortium (netpreserve.org).

Tools for accessing web archives

With increases in research interest, research ready tools available for scholars to utilize have grown in numbers. Some basic analysis can be conducted using guidelines provided by the Internet Archive or by using the WARC metadata format in conjunction with basic programming on a laptop. Two notable tools that have significantly improved researcher access in recent years; these tools take advantage of advances in metadata formats. These tools are open source and provide documentation, but have some technical barriers and thus require a time investment to use.

The Archives Unleashed Toolkit (formerly Warcbase) (http://www.archivesunleashed.com) is a package of tools designed using the WARC format in conjunction with numerous advanced programming languages including Spark and HBase. The suite of scripted tools provides a scalable platform for accessing and analyzing web archive data in a variety of research contexts (Lin, Milligan, Wiebe, & Zhou, 2017). The Archives Unleashed Toolkit is intended to enable microanalysis of collections of web archives (Lin, Kraus, & Punzalan, 2014). The Archives Unleashed Toolkit has been applied in a number of contexts, such as research studies the growth of communities on the early Web's Geocities platform. The package provides the user with the ability to search for specific sets of URLs, to extract text, and to build social network analysis graph files, among other features (Maemura, Becker, & Milligan, 2016)

ArchiveSpark takes advantage of the WAT format and also uses Spark and HBase programming to enable access to web archives. ArchiveSpark is intended to work with large data sets, and uses the features of the WAT metadata to create easy-to-search indexes. The package offers many of the features as The Archives Unleashed Toolkit; it requires some additional technical skills to setup but may enable faster processing of some data types (Holzmann, Goel, & Anand, 2016).

A method for using of web archives

In order to establish a stronger body of work for scholarship using web archives, clear methodological guidelines are needed. The following aggregates lessons from prior work, and outlines an approach for utilizing web archives in the context of communication research.

Using web archives in communication research

The following provides a generic methodological approach for using web archive data in communication research, with a number of examples provided to illustrate the approach. Each step is described in detail, and the following section then addressed limitations of this approach, and of using web archives in general.

(1) Determine an appropriate set of uniform resource locators (URLs) and/or an appropriate dataset, as well as an appropriate time range.
(2) Collect the necessary data or secure remote access to the data.
(3) Use existing tools and packages to convert the data to a research ready format.
(4) Identify relevant and non-relevant clusters in the data; filter and remove irrelevant data.

Each of these steps is discussed in the following as a means of providing an initial approach to engaging with archived web data in computational communication research.

Determining appropriate data

Web archives are often vast; the Internet Archive contains more than 50 PB of data, pushing the limits of many supercomputing centers. Thus, the first step is to determine the appropriate data, both in terms of specific URLs of web domains, as well as the time range for data extraction. As Shaw (2017, p. 821) notes, theory can be a key guide in developing studies. In particular, "a theory— rather than results— driven approach should generate a less contorted, more coherent set of predictions that emanate from or build upon the underlying perspective."

Consider, for example, a researcher who wants to use community websites from New Jersey, New York, and Connecticut in order to understand how community cohesiveness and community discourse changed from before to after Superstorm Sandy. Communicative theories on resilience emphasize the importance of local communities as information hubs, providing critical information to citizens during major disasters (Chewning, Lai, & Doerfel, 2012). As a starting point for research, this framing directs the researcher to community based websites, as well as local news websites and local information portals, among others.

Given the temporal nature of Web archive research, it is subsequently important to determine the appropriate time range for data collection. Theory and research questions help to answer this; a study looking at recovery would likely want to focus on websites after the superstorm hit, but websites seeking to compare changes pre- and post-Sandy would want to extract a wider scope of data. Superstorm Sandy made landfall in New York City on October 29, 2012, providing a focal point for data collection.

Collecting or accessing data

With the above constraints, a next step is to aggregate all the relevant URLs, and then to query an available Web archive. In this case, targeted keyword searching is a logical starting point for aggregating relevant URLs. Searching with geographic phrases as well as event relevant phrases helps to narrow the potential list of contents. For instance, a team of graduate assistants working over a three-month period in 2013 generated a list of 665 relevant URLs of web domains related to Superstorm Sandy using the aforementioned community frame.

There are many repositories containing archived web data relevant to Superstorm Sandy. For instance, many university libraries created specific archives focused on recording content related to Superstorm Sandy. Cornell University has created a Climate Science web archive containing information on flood and disaster recovery.[4] Virginia Tech has a large archive of webpages focused on tragedy and recovery, which includes extensive content from Superstorm Sandy.[5]

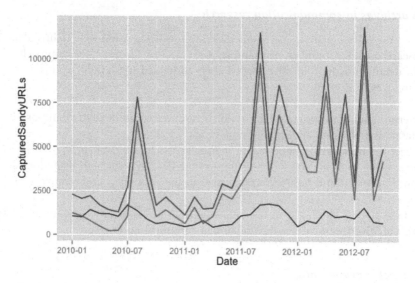

Figure 1. Captured and actual uniform resource locators in superstorm sandy subset (2010–2012).

The researcher must decide what types of archives to work with, and often must negotiate access directly with the archive. An example of a collection of archived web data from Superstorm Sandy is illustrated in Figure 1. The figure focuses on a collection generated in partnership with the Internet Archive and using the aforementioned list of 665 URLs of web domains to generate a subset of archived Web data. The total collection covers a period from 2008–2013, and includes more than 500 million unique URLs extracted from the 665 web domains specified above. The figure shows the number of captured archived pages in each month between the focal period of 2010–2012.

More broadly, scholars elsewhere have spent significant time investigating approaches for archiving web data related to events. For instance, a team of scholars at Virginia Tech have developed techniques for using social media such as Twitter to detect the occurrence of an event. Subsequently, links mentioned in tweets are harvested to create a seed list for future web archiving related to a given event (Atefeh & Khreich, 2015; Kavanaugh et al., 2012).

Converting data to a research ready format

The next two steps in working with web archive data involve converting the data to a research ready format and filtering the data to remove unnecessary content. Depending on the tools being used, and the size of the dataset, the conversion and filtering can be reversed.

Web archive formats can be read with relative ease using the above packages, but converting the data to text files, tables, database formats (for SPSS), or formats for network analysis provide ways of drastically reducing the data size and simultaneously transforming the data into a format that is easier to analyze in conventional analyses. Researchers working in computational social science have frequently pointed to social network analysis as an important method for engaging with large scale data. Freelon, Lynch and Aday (2015) demonstrated the use of social network analysis as a tool for examining large-scale Twitter data and identifying key communities. Others have used large-scale network analysis to analyze patterns of social relationships (Welles & Contractor, 2015) or to look at interactions between candidates and citizens during political cycles (Bode et al., 2015).

Scripts available at (http://archivesunleashed.com/data/ and http://archivehub.rutgers.edu/downloads) provide research-ready tools for taking web archive data and transforming the data from WARCs or ARCs to link lists that record all the outbound links from a given webpage. The output provides a text file that contains lists of the links, dates, and descriptive text from the webpage. Other tools, such as WarcBase, also provide similar flexibility with broader scalability. The data from Superstorm Sandy, generated using the above process, are also available at the above URL.

Filtering data

There are established processes for removing spam from web archives (Erdélyi, Benczúr, Masanés, & Siklósi, 2009), filtering irrelevant pages (Abiteboul, Cobéna, Masanes, & Sedrati, 2002), as well as other advanced approaches to filtering large-scale Web archives (Kimpton & Ubois, 2006). One approach of moving from high-performance computer or services such as Amazon Web Services to research ready platforms is that it may be easier to filter data based on known spam lists and irrelevant data.

Most web archives collected *all* data within a given domain. Depending on how the data are collected, it is possible that many pages will be 3xx or 4xx error pages. 3xx errors refer to webpages that redirect to other web domains, or require additional action from the user. 4xx errors generally indicate that content was not found or there was some other critical error in retrieving the webpage. Basic filtering is a first step, and can help to reduce the data further. In addition, it is important to think about the unit of analysis for research. For instance, a researcher might be interested in studying the way a domain, such as http://www.nytimes.com, changed over time. The researcher may only be interested in the homepage (www.nytimes.com), but an archive is likely to include multiple levels of data, including story specific URLs such as:

https://www.nytimes.com/2017/07/07/opinion/how-to-make-congress-bipartisan.html?action=click&pgtype=Homepage&clickSource=story-heading&module=opinion-c-col-right-region&region=opinion-c-col-right-region&WT.nav=opinion-c-col-right-region

which is a URL pointing to a single story. Removing such data can further help to reduce the dataset to focus in on relevant content. Alternatively, retaining such data can be useful for examining the structure and scale of the full web domain.

Sample datasets

As a test of this approach to extracting data, the outlined method was used to create sample datasets for researcher use. These datasets are available at (http://archivesunleashed.com/data/ and http://archivehub.rutgers.edu/downloads/). The datasets cover topical areas of potential interest to communication researchers, and were created by applying the above methodology to curate, prepare and filter subsets of archived seb data. There are six complete datasets available on the website; those six datasets are in a social network analysis format (linklist). The topics were determined by an extensive literature search that identified topical areas of communication research where scholars were engaged in longitudinal social network analysis. The six datasets, summarized in Table 1, cover U.S. Media, Occupy Wall Street, the U.S. Senate, the U.S. House of Representatives, Hurricane Katrina, and Superstorm Sandy. The datasets are provided in tandem with this article as a proof of concept and as material for others to use in future research.

These datasets are topically oriented, and were created using the approach outlines in the preceding pages. These are new dataset, and much of the research conducted using these datasets is still in progress. In part, there were numerous challenges associated with creating the datasets mentioned above. First, the raw data is approximately 38 TB in size; much of the work on these datasets required a substantial high-performance computing system in order to analyze and create the subsets presented here. This underscores an existing challenge; working with raw data often still

Table 1. Overview of curated datasets use method for extracting data.

Dataset	Research Potential	Dates	Captured Webpages	Unique URLs
US Media	Previous communication studies of news media organizations (Greer & Mensing, 2006; Weber, 2012; Weber & Monge, 2014) focused on evolutionary patterns	2008–2012	1,315,132,555	539,184,823
Occupy Wall Street	Previous research on NGOs in the online environment (Bach & Stark, 2004; Shumate, 2003, 2012; Shumate, Fulk, & Monge, 2005) uses hyperlink data to study the formation and role of alliances between SMOs	2010–2012	247,928,272	113,259,655
US Senate	Studies of the growth of political activity in online environments (Adamic & Glance, 2005; Bode et al., 2015; Bruns, 2007) often focused on polarization & media discourse	2005–2013 (109th–112th Congresses)	26,965,770	8,674,397
US House			51,840,777	12,410,014
Hurricane Katrina	Online networks and organizational resilience(Chewning et al., 2012; Taylor & Doerfel, 2003)in the wake of disasters; additional work on information dissemination	2003–2012	1,694,236	663,740
Superstorm Sandy		2003–2013	41,703,112	20,013,455

requires significant computing resources. Second, significant work went in to verifying the accuracy of these datasets, as discussed in the following section. Third, the datasets were filtered to remove as much unnecessary content as possible, including advertising and other potentially unwanted content. Nevertheless, such datasets have significant potential as a tool for future scholarship. For instance, one recent study leveraged much of the early data on news media in this data collection in order to illustrate the way in which early online newspaper websites had a propensity to mimic and imitate one another (Weber, Ognyanova, & Kosterich, 2017).

Limitations of web archives

This work has established the relevance and utility of web archives to computational communication research. In turn, one methodological framework for research with web archives was outlined, and the limitations to this approach were discussed. The amount of data in web archives is large, and there is potential for new and innovative communication research in this domain. The approaches outlined heretofore help bring computational communication research to scale. At the same time, working with web archives brings to bear numerous challenges.

One of the central problems in using web archives for research is that it is difficult to ensure that every single page or record is captured. Web archives are often fragmented. The challenge of fragmentation and completeness of a web archive is referred to as degradation of web archives. Degradation refers to the fact that archived data sources become less accurate as a user transverses back through time. A number of attempts have been made to measure the degree of degradation. For instance, Brunelle et al. (2014) created a damage measure to indicate the amount of data missing from archived webpages sources. In a similar vein, Spaniol et al. (2009) proposed a coherence model that focuses on the degree to which a subsection of an archive is complete, and the degree to which that subset captures changes to webpages over time.

The challenges of degradation can be broken down into two key aspects; accuracy and completeness. These prior approaches focus on coherence as a way to measure the completeness of a page, but they do not focus on the entirety of a dataset. The coherence model is a bit broader, in that it focuses on change across a subset of webpages.

Accuracy of web archives

The process of web archiving is generally accurate, in that a capture of a webpage provides the user with an archived record of that webpage at a point in time. The accuracy of archiving is less clear when the scope is expanded to topical areas or domains. For instance, it is difficult to know if a web archive of Occupy Wall Street websites accurately captures the full breadth of the Occupy Wall Street movement on the Web. In order to assess the accuracy of a Web archive, the optimal approach is to compare an archive to a known record of the topic. Unfortunately, it is often difficult to know what the known domain is and what webpages are in that domain. An analysis of a random sampling of archives of popular websites found that fewer than 30% of websites were archived more than once a month; the quality of archives varies widely (Ainsworth, Alsum, Salah Eldeen, Weigle, & Nelson, 2011).

Alternatively, it is easier to make a comparison to other sources of information on a given topic. For example, Milligan, Ruest, and Lin (2016) examined a web archive of websites focused on the 2015 Canadian election, and compared the URLs in the web archive to the URLs mentioned in tweets relevant to the election. The authors found that there was a 10% overlap between the two datasets. These findings point to the need to approximate the completeness of a web archive used in research, and further to ensure that the data collected focuses on the specific research questions being asked.

Completeness of data

Web archives are not identical copies of the live web. Rather, a web archive is an assembled corpus of snapshots of a website, and represent a subjective reconstruction based on what was captured during the archiving process (Brügger, 2012). Another way of looking at web archives is to think about completeness of a web archive based on the subset of data being used by a researcher. Consider, for example, the prior example of a subset of websites based on Superstorm Sandy. As illustrated in Table 1, that dataset contains website records from 2003–2013. This archive includes 41,703,112 webpages from 20,013,455 unique URLs representing the 665 initial domains.

Each webpage in the archive contains a set of outbound hyperlinks. Looking at a subset of data from 2010–2012, there were 142,377 links out to other webpages; only 24% of those linked to webpages were present in the subset. This difference is illustrated in Figure 1. Knowing the

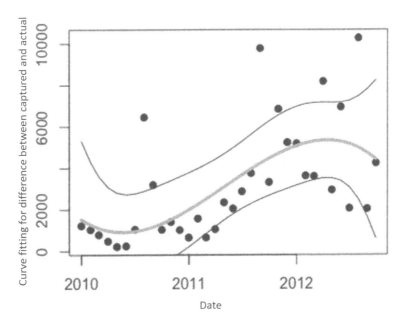

Figure 2. Captured uniform resource locators in superstorm sandy subset (2010–2012).

difference between actual URLs and captured URLs provided a way to assess (a) the degree of completeness and (b) whether or not the error is random. Figure 2 provides an illustration of polynomial curve-fitting to illustrate whether or not the degree of error can be predicted. In this case, the number of missing pages increased significantly following the storm's impact, but the curve-fitting is far less accurate in the later time period, suggesting more randomness to the degree of error.

The issue of dataset completeness is one that has plagued researchers for decades. Paleobiologists have struggled to understand the completeness of fossil records (Ksepka & Boyd, 2012). Evolutionary scholars similar struggle with life history data (Penone et al., 2014). In another instance, physicists struggling with the completeness of archived data on earthquakes have set strict thresholds for censoring datasets for analysis (Stucchi, Albini, Mirto, & Rebez, 2004); a similar approach could be taken to trimming Web datasets to what is perceived to be the most complete subset of data related to a given topic.

More to the point, and relevant to the above example, historians have long been aware of the challenges of a selection bias (Lustick, 1996). The example of records tracing the unfolding of Superstorm Sandy is dependent on the creation of an initial seedlist; the degree to which the seedlist creates an accurate or complete representation creates a potential bias in terms of the shape of the subsequent dataset. Even in cases where there is a general agreement that a database accurately captures a target population, questions in historical research often exist with regards to the reliability of variables and other associated measures (Bean, May, & Skolnick, 1978).

Finally, information scientists suggest focusing on a variety of measures of relevance and completeness in order to assess the degree to which a collected dataset matches against a target set of keywords or search terms (Gordon & Pathak, 1999; Leighton & Srivastava, 1999). The development of metrics for the accuracy and completeness of web archive subsets will thus be a key step towards improving the reliability of subsequent statistical tests based on data collected in this manner.

Ethical boundaries

Ethical concerns should not be overlooked. For instance, web data are often archived without explicit permission from the creator of a webpage. Robots.txt files are bits of text that may specify a webpage not be archived, but such requests are not always honored. Beyond ethical questions, there are practical challenges associated with web archives. Boyd and Crawford point to a number of key ethical concerns that researchers should be aware of when working with web archive data (Boyd & Crawford, 2012). They call attention to the need to consider the provenance of data, the need to give large-scale data context, and the importance of considering the appropriateness of using collected online data. This points to the central issue of collection strategies; website owners are rarely asked for permission when archivists are collected and aggregating data, but identifying information is often retained.

In European countries, and elsewhere, intellectual property rights further complicate the collection and use of archiving data. Some countries, such as France, have legal mandates the explicitly address the right to archive content. Elsewhere, such as in Australia, there is a process in place for asking permission to archive (Day, 2003). Some have proposed changing crawling strategies to more clearly respect and address hidden legal concerns (Kim & Lee, 2007), but change has been slow. Moreover, the Web is international in nature, and although there are country specific domains, much content resides on the .com domain, and it is challenging to know the exact nature of property rights when origins are unclear (Lor, Britz, & Watermeyer, 2006). Ultimately, this means that much of the responsibility with regards to addressing ethical and legal concerns falls on the researcher. In the United States, Institutional Review Boards (IRBs) at most universities are a resource that can help to develop strategies for addressing these concerns. More broadly, scholars examining the web archiving process have started an important conversation regarding how to handle these issues in the future (Dougherty et al., 2010; Ogden, 2016).

Other limitations

As the above examples illustrate, there are a number of challenges associated with using web archiving in computational communication research. Cognizance of these challenges provides a path for developing new approaches to working with this datasets in a meaningful way. There are additional limitations worth noting. For instance, the lack of archiving of social media content is another significant limitation of current web archiving approaches. There are swaths of archived Twitter data available in various locations, but social media data from popular websites such as Facebook and Instagram are tough to collect due to the proprietary nature of content on those websites.

An unbounded research space

The promise of web archives for research is significant, particularly within communication. It is important to remember that the Web is a pervasive technological platform, and there is a wide range of scholarship addressing related topics. Historians working with web content have used online repositories to study the history of the Cold War, and broadly argued for the Web as a space of historical study (Brügger, 2009; Price, 1995). Similarly, anthropologists and sociologists have engaged with historical Web content as a space of scholarly study, arguing for the Web as an object both of sociological study (Beer & Burrows, 2007), and as a place for sociological and anthropological study (Bainbridge, 1995). Scholars would be well advised to reach across disciplinary boundaries, and to consider lessons learned by scholars working in related areas.

Moreover, future research should continue to explore the challenges associated with web archive data, and take advantage of the potential for scholarship in this area. The methods outlined up to this point provide a generic process for engaging with web archives in computational communication research. Next steps in analysis should be guided by the researcher's theoretical questions, as specific methods for analyzing data will depend on specific research questions. For instance, those interested in studying communities of websites may want to use clustering techniques to examine community formation. For instance, methods of community detection are well suited for web data in their power to detect tight knit clusters in large domains of relatively sparse connectivity (Newman, 2006). Alternatively, one may find it appropriate to compare changes in community composition over time; thus, Jacard's measure of change would be an appropriate way to look at community change between time periods (Murata, 2003). Ultimately, there are countless paths of potential analysis, and determining the right approach is one of the significant challenges of working with this type of data.

Conclusion

Web archives provide a unique perspective on the changing patterns of societal communication, at both a macro and micro level, and promise to enable new forms of research (Milligan, 2016). The field of communication is well situated within the broad scope of scholarly disciplines to set a theoretical research agenda for leveraging web archives in research. Yet as Parks (2014, p. 355) noted in a special issue of *Journal of Communication*, "Big Data research is still in its infancy in communication." Explorations of new regimes in research often begin with an exploration of methods, but advancing a new regime within a field involves engagement with theory. From this point of view, communication research may take a leadership role; previous research lays a strong methodological basis for communication studies, and as an inherently interdisciplinary field of exploration, communication scholars can bring a strong theoretical compass to web archives.

Notes

1. It is worth noting that Twitter archives are not explicitly web archives. The distinction is somewhat fine grained, and the use of archived Twitter data is quite common, therefore a number of Twitter examples are included in this article. For a discussion of the limitations of these data, see Driscoll and Walker (2014).
2. http://archive.org/web/researcher/ArcFileFormat.php.
3. https://www.iso.org/standard/44717.html.
4. https://www.archive-it.org/organizations/529?sort=f_sort_title.desc&show=Sites&fc=meta_Subject%3AEmergency+planning.
5. https://archive-it.org/explore?q=superstorm+sandy&show=Sites&fc=organizationName%3AVirginia+Tech%3A+Crisis%2C+Tragedy%2C+and+Recovery+Network.

Funding

This research was supported in part by a grant from the National Science Foundation, Directorate for Social, Behavioral and Economic Sciences (Award #1244727).

References

Abiteboul, S., Cobéna, G., Masanes, J., & Sedrati, G. (2002). A first experience in archiving the french web. In M. Agosti, & C. Thanos (Eds.), *Research and advanced technology for digital libraries: 6th European conference, ECDL 2002 Rome, Italy, September 16 -18,2002 proceedings* (pp. 1–15). Berlin, Heidelberg: Springer Berlin Heidelberg.

Adamic, L. A., & Glance, N. (2005). *The political blogosphere and the 2004 U.S. election: Divided they blog.* Paper presented at the 3rd International Workshop on Link Discovery, Chicago, IL.

Agarwal, S. D., Bennett, W. L., Johnson, C. N., & Walker, S. (2014). A model of crowd enabled organization: Theory and methods for understanding the role of twitter in the occupy protests. *International Journal of Communication*, 8(27), 646–672.

Agata, T., Miyata, Y., Ishita, E., Ikeuchi, A., & Ueda, S. (2014, 8–12 September). *Life span of web pages: A survey of 10 million pages collected in 2001.* Paper presented at the 14th annual international ACM/IEEE joint conference on Digital libraries, London, United Kingdom.

Ainsworth, S. G., Alsum, A., Salah Eldeen, H., Weigle, M. C., & Nelson, M. L. (2011). *How much of the web is archived?* Paper presented at the 11th annual international ACM/IEEE joint conference on Digital libraries, Ottawa, Ontario, Canada.

AlNoamany, Y., AlSum, A., Weigle, M. C., & Nelson, M. L. (2014). Who and what links to the Internet Archive. *International Journal on Digital Libraries*, 14(3–4), 101–115. doi:10.1007/s00799-014-0111-5

Arms, W., Huttenlocher, D., Kleinberg, J., Macy, M., & Strang, D. (2006). *From wayback machine to Yesternet: New opportunities for social science.* Proceedings of the 2nd International Conference on e-Social Science (Vol. 1).

Atefeh, F., & Khreich, W. (2015). A survey of techniques for event detection in twitter. *Computational Intelligence*, 31(1), 132–164. doi:10.1111/coin.12017

Bach, J., & Stark, D. (2004). Link, search, interact: The co-evolution of NGOs and interactive technology. *Theory, Culture and Society*, 21(3), 101–117. doi:10.1177/0263276404043622

Bainbridge, W. S. (1995). Sociology on the World Wide Web. *Social Science Computer Review*, 13(4), 508–523. doi:10.1177/089443939501300406

Bean, L. L., May, D. L., & Skolnick, M. (1978). The mormon historical demography project. *Historical Methods: A Journal of Quantitative and Interdisciplinary History*, 11(1), 45–53. doi:10.1080/01615440.1978.9955216

Beer, D., & Burrows, R. (2007). Sociology and, of and in web 2.0: Some initial considerations. *Sociological Research Online*, 12(5), 17. doi:10.5153/sro.1560

Bode, L., Hanna, A., Yang, J., & Shah, D. V. (2015). Candidate networks, citizen clusters, and political expression. *The Annals of the American Academy of Political and Social Science*, 659(1), 149–165. doi:10.1177/0002716214563923

Boyd, D., & Crawford, K. (2012). Critical questions for big data. *Information, Communication & Society*, 15(5), 662–679. doi:10.1080/1369118X.2012.678878

Brügger, N. (2009). Website history and the website as an object of study. *New Media & Society*, 11(1–2), 115–132. doi:10.1177/1461444808099574

Brügger, N. (2012). Historical network analysis of the web. *Social Science Computer Review*, 31(3), 306–321. doi:10.1177/0894439312454267

Brügger, N. (2016). Introduction: The Web's first 25 years. *New Media & Society*, 18(7), 1059–1065. doi:10.1177/1461444816643787

Brunelle, J. F., Kelly, M., Salah Eldeen, H., Weigle, M. C., & Nelson, M. L. (2014, 8-12 September). *Not all mementos are created equal: Measuring the impact of missing resources.* Paper presented at the 14th annual international ACM/IEEE joint conference on Digital libraries, London, United Kingdom.

Bruns, A. (2007). Methodologies for mapping the political blogosphere: An exploration using the issuecrawler research tool. *First Monday, 12*(5). doi:10.5210/fm.v12i5.1834

Cappella, J. N. (2017). Vectors into the future of mass and interpersonal communication research: Big data, social media, and computational social science. *Human Communication Research*, n/a-n/a. doi:10.1111/hcre.12114

Chewning, L. V., Lai, C.-H., & Doerfel, M. L. (2012). Organizational resilience and using information and communication technologies to rebuild communication structures. *Management Communication Quarterly*. doi:10.1177/0893318912465815

Cohen, D. J. (2005). The future of preserving the past. *CRM Journal, 2*(2), 6.

Colleoni, E., Rozza, A., & Arvidsson, A. (2014). Echo chamber or public sphere? Predicting political orientation and measuring political homophily in twitter using big data. *Journal of Communication, 64*(2), 317-332. doi:10.1111/jcom.12084

Day, M. (2003). Preserving the fabric of our lives: A survey of web preservation initiatives. *Lecture Notes in Computer Science*, 461-472.

Dougherty, M., Meyer, E. T., Madsen, C. M., Van Den Heuvel, C., Thomas, A., & Wyatt, S. (2010). *Researcher engagement with web archives: State of the art.* Retrieved from https://papers.ssrn.com/sol3/papers.cfm?abstract_id=1714997

Driscoll, K., & Walker, S. (2014). Big data, big questions| Working within a black box: Transparency in the collection and production of big twitter data. *International Journal of Communication, 8*, 20.

Erdélyi, M., Benczúr, A. A., Masanés, J., & Siklósi, D. (2009). *Web spam filtering in internet archives.* Paper presented at the 5th International Workshop on Adversarial Information Retrieval on the Web (AIRWeb '09), New York, NY.

Foot, K. (2006). Web sphere analysis and cybercultural studies. In D. Silver, & A. Massanari (Eds.), *Critical Cyberculture Studies* (pp. 88-96). New York, NY: New York University Press.

Foot, K., & Schneider, S. M. (2006). *Web campaigning (acting with technology).* Cambridge, MA: The MIT Press.

Foot, K., Warnick, B., & Schneider, S. M. (2005). web-based memorializing after September 11: Toward a conceptual framework. *Journal of Computer-Mediated Communication, 11*, (1), 72-96. doi:10.1111/j.1083-6101.2006.tb00304.x

Freelon, D., Lynch, M., & Aday, S. (2015). Online fragmentation in wartime. *The Annals of the American Academy of Political and Social Science, 659*(1), 166-179. doi:10.1177/0002716214563921

Gomes, D., Miranda, J., & Costa, M. (2011). A survey on web archiving initiatives. *Research and Advanced Technology for Digital Libraries*, 408-420.

Gordon, M., & Pathak, P. (1999). Finding information on the World Wide Web: The retrieval effectiveness of search engines. *Information Processing & Management, 35*(2), 141-180. doi:10.1016/S0306-4573(98)00041-7

Green, B. B., Cook, A. J., Ralston, J. D., Fishman, P. A., Catz, S. L., Carlson, J., ... Thompson, R. S. (2008). Effectiveness of home blood pressure monitoring, Web communication, and pharmacist care on hypertension control: A randomized controlled trial. *JAMA : the Journal of the American Medical Association, 299*(24), 2857-2867. doi:10.1001/jama.299.24.2857

Greer, J. D., & Mensing, D. (2006). The evolution of online newspapers: A longitudinal content analysis, 1997-2003. In X. Li (Ed.), *Internet newspapers: The making of a mainstream medium* (pp. 13-32). Mahwah, NJ: Lawrence Erlbaum Associates.

Hockx-Yu, H. (2014). Access and scholarly use of web archives. *Alexandria, 25*(1-2), 113-127. doi:10.7227/ALX.0023

Holzmann, H., Goel, V., & Anand, A. (2016, June 19-23). *ArchiveSpark: Efficient Web archive access, extraction and derivation.* Paper presented at the 2016 IEEE/ACM Joint Conference on Digital Libraries (JCDL).

Kavanaugh, A. L., Fox, E. A., Sheetz, S. D., Yang, S., Li, L. T., Shoemaker, D. J., ... Xie, L. (2012). Social media use by government: From the routine to the critical. *Government Information Quarterly, 29*(4), 480-491. doi:10.1016/j.giq.2012.06.002

Kelleher, C., Sangwand, T. K., Wood, K., & Kamuronsi, Y. (2010). The human rights documentation initiative at the university of Texas libraries. *New Review of Information Networking, 15*(2), 94-109. doi:10.1080/13614576.2010.528342

Khannanov, A. (2003). *Internet in education: Support materials for educators.* Retrieved from. http://iite.unesco.org/publications/3214612/

Kim, H.-J., & Lee, H.-W. (2007). Development of metadata elements for intensive web archiving. *Journal of the Korean Society for Information Management, 24*(2), 143-160. doi:10.3743/KOSIM.2007.24.2.143

Kimpton, M., & Ubois, J. (2006). Year-by-year: From an archive of the internet to an archive on the internet. In J. Masanés (Ed.), *Web archiving* (pp. 201-212). Berlin, Heidelberg: Springer Berlin Heidelberg.

Kraut, R., Kiesler, S., Boneva, B., Cummings, J., Helgeson, V., & Crawford, A. (2002). Internet paradox revisited. *Journal of Social Issues, 58*(1), 49-74. doi:10.1111/1540-4560.00248

Ksepka, D. T., & Boyd, C. A. (2012). Quantifying historical trends in the completeness of the fossil record and the contributing factors: An example using Aves. *Paleobiology, 38*(1), 112-125. doi:10.1666/10059.1

Lazer, D., Pentland, A., Adamic, L. A., Aral, S., Barabasi, A.-L., Brewer, D., ... Van Alstyne, M. (2009). Computational social science. *Science, 323*, 721–723. doi:10.1126/science.1167742

Leighton, H. V., & Srivastava, J. (1999). First 20 precision among World Wide Web search services (search engines). *Journal of the Association for Information Science and Technology, 50*(10), 870.

Lin, J. (2015). *Scaling down distributed infrastructure on wimpy machines for personal web archiving*. Paper presented at the International Conference on World Wide Web, Florence, Italy.

Lin, J., Gholami, M., & Rao, J. (2014). *Infrastructure for supporting exploration and discovery in web archives*. Paper presented at the WWW '14 Companion Proceedings of the 23rd International Conference on the World Wide Web, Seoul, Korea.

Lin, J., Kraus, K., & Punzalan, R. (2014). Supporting "distant reading" for web archives. Paper presented at Digital Humanities 2014, Lausanne, Switzerland.

Lin, J., Milligan, I., Wiebe, J., & Zhou, A. (2017). Warcbase: Scalable analytics infrastructure for exploring web archives. *Journal Computation Cultural Herit, 10*(4), 1–30. doi:10.1145/3097570

Lomborg, S. (2012). Researching communicative practice: Web archiving in qualitative social media research. *Journal of Technology in Human Services, 30*(3–4), 219–231. doi:10.1080/15228835.2012.744719

Lor, P. J., Britz, J., & Watermeyer, H. (2006). Everything, for ever? The preservation of South African websites for future research and scholarship. *Journal of Information Science, 32*(1), 39–48. doi:10.1177/0165551506059221

Lustick, I. S. (1996). History, historiography, and political science: Multiple historical records and the problem of selection bias. *American Political Science Review, 90*(3), 605–618. doi:10.2307/2082612

Maemura, E., Becker, C., & Milligan, I. (2016, December 5–8). Understanding computational web archives research methods using research objects. Paper presented at the 2016 IEEE International Conference on Big Data (Big Data), Washington, DC, USA.

Manovich, L. (2011). *Trending: The promises and the challenges of big social data*. doi:10.5749/minnesota/9780816677948.003.0047

Masanès, J. (2006). Web archiving: Issues and methods. *Web Archiving*, 1–53.

Meyer, E. T., Schroeder, R., & Cowls, J. (2016). The net as a knowledge machine: How the Internet became embedded in research. *New Media & Society, 18*(7), 1159–1189. doi:10.1177/1461444816643793

Mi, C., Shan, X., Qiang, Y., Stephanie, Y., & Chen, Y. (2014). A new method for evaluating tour online review based on grey 2-tuple linguistic. *Kybernetes, 43*(3–4), 601–613. doi:10.1108/k-06-2013-0123

Milligan, I. (2016). Lost in the infinite archive: The promise and pitfalls of web archives. *International Journal of Humanities and Arts Computing, 10*(1), 78–94. doi:10.3366/ijhac.2016.0161

Milligan, I., Ruest, N., & Lin, J. (2016). *Content selection and curation for Web archiving: The gatekeepers vs. the masses*. Paper presented at the 16th ACM/IEEE-CS on Joint Conference on Digital Libraries, Newark, NJ.

Murata, T. (2003). Visualizing the structure of Web communities based on data acquired from a search engine. *IEEE Transactions on Industrial Electronics, 50*(5), 860–866. doi:10.1109/TIE.2003.817486

Newhagen, J. E., & Rafaeli, S. (1996). Why communication researchers should study the internet: A dialogue. *Journal of Computer-Mediated Communication, 1*(4). doi:10.1111/j.1083-6101.1996.tb00172.x

Newman, M. E. J. (2006). Modularity and community structure in networks. *Proceedings of the National Academy of Sciences, 103*(23), 8577–8582. doi:10.1073/pnas.0601602103

Niu, J. (2012). An overview of web archiving. *D-Lib Magazine, 18*(3/4). doi:10.1045/dlib.magazine

Ogden, J. (2016). *Interrogating the politics and performativity of web archives*. At JCDL2016: Joint Conference on Digital Libraries 2016: Doctoral Consortium, Newark, NJ, USA.

Parks, M. R. (2014). Big data in communication research: Its contents and discontents. *Journal of Communication, 64*(2), 355–360. doi:10.1111/jcom.12090

Penone, C., Davidson, A. D., Shoemaker, K. T., Di Marco, M., Rondinini, C., Brooks, T. M., ... Costa, G. C. (2014). Imputation of missing data in life-history trait datasets: Which approach performs the best? *Methods in Ecology and Evolution, 5*(9), 961–970. doi:10.1111/2041-210X.12232

Price, G. (1995). The World Wide Web and the historian. *History and Computing, 7*(2), 104–108. doi:10.3366/hac.1995.7.2.104

Qin, J., Zhou, Y., Reid, E., Lai, G., & Chen, H. (2007). Analyzing terror campaigns on the internet: Technical sophistication, content richness, and Web interactivity. *International Journal of Human-Computer Studies, 65*(1), 71–84. doi:10.1016/j.ijhcs.2006.08.012

Rackley, M. (2000). *Internet archive encyclopedia of library and information science* (3rd ed., pp. 2966–2976). London, UK: Taylor & Francis.

Reyes, A. (2014). Linguistic anthropology in 2013: Super-new-big. *American Anthropologist, 116*(2), 366–378. doi:10.1111/aman.12109

Robinson, L., Cotten, S. R., Ono, H., Quan-Haase, A., Mesch, G., Chen, W., ... Stern, M. J. (2015). Digital inequalities and why they matter. *Information, Communication & Society, 18*(5), 569–582. doi:10.1080/1369118X.2015.1012532

Ruths, D., & Pfeffer, J. (2014). Social media for large studies of behavior. *Science, 346*(6213), 1063. doi:10.1126/science.346.6213.1063

Salah Eldeen, H. M., & Nelson, M. L. (2012). Losing my revolution: How many resources shared on social media have been lost?. In *Theory and practice of digital libraries* (pp. 125–137). Springer.

Shah, D. V., Cappella, J. N., Neuman, W. R., Shah, D. V., Cappella, J. N., & Neuman, W. R. (2015). Big data, digital media, and computational social science. In Zaphiris P., Buchanan G., Rasmussen E., Loizides F. (eds.), Theory and Practice of Digital Libraries. TPDL 2012. Lecture Notesin Computer Science, vol. 7489. Berlin, Heidelberg: Springer.

Shaw, J. D. (2017). Advantages of starting with theory. *Academy of Management Journal, 60*(3), 819–822. doi:10.5465/amj.2017.4003

Shumate, M. (2003). *The coevolution of a population with a community, organizations and the evironment: The emergence, evolution, and impact of HIV/AIDS NGOs*. (Doctor of Philosophy). Los Angeles, CA: University of Southern California.

Shumate, M. (2012). The Evolution of the HIV/AIDS NGO Hyperlink Network. *Journal of Computer-Mediated Communication, 17*(2), 120–134. doi:10.1111/j.1083-6101.2011.01569.x

Shumate, M., Fulk, J., & Monge, P. (2005). Predictors of the international HIV-AIDS INGO network over time. *Human Communication Research, 31*, 482–511. doi:10.1111/j.1468-2958.2005.tb00880.x

Spaniol, M., Denev, D., Mazeika, A., Weikum, G., & Senellart, P. (2009). *Data quality in web archiving*. Paper presented at the Proceedings of the 3rd workshop on Information credibility on the web, Madrid, Spain.

Stevens, J. (2004). Long-term literary E-zine stability: Issues and access in libraries. *Technical Services Quarterly, 22*(1), 21–32. doi:10.1300/J124v22n01_03

Stucchi, M., Albini, P., Mirto, M., & Rebez, A. (2004). Assessing the completeness of Italian historical earthquake data. *Annals of Geophysics, 47*(2–3). doi:10.4401/ag-3330

Taylor, M., & Doerfel, M. L. (2003). Building interorganizational relationships that build nations. *Human Communication Research, 29*(2), 153–181. doi:10.1111/j.1468-2958.2003.tb00835.x

Topps, D., Helmer, J., & Ellaway, R. (2013). YouTube as a platform for publishing clinical skills training videos. *Academic Medicine, 88*(2), 192–197. doi:10.1097/ACM.0b013e31827c5352

Weber, M., Ognyanova, K., & Kosterich, A. (2017). Imitation in the quest to survive: Lessons from news media on the early web. *International Journal of Communication, 11*(2017), 5068–5092.

Weber, M. S. (2012). Newspapers and the long-term implications of hyperlinking. *Journal of Computer-Mediated Communication, 17*(2), 187–201. doi:10.1111/j.1083-6101.2011.01563.x

Weber, M. S., & Monge, P. (2014). Industries in turmoil: Driving transformation during periods of disruption. *Communication Research*, 1–30. doi:10.1177/0093650213514601

Weber, M. S., & Nguyen, H. (2015). Big Data? Big Issues: Degradation in Longitudinal Data and Implications for Social Sciences. Paper presented at the WebSci 2015, Oxford, UK.

Welles, B. F., & Contractor, N. (2015). Individual motivations and network effects. *The Annals of the American Academy of Political and Social Science, 659*(1), 180–190. doi:10.1177/0002716214565755

Williams, K. C. M. (2000). Reproduced and emergent genres of communication on the World Wide Web. *The Information Society, 16*(3), 201–215. doi:10.1080/01972240050133652

Wouters, P., Hellsten, I., & Leydesdorff, L. (2004). Internet time and the reliability of search engines. *First Monday, 9*, 10.

Zeng, R., & Greenfield, P. M. (2015). Cultural evolution over the last 40 years in China: Using the google ngram viewer to study implications of social and political change for cultural values. *International Journal of Psychology, 50*(1), 47–55. doi:10.1002/ijop.12125

Zhou, Y., Reid, E., Qin, J., Chen, H., & Lai, G. (2005). US domestic extremist groups on the Web: Link and content analysis. *IEEE Intelligent Systems, 20*(5), 44–51. doi:10.1109/MIS.2005.96

Disentangling User Samples: A Supervised Machine Learning Approach to Proxy-population Mismatch in Twitter Research

K. Hazel Kwon, J. Hunter Priniski, and Monica Chadha

ABSTRACT
This study addresses the issue of sampling biases in social media data-driven communication research. The authors demonstrate how supervised machine learning could reduce Twitter sampling bias induced from "proxy-population mismatch". Particularly, this study used the Random Forest (RF) classifier to disentangle tweet samples representative of general publics' activities from non-general—or institutional—activities. By applying RF classifier models to Twitter data sets relevant to four news events and a randomly pooled dataset, the study finds systematic differences between general user samples and institutional user samples in their messaging patterns. This article calls for disentangling Twitter user samples when ordinary user behaviors are the focus of research. It also builds on the development of machine learning modeling in the context of communication research.

"Just because Big Data presents us with large quantities of data does not mean that methodological issues are no longer relevant. Understanding sample, for example, is more important now than ever" (boyd & Crawford, 2012, p. 668).

Data-driven research has gained unprecedented popularity among communication scholars in the past few years. As the recent establishment of a Computational Methods interest group and the preconference workshop on computational techniques tools at the International Communication Association (ICA) conference in 2017 demonstrate (http://www.icahdq.org), communication scholarship has kept pace with the recent advancement of the computational social science paradigm. Social media platform Twitter, especially, has become one of the most popular data feeds for computational communication researchers who pursue "unobtrusive methods," (Burrows & Savage, 2014, p.2) to understand public opinions and behavioral tendencies of social media users in various social and political contexts. Indeed, social media research has offered fruitful insights on digitally mediated communicative practices, and new directions for research and theory-building.

Simultaneously however, data-driven research has raised concerns about its sampling procedure and whether it accurately represents the population or topic it claims to study. Critics have pointed out that existing computational models and their findings can not only pose biases toward issue experts, professionals, dedicated users, or certain demographic groups but also have low accuracy when they claim to represent the general body of "ordinary" users (Boyd & Crawford, 2012; Cohen & Ruth, 2013; Hargittai, 2015). In the same vein, communication research that examines large-scale data often does not disentangle the samples representative of "ordinary" publics from those of "specialized" actors. Rather, different types of users are mixed in an aggregated data structure that would treat them as a single population. Although studies have extensively discussed the roles of diverse social actors (e.g., elite vs. non-elite users) in shaping discourses in social media space (e.g., Himelboim, McCreery, & Smith, 2013; Papacharissi, 2015), a systematic procedure to unravel different types of social actors from the large data chunk has rarely been implemented into the sampling stage of such studies.

The current study extends the discussion on sampling biases in computational communication research. The underlying motivation of this study is to examine a machine-learning solution to improve sampling techniques for Twitter research, one of the most popular data venues for computational communication scholarship. Twitter sampling has introduced a variety of selection biases, caused by different issues such as proprietary restrictions (Burrows & Savage, 2014; Driscoll & Walker, 2014), algorithmic contamination (González-Bailón, Wang, Rivero, Borge-Holthoefer, & Moreno, 2014; Salganik, 2017), noise from non-organic activities such as bots and astroturfing (Chu, Gianvecchio, Wang, & Jajodia, 2012; Ratkiewicz et al., 2011), and observational errors (boyd & Crawford, 2012; Hargittai, 2015; Salganik, 2017). Whereas some of these issues are beyond the individual researchers' control, others may be amenable by implementing rigorous sampling procedures and data preprocessing.

The purpose of this article is a methodological contribution, and it is organized as follows. In the following section, we discuss various social media sampling issues based on three concerns: predefined sampling frame, engineered noises, and proxy misspecification. After introducing the three concerns, the study narrows the focus down onto one specific issue related to proxy misspecification, the so called "proxy-population mismatch." It also is referred to as the "[unverified] quantitative relation between the proxy and the original populations studied" (Ruths & Pfeffer, 2014, p. 1064). Next, we introduce the research design in which we demonstrate the use of supervised machine learning as one approach to mitigate the proxy- population mismatch issue. As an example, we apply Random Forest classification models to separate ordinary users—whom communication scholars traditionally envision as constituents of the general publics and are referred to as *general public users* in this article—from the specialized actors who altogether we classify as *institutional users*. After explaining how we developed the model, we empirically examine whether the tweet sample representative of the general publics is indeed systematically different from the sample that represents institutional users. Based on the results, the conclusion section reiterates the need to couple data-preprocessing with systematic "slicing" of the dataset (Woodford, Walker, & Paul, 2013) to avoid confounding errors induced from proxy-population mismatch.

Background

Biases in social media data-driven research

Sampling of social media data, unfortunately, has not always been transparent. Literature has discussed various sources for biases in social media data-driven research, which we recap into three concerns: (1) predefined sampling frame, (2) noise from engineered activities, and (3) proxy misspecification. Note these three problems may not cover the exhaustive list of sources of biases and are not necessarily exclusive of one another either. Regardless, distinguishing these problems is helpful to elucidate sources of biases that can be improved through more systematic sampling or preprocessing procedures.

Predefined sampling frame. The first type of bias is induced from the use of a predefined sampling frame. Conventional social research, including communication studies, begins by setting up the research purpose and defining the "target population" (Salganik, 2017). Choosing the sampling frame—a pool of potential samples representative of the population—usually comes next. In social media data-driven research, however, the sampling frame is often predefined irrespective of the research purpose.

A primary reason for computational research using a predefined sampling frame is data inaccessibility, often attributed to the *proprietary restrictions* imposed by social media companies. Researchers may investigate a certain platform as an empirical site not always because the selected platform is the best representation of the phenomena under investigation but rather it allows easier access to data than other platforms (Schroeder, 2014). Twitter, for example, has undeniably become the most popular data source than other social media platforms for computational communication studies. This is not only due to Twitter's role in facilitating public communication but also the "relatively easy access to the data" enabled by the platform's application programing interfaces (API) policy (Gonzalez-Balion et al., 2014, p. 16). Conversely, private communication in more restrictive platforms such as Facebook or Snapchat is not accessible to majority of researchers, and thus precluded from the sampling frame regardless of the empirical relevance of such data to the research purpose or target population.

Furthermore, the same company's data policy varies from time to time, making the replication of a previous sampling procedure implausible even within a single platform context. This problem is referred to as *"system drift"* (Salganik, 2017). For example, studies that used ego network samples from Facebook (e.g., Brooks, Hogan, Ellison, Lampe, & Vitak, 2014; Kwon, Stefanone, & Barnett, 2014) may not be replicable anymore due to the companies' restrictions on the Application Program Interface (API) that previously enabled the collection of network data. Similarly, access to Twitter data has become increasingly limited over time. Unless data are purchased via the commercial "firehose" service, the currently available Twitter public API allows access to only 1% of all the tweets generated, for which "the methods that Twitter employs…is unknown" (Morstatter, Pfeffer, Liu, & Carley, 2013, p. 1). Additionally, studies have attested to systematic differences in measurements among the different API-based datasets (Driscoll & Walker, 2014; Gonzalez-Bailon et al., 2014; Morstatter et al., 2013).

Engineered noises. The second type of sampling bias arises due to the artificially planned activities that affect data creation or distribution, which together, we refer to as engineered noises. Engineered noises occur mainly from two factors: First, *"algorithmic confounding"* or "the ways that the goals of system designers can introduce patterns into data" (Salganik, 2017). For example, the distribution of a friend's network size on Facebook shows an anomalous peak at around 20 friends (Ugander, Karrer, Backstrom, & Marlow, 2011). Scholars familiar with the "social brain hypothesis" would interpret this anomaly as a spillover of the "sympathy group"–a grouping of maximum 20 individuals with whom one can maintain meaningful relations and contact on a regular basis (Zhou, Sornette, Hill, & Dunbar, 2005, p. 440)–on Facebook. In fact, this anomaly arises from the company's algorithmic curation that encourages "low friend count individuals" to connect with more friends "until they reach 20 friends" (Ugander et al., 2011, p.3).

Second, *non-organic activities* such as the use of bots and astroturfing also produce engineered noises. Studies estimate that 7% of Facebook accounts, and 9–15% of Twitter accounts are composed of bot-accounts (Varol, Ferrara, Davis, Menczer, & Flammini, 2017). Bot-assisted activities can manipulate public opinion (Ratkiewicz et al., 2011), contaminate social sharing processes (Lee, Eoff, & Caverlee, 2011), and disrupt information propagation (Abokhodair, Yoo, & McDonald, 2015). Sampling biases introduced from nonorganic activities could mislead our interpretation of the bottom-up processes underlying online public discourse. The noise from non-organic activities could be especially problematic when the research goal is to explore spontaneously emergent, grass-root phenomena in social media.

Proxy misspecification. In addition to the issues of predefined sampling frame and engineered noises discussed above, proxy misspecification can create another layer of errors. Particularly, defining proxies can vary, contingent upon how researchers set the data collection parameters such as keywords, time windows, locations, and others. That is, *misspecified or insufficient search parameters* could result in misrepresentation of the population under investigation. For example, González-Bailón et al. (2014) compared three different data collection methods on Twitter during the Indignados movement in 2012: SearchAPI using six hashtag search keywords; StreamAPI using the same six hashtag keywords; and StreamAPI using an extensive list of 70 keywords. Their network analysis results revealed that the effect of search parameters was "more prominent" than the API effect in creating biases in network statistics (González-Bailón et al., 2014, p. 24).

Finally, another important issue that falls in line with the problem of proxy misspecification is called *"proxy-population mismatch"*, which is the focus of the current study. Proxy-population mismatch refers to a gap between the proxy and real populations due to lack of understanding of the nature of the proxy (Hargittai, 2015; Hargittai & Litt, 2011). The proxy-population mismatch has been explained as a methodological challenge, as Ruths and Pfeffer (2014) state:

"Social media research question defines a population of interest: e.g., voting preference among California university students. However, because human populations rarely self-label, proxy populations of users are commonly studied instead, for example, the set of all Facebook users who report attending a UC school. However, the quantitative relation between the proxy and original populations studied, typically, is unknown—a source of potentially serious bias" (p. 1064).

Cohen and Ruth (2013) tap into this issue by re-examining predictive models of political orientations on Twitter. They found that the prediction tasks were largely successful when the samples were drawn from the population of politicians or politically active users. However, the same approach revealed much poorer outcomes when "more normal, less politically vocal" users were under investigation (p. 98). Their finding suggests that analytic efforts to understand social media users' attributes can overestimate the attribute tendency due to the bias toward specialized users who would explicitly display the attribute markers. In other words, random sampling from 'all' available Twitter data pool could be misleading in some contexts because the assumption that all Twitter users should be the proxy of ordinary social media users has not been verified. Other scholars have similarly contended that the social media population is not a proxy for the general population and the former is biased toward certain demographics and topical interests, recommending social media data-driven studies to be explicit about the research scope and the potential proxy-population mismatch (Hargittai, 2015; Hargittai & Litt, 2011).

Summary. Data-driven research is not free from sampling and measurement challenges. Some of the challenges are entwined with the social media company's policies and decision-making that are often unknown to, or beyond the control of, academic researchers. Some other issues arise due to the social media platform's inherent characteristics or third-party interruptions. Researchers may only reflexively respond to such issues, for example, by acknowledging data limitations and explicating the scope of the research (Hargittai, 2015). Meanwhile, some other methodological issues could be addressed by developing a rigorous research design. Extensive domain knowledge and effortful data collection and preprocessing techniques could improve the representativeness of samples. For example, there have been recent endeavors to disambiguate bots from a large-scale data corpus (e.g., Abokhodair et al., 2015; Chu et al., 2012; Varol et al., 2017). Cohen and Ruth (2013) demonstrated the use of machine-assisted sampling to help reduce errors introduced not only by bot activities but also by other sources of proxy-population mismatch. This study taps into this proxy-population mismatch issue, specifically addressing the question whether the general publics' activities on Twitter can be captured in a manner that represents the target population more accurately.

An example of proxy-population mismatch: proxy for general public users in Twitter

Twitter is a multifarious information stream that blends various groups of users, ranging from institutions, organizations, elites, to ordinary, non-elite individuals (Hermida, 2010). Examining all publicly available Twitter data has been useful in manifesting such diversities in social media communication networks (e.g., Jackson & Foucault Welles, 2015; Papacharissi, 2015). However, bundling all types of users and their activities into a single 'sampling basket' may not be the ideal approach when the research objective is to understand behaviors of *general publics* –a collective of individual citizens distinct from media elites, government, or other institutional entities.

Table 1. Examples of journal of communication articles based on quantitative Twitter analyses.

Article	Target Population	Twitter Data Access	Sampling Parameters	Separated between ordinary and institutional users?
Colleoni et al. (2014)	Twitter users who engage in political discourses	Secondary	Political users identified by using machine learning techniques from the secondary large-scale Twitter data of 2009.	No
Emery et al. (2014)	Online viewers of the Tips campaign	Firehose	Publicly available tweets collected using 36 search keywords during the campaign period; Used machine learning techniques to disambiguate Tips campaign relevant tweets.	No
Murthy et al. (2015)	General Twitter users	StreamAPI	Globally available tweets at any given time during the summer of 2013	No
Shin and Thorson (2017)	Users who share fact-checking messages in Twitter	Firehose	Publicly available political tweets searched by the list of 427 keywords during the 2012 presidential election; Used 194 tweets posted by three fact-checking websites to identify users who re-tweeted or commented on these tweets.	No
Vargo et al. (2014)	Supporters of presidential candidates	StreamAPI	Tweets made by supporters of Obama and Romney, identified by sentiment analysis coupled with machine learning, and tweets made by media accounts	Partly Yes (separated tweets sent from a predefined list of media accounts)

Table 1 lists a few exemplary studies published in one of the flagship journals in the communication discipline (*Journal of Communication*) that quantitatively analyzed Twitter data to understand communication patterns of social media publics. The list is far from exhaustive; the articles are high-quality publications that offer insightful findings using innovative data sources and methodological approaches. The intention is thus not to discredit the value of these studies but to accentuate a couple of points resonant with the issue of proxy-population mismatch.

First, the studies listed in Table 1 alluded to their population of interest as online "citizens" (Vaccari, Chadwick, & O'Loughlin, 2015), "viewers" (Emery, Szczypka, Abril, Kim, & Vera, 2014), "audiences" (Vargo, Guo, McCombs, & Shaw, 2014), "[information] consumer" (Shin & Thorson, 2017), or simply, "users" (Colleoni, Rozza, & Arvidsson, 2014). To represent these populations, they considered all publicly available Twitter data, searched by the researchers' filtering parameters. The actual data structure of Twitter, however, is likely to contain information produced by organizational, non-personal, or institutional activities. Therefore, assuming that all searched tweets represent a single population could neglect to account for a potential mismatch between the proxy—publicly accessible data in Twitter—and the population of interest—citizens, audiences, or ordinary users constituting the general public.

Second, some of these studies classified their data into subgroups, for example in terms of political orientations (Himelboim et al., 2013; Shin & Thorson, 2017; Vargo et al., 2014) or device types (Murthy, Bowman, Gross, & McGarry, 2015). The analytic focus then is to investigate differential effects of the sub-groups on shaping the patterns of tweet activities. Investigating subgroup effects has indeed resulted in shrewd lessons about social media use patterns. Nevertheless, the possibility of confounding effects due to the inherent differences within the proxies should not be neglected. For example, Shin and Thorson (2017) studied political fact-checking information diffusion, and underscored the role of "consumers' voluntary sharing and commenting behavior" in "increasing visibility of [fact-checking] messages," (p. 15). Meanwhile, less highlighted was the possibility that political fact-checking information could be disseminated not just by individual consumers' voluntary sharing but also by strategic, coordinated political efforts. If the sample data contained a significant portion of strategic actors beyond the ordinary citizen population, the emphasis on voluntary sharing could be an overstatement. Another exemplary study (Murthy et al., 2015) showed the effect of devices (mobile-based vs. web-based) on shaping linguistic styles in tweets. In discussing their findings, however, Murthy et al. (2015) cautiously suggest the possibility of spurious inference, highlighting "the value of keeping the question open as to whether the type of people who tweet from mobile devices are qualitatively different from those who tweet from web-based platforms," (p. 834). That is, if ordinary users are likely to use mobile devices to send their tweets and institutional actors send their tweets via web platforms, or vice versa, the linguistic difference could be produced not due to device affordances but rather the distinct natures of populations—the general populace versus institutional actors.

To summarize, communication activities on Twitter are social and non-social, and spontaneous and strategic. When the focus of research lies on naturally occurring communication among ordinary individual users, the assumption that all publicly available Twitter data should be the proxy population could engender an issue of proxy-population mismatch, and lead to a misinterpretation of findings. To address this concern, the study explicated here explores the use of computerized processes to help researchers resolve the issue of proxy-population mismatch and thus proposes the first RQ.

RQ1: Could machine learning help disentangle the separate populations, specifically one representative of *general public users* from those comprising specialized user accounts such as media elites, government, and other institutional entities, organizational agents, and non-personal users?

In addition to effectively separating the two sample groups, we tested for differences in the tweeting patterns of general public users and institutional users. We conducted post-hoc tests with descriptive statistics of popularly studied characteristics of tweet messages, such as retweeting, the use of external informational source (URL), hash-tagging, and language uses (analytic and affective). The post-hoc tests intend to address whether there is indeed a possibility of sampling bias if these two groups are treated as one single population. Hence, the following hypotheses are proposed.

H1: The group of general users will show a different pattern of retweeting than institutional users.

H2: The group of general users will show a different pattern of using external information (URL) than institutional users following violent events.

H3: The group of general users will show a different pattern of hashtag use than institutional users.

H4: The group of general users will show a different pattern of analytic language use than institutional users following violent events.

H5: The group of general users will show a different pattern of affective language use than institutional users.

Additionally, we tested for differences in the tweeting patterns between the two populations based on the type of device used to tweet the message (Murthy et al., 2015). Only a couple of datasets include the related data field, and thus the following hypothesis is tested with the related datasets.

H6: The group of general users will show a different pattern than institutional users based on the device used to tweet the message.

Research design

Case studies: tweets on violence news

In this study, specialized actors have been grouped together and labeled as *institutional users*. For empirical exploration, we used four Twitter datasets that were collected after four violence-related news events: Mass shooting in Mesa, Arizona, a city in the metro-Phoenix area, in March 26, 2015 (Mesa), Boston Marathon Bombing in April 15, 2013 (Boston), Brussels Airport Attacks in March 22, 2016 (Brussels), and Quebec Mosque Attack in January 29, 2017 (Quebec).

One of the authors had previously collected the four Twitter datasets after the aforementioned news events as part of a larger research initiative. We used these news events as our empirical contexts for a few reasons. First, the episodic nature of such news tends to engender public responses within a short period time, and is, thus, relatively free from the temporal confounders. Second, terror news appeals to both, general publics and institutional actors, and thus may be advantageous for representing both populations. Third, violent incidents are usually breaking news events, that are less likely to involve planned activities than organized or longer-lasting news events such as political campaigns or social movements. Lastly, these four datasets represent different spatial scopes—local, national, and international—and, thus, the comparison of these datasets is opportune for exploring whether the machine-assisted sampling technique is applicable across different geographical scales.

The data for Mesa and Brussels were collected via NodeXL, a StreamAPI-based collection tool (Smith et al., 2010). Boston and Quebec data were collected by directly using StreamAPI. Mesa data contained tweets from March 18 (the day of the incident) through March 26, 2015, searched with the keywords *#MesaShooting*, and '*Mesa & Shooting*'; the coverage of Boston data was more sporadic, including April 15 (the day the bombing occurred), April 19–20, and April 24–April 29, 2013, searched with the keywords *#BostonMarathon*, '*Boston & Marathon*', and *Boston*. Brussels data was collected over a span of almost two weeks, from March 22 (the day of the bombing) to April 3, 2016; the keywords used in the tweet collection were *#BrusselsAttacks* and *Brussels*. Quebec data contained tweets from January 19 (the day of the shooting) to February 14, 2017, searched with the keywords *#QuebecAttacks*, *#QuebecShooting*, '*Quebec & Mosque*', and *Quebec*. To minimize cultural differences, we limited the investigation to English language tweets that originated from U.S.-based accounts. To identify the U.S.-based tweets, we developed a Twitter geo-tagging tool, using the four sources of geographic information associated with a tweet: tweet coordinates, tweet place, location in user profile, and tweet text, based on the "Carmen" library (Dredze, Paul, Bergsma, & Tran, 2013). As a result, the total number of tweets investigated was 7898, created by 4,345 unique users for Mesa, 14,211 tweets created by 9,562 unique users for Boston, 13,660 tweets created by 9,980 unique users for Brussels, and 151,928 tweets created by 87,225 unique users for Quebec. Note that these users are rarely single-tweet users in the datasets; the number of users who tweeted less than five times since the start date of their membership were only 14 users in Mesa, 26 users in Brussels, and 101 users in Quebec dataset (We did not have user status information for the Boston dataset).

Given that all data were drawn from news events similar in nature (i.e., violence news), we additionally created and analyzed a random dataset to enhance the generalizability of the results. This additional dataset included randomly pooled profile texts and tweets via StreamAPI for one week from September 22–28, 2017, at various times each day. Only tweets and profiles written in English from U.S.-based accounts were included ($N = 175420$).

For the post-hoc tests, retweet status, number of hashtags, and the use of URL were coded from the tweet messages. The use of analytic and affective languages was measured using Pennebaker, Booth, Boyd, & Francis, 2015 a tested lexicon-based sentiment analysis software (Pennebaker et al., 2015). Only two of our datasets (Boston and Quebec) contained information about tweeting devices and thus we looked at these two events for examining differences in the device popularity between the two populations. We replicated the process put forth by Murthy et al. (2015) to code the device types.

Technical description of random forest classification as a case for supervised machine learning in data preprocessing

Supervised Machine Learning modeling enables automatic classification of documents by feeding given algorithms with previously categorized data, also called the "training set". The algorithms can then apply the rules of the categorized data in the training set to uncategorized data in a "testing set". In this study, our goal was to classify two classes of Twitter users: general public users and institutional users. Specifically, given a training set of linguistic features extracted from Twitter profile descriptions, the Machine-Learning (ML) task was to approximate a function that successfully maps the linguistic features from the profile descriptions to the proper classes: general or institutional user. The model performance was then evaluated by applying the trained algorithm to a testing set, which would result in quality assurance metrics such as accuracy, precision, recall rates, and F-score.[1]

There are several popular classifier algorithms in Machine Learning. Random Forest (RF) classification is among the most popular and is the focus of this study. The RF classifier is a member of a class of learning algorithms known as Ensemble Learners that aggregate the results of many variating, 'weaker' learning functions to derive a final classification. Specifically, the RF classifier constructs multiple different decision trees that classify the data into the desired samples or categories and derives a final decision by aggregating all the trees' decisions. Hence, the model as a whole is analogously understood as a "forest," where many individual decision "trees" are grown. Based on the functions and trained dataset, each tree "votes" for a classification. The final decision or classification chosen by the forest is the one that receives the most votes. The RF classifier is particularly appropriate when the classes are not linearly separable. We assume that ordinary users are a heterogeneous collection of individuals, and thus our classification problem is not linearly separable (Figure 1). Although we chose the RF classifier for the prediction task given the linearly non-separable data condition, it does not mean that RF is superior to other algorithms. Accordingly, we present the results from other popular classifiers along with the RF results in the following section, that allow for an objective comparison of model performances across different classifiers.

In the RF classifier, each decision tree grows from a "root" node (no incoming edges, only outgoing edges), to "branch" nodes (has an incoming and an outgoing edge), and to "leaf or terminal" nodes (only has incoming edges). The process of splitting nodes is equivalent to the process of feature partitioning, resulting in one of the terminal nodes serving as the predicted class. In each tree, the nodal splits follow a random process, which is why the algorithm is called a *Random*

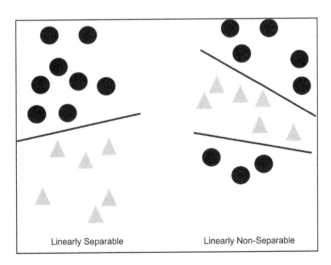

Figure 1. Example of linearly separable and non-separable data structures.

Forest (Breiman, 2001). Furthermore, each decision tree does not partition the data on the same set of features. Each tree is constructed from a random subset of features representing the data. The splitting or partitioning process continues recursively until the recursion reaches the best "split" that no longer makes the probability of a correct classification for the data much larger than the previous iteration (Loh, 2011). The decision on the "best" split is based on Gini impurity (GI)—the frequency measure for the inconsistent classification by a given feature set (Breiman, 1984).[2] Whereas the lowest Gini impurity would render perfect accuracy for group classification in an ideal world, the real data typically has an overfitting issue when the trees grow fully (unpruned) until each leaf node corresponds to the lowest impurity. Therefore, to avoid overfitting, a common practice is to "prune" trees, i.e., discontinue splitting once the decrease in GI from one split to the next is smaller than a given threshold (Breiman, 2001). Once individual trees make decisions after the partitioning, the forest derives the final prediction by aggregating the results using a method known as Bagging or **Bootstrap Aggregating** (Breiman, 2001). Figure 2 summarizes the RF classifier algorithm.

Classification of Twitter user samples

In each dataset (Mesa, Boston, Brussels, and Quebec), Twitter users were classified as either general public users or institutional users according to the five steps described below. After many trials and tests, this article presents the most successful procedure.

Step 1: rule-based annotation

In a supervised ML model, a machine learns from a training set and tests its learnt algorithms against a testing set. In this study, prepping the training and testing sets required the categorization of some profile texts as belonging to either general public or institutional users. Therefore, we randomly selected and labeled 1,000 user profile texts from the Mesa dataset, 2,000 from Boston, 2,000 from Brussels, and 2,000 from Quebec, a total of 7,000 texts.

As diverse and heterogeneous as general publics are, it could be daunting to consider every instance of ordinary user profiles. Instead, a more plausible approach was to adopt a process of elimination by which we labeled a profile as the positive class of the general user (=1) if it did *not* fall in any of the predefined non-ordinary user categories, namely: media organizations, journalism personnel, group, or organizational profiles, strictly professional career accounts with clear indication of organizational information, political/politicians account, and promotional account. The profiles falling in any of these categories were labeled as the negative class, which was the

Random Forest Classification Algorithm

Let our training set be $D = ((X_1, y_1), (X_2, y_2), \ldots, (X_n, y_n))$. (X_i, y_i) is a feature vector and its classification. $X_i \in X^d$, $y_i \in \{0,1\}$, where d is the number of features.

<u>Construct T random decision trees</u>

For $i = 1, 2, 3, \ldots, T$ decision trees:

    Sample with replacement a $D_i = (X_i, y_i)$ from D:

    Uniformly and randomly select M features of X_i (**note:** m << d):

    Classification tree $T_f \leftarrow$ **For** each $m \in M$: calculate **Gini**(m)

<u>Aggregate results for prediction</u>

Given a new $x' \notin D$ (test-set)

    Classification for $x' \leftarrow$ Majority vote of the B decision trees.

Figure 2. Summary of the RF classification algorithms.

institutional user (=0). Two graduate student coders annotated the selected profiles (Cohen's Kappa = .72), resolving disagreement through discussions when it occurred. The detailed description of this coding framework is found in our sister paper (Kwon, Chadha, & Pellizzaro, 2017).

Step 2: data preprocessing

The 7,000 labeled profile texts were pre-processed by (i) removing non-English and non-alphabetic characters, (ii) casting all letters in lower case, (iii) unifying all URLs into a single feature called "*http*", (iv) unifying Instagram links into a single feature "*ig*", and (v) removing stop-words based on the NLTK dictionary. We retained some stop-words like first-person pronouns, considering the possibility of a plural pronoun (such as "we") resulting in difference from a singular classifier (such as "I"). We did not employ stemming because the process led to lower accuracy results in all datasets. The labeled profile texts were then separated into two sets: a training set (80% of the total labeled data) and a testing set (20%), resulting in four training sets and four testing sets, each of which represented the corresponding Twitter dataset (Mesa, Boston, Brussels, and Quebec).

Step 3: feature extraction

The *sci-kit learn* package in Python was used to create the bag-of-words model, which turned each profile document into a feature vector. To avoid overfitting, we restricted—or "pruned"—the length of the feature vector to 500 most commonly used terms, which we chose based on term frequency (TF), by the raw count of a term. While we also tried to select 500 features based on term frequency-inverse document frequency (TF-IDF), the results remained largely the same. Previously, we tried to include bi-gram features and part-of-speech tagging; however, the model performance did not improve notably while the cost of computing time was greater. Accordingly, we decided to adhere to the simplest approach, which was to generate features based on TF. We then vectorized each profile text by representing it as a sparse (with mostly zeroes), 500-count frequency long vector.

Step 4: classification learning

The RF classifier was fed with each training set. For illustrative purpose, we take two examples of raw profile texts from the Mesa dataset. The first one was labeled as 'institutional user profile' (= 0), and the second one was labeled as "general public user profile" (=1).

Text 1 (institutional): Journalist and Reporter for AZ Republic.

Text 2 (general public): Love America. Bless God and go Cardinals! ig:instagram/ID

After preprocessing, each text would become: "*journalist reporter az republic*" and "*love america bless god go cardinals ig*". Let us assume that decision trees were constructed from the training set and the feature vectors used to partition the data were *journalist, ig, reporter, america, god*. Next, let us suppose that a text that included the features *journalist* or *reporter* was highly likely to be an institutional account, and conversely, a text containing the features *ig* (abbreviation for Instagram), *america*, or *god*, was more likely to belong to a general public user. Figure 3 presents a simplified example of the two decision trees concerned with these features for each text. These decision trees were iterated through recursive partitioning until they reached the best splits. The partial decisions derived from these decision trees were then aggregated for the final classification prediction. We used the *scikit-learn Random Forest module* in Python for the classification learning, with the number of trees set to 100.

Step 5: validation and automatic classification

After feeding the classifier with the training set data, a testing data set was used to validate the model's performance in accuracy, precision, and recall rates. The Results section below presents the RF-based validation results along with the results from other popular algorithms

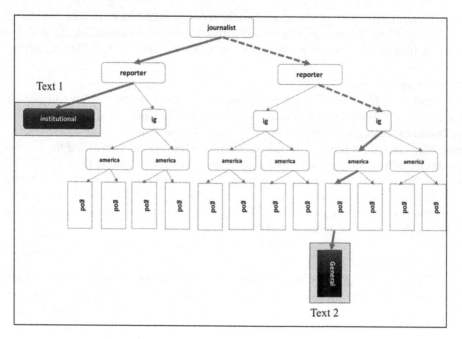

Figure 3. An example of two decision trees concerned with the features *journalist, ig, reporter, america, god* (a decision tree for text 1 = "journalist and reporter for az republic."; and another decision tree for text 2 = "love america. bless god and go cardinals! ig: instagram/id."). Bold line indicates the feature exists in the text; dotted line indicates the feature does not exist in the text. Each tree ends with a different class as the leaf node.

including SVM, Multinomial Naïve Bayes, and Logistic Regression. After the validation, the learnt RF algorithm was used to classify the rest of the unlabeled profiles as either general public users or institutional users. That is, two sample groups were created based on the machine-generated classification, and the differences between the two groups were examined using descriptive statistics.

Results

Validation of human annotation outputs

As our approach for annotation was rule-based, we needed to validate the annotation outputs by manually reviewing actual user profile pages on Twitter where available. We could examine user profile pages for all datasets but Boston, for which we did not include the profile URLs field when collecting the data in 2013. The annotation outputs and manually checked labels matched highly, at 85.4% agreement. Some profiles (11%), however, were either suspended or did not exist any more, thus were impossible to validate. There were 3.6% unmatched profiles out of the profiles that were manually reviewed. The mismatch arose for several reasons, for example ambiguity about whether the account was a political promotional bot or belonged to a real human; amateur media/art/entertainment promotional accounts; freelance journalist profiles that had a journalistic profile description but the actual Twitter use was more personal; the accounts where tweets were either absent or had disappeared; a real person's account with no or little textual information in the profile description section. Figure 4 shows a few example profiles that showed inconsistency between the rule-based annotation and manual check of the accounts. Considering that the rule-based annotation resulted in only a small proportion of misclassification, we maintained our coding rules as a reasonable strategy for the purpose of this study.

(a) Annotated as institutional (i.e., promotional account); The actual profile was used primarily for personal tweets.

(b) Annotated as personal; The actual profile was used primarily for political promotion, giving suspect whether it is a bot.

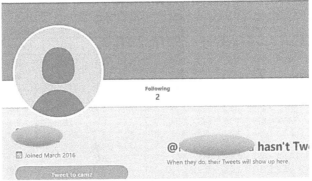

(c) Previous had profile description annotated as a general user; The actual profile is unverifiable.

Figure 4. Examples of mismatched profiles (identifiable information shaded).

Validation of model performance

The hand-coded annotation resulted in 19.6% institutional users in Mesa data ($N = 196$ out of 1,000), 38.6% in Boston ($N = 771$ out of 2,000), 26.4% in Brussels ($N = 527$ out of 2,000), and 9.9% in Quebec ($N = 527$ out of 2,000); the machine-generated annotation included 16.4% in Mesa ($N = 1296$ out of 7,898), 32% in Boston ($N = 4547$ out of 14,211), 21.4% in Brussels ($N = 2929$ out of 13,660), and 7.2% in Quebec ($N = 11,046$ out of 151,928).

Next, the ML model performance was validated for each case, resulting in satisfactory recall rates ranging from 87.7–97.9%; precision rate ranging from 83.6–95.3%; accuracy ranging from 83–94.2%, and F1 score ranging from .86–.97. The RF results were similar to the results drawn from the other popular ML algorithms.

To examine the possibility of using labeled data in multiple news event contexts, we conducted cross-validations by using different news events' testing data sets. For example, the model trained with the Mesa training set was validated using the Boston, Brussels, and Quebec testing sets. Accordingly, nine additional pairs of training-testing-sets were examined for cross-validations. The overall results of cross-validations were high with the exception of the Boston dataset that provided lower scores for recall, precision, accuracy, and F1.

To assess generalizability, the same validation process was run with the Random dataset, comprising randomly selected tweets on uneventful days. Hand-coded random data included 18.1% institutional users (406 out of 2,247); the machine-based annotation included 17.68% (27,051 out of 152,983). Overall, the model performed slightly poorly with Random data, resulting in 74.3% for accuracy, 86.7% for precision, 82.7% for recall, and .85 for F1 measure. Cross-validations also suggest the model trained with Random data performed weakly in predicting classifications in other datasets. The results suggest an advantage of training the model with labeled data generated within a well-defined topical domain. Table 2 and Figure 5 presents the results for both within- and cross-validations of RF models, in comparison with other classifier results.

The list of feature coefficients quantifies the importance of features in predicting the user classes: a feature with a larger coefficient size plays a more important role in discriminating the two classes than one with a smaller coefficient. The results of RF coefficients, however, do not inform the features' directionality, i.e., which features are associated with the general user class, and which with the institutional user class. For this reason, we compared the RF-derived coefficients alongside the Logistic Regression (LR)-derived coefficients, which allow us to interpret the features' directionality. The list of top 50 feature coefficients is presented in Figure 6.

Table 2. Random Forest model validation results in comparison with other classifier algorithms. (Bolds = within data validation).

Train	Test	Random Forest				Logistic Regression				Multinomial Naïve Bayes				Support Vector Machine			
		A	P	R	F1	A	P	R	F1	A	P	R	F1	A	P	R	F1
Mesa	Mesa	**.942**	**.953**	**.979**	**.966**	.913	.922	.979	.950	.890	.950	.917	.933	.919	.946	.959	.952
	BMB	.655	.628	.989	.768	.675	.641	.992	.779	.763	.721	.962	.824	.692	.660	.966	.784
	Brussels	.774	.767	.983	.861	.789	.780	.983	.869	.808	.831	.920	.873	.794	.795	.958	.869
	Quebec	.887	.894	.989	.939	.887	.894	.989	.939	.846	.914	.911	.913	.864	.898	.954	.925
	Random	.802	.848	.933	.889	.833	.848	.978	.908	.765	.850	.878	.864	.777	.846	.900	.872
Boston	Boston	**.830**	**.836**	**.877**	**.856**	.843	.804	.962	.876	.814	.776	.954	.856	.841	.823	.923	.870
	Brussels	.736	.876	.736	.800	.796	.860	.854	.857	.836	.851	.934	.891	.759	.858	.795	.825
	Mesa	.850	.969	.848	.904	.843	.804	.962	.876	.836	.851	.934	.891	.850	.976	.841	.904
	Quebec	.806	.923	.851	.886	.851	.907	.926	.916	.846	.914	.911	.913	.793	.906	.854	.879
	Random	.685	.852	.760	.803	.789	.852	.909	.880	.733	.854	.825	.839	.757	.857	.856	.856
Brussels	Brussels	**.828**	**.874**	**.889**	**.881**	.861	.872	.944	.907	.838	.883	.892	.888	.826	.856	.910	.882
	Boston	.794	.762	.935	.840	.781	.737	.966	.836	.830	.801	.939	.864	.785	.744	.958	.838
	Mesa	.867	.942	.897	.919	.919	.940	.966	.952	.890	.970	.897	.932	.902	.957	.924	.940
	Quebec	.869	.919	.934	.926	.887	.911	.966	.938	.846	.921	.903	.912	.861	.913	.931	.922
	Random	.704	.859	.778	.817	.773	.847	.894	.870	.745	.857	.838	.848	.741	.849	.844	.847
Qubec	Quebec	**.889**	**.914**	**.966**	**.939**	.902	.906	.991	.947	.889	.923	.954	.938	.887	.916	.960	.937
	Brussels	.811	.827	.931	.876	.794	.784	.983	.872	.764	.780	.934	.850	.831	.824	.972	.892
	Boston	.770	.732	.950	.827	.699	.661	.985	.791	.748	.706	.966	.816	.737	.694	.973	.810
	Mesa	.879	.903	.959	.930	.890	.904	.972	.937	.873	.936	.910	.923	.867	.901	.945	.923
	Random	.792	.848	.919	.882	.843	.848	.991	.914	.791	.850	.914	.881	.820	.849	.958	.900
Random	Random	**.743**	**.867**	**.827**	**.847**	.835	.862	.962	.909	.762	.854	.871	.863	.778	.861	.885	.873
	Brussels	.616	.751	.714	.732	.712	.740	.940	.828	.683	.743	.870	.802	.695	.745	.891	.811
	Boston	.586	.636	.764	.694	.633	.632	.962	.763	.616	.636	.876	.737	.633	.638	.927	.756
	Mesa	.704	.863	.755	.806	.757	.826	.888	.856	.727	.846	.812	.829	.726	.825	.841	.833
	Quebec	.677	.897	.725	.802	.813	.904	.887	.895	.733	.903	.788	.842	.757	.902	.820	.859

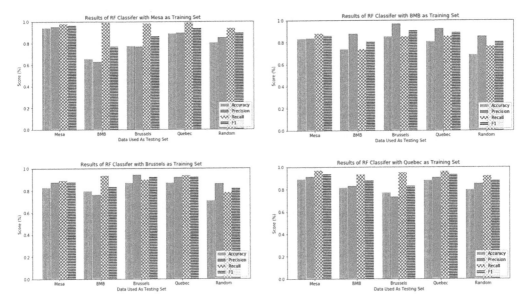

Figure 5. Visual summary of random forest model validation results.

The review of feature coefficients suggested that majority of high-ranked features were indicative of institutional users; and several of these features showed large coefficient sizes across all four datasets. For example, media channels (e.g., *channel, station, tv, network*) and journalism careers (e.g., *news, reporter, journalist, anchor*), and industry-related terms (e.g., *co, com, manager*) were ranked highly and associated with the institutional user class, with negatively signed coefficients. The presence of a hyperlink in the profile was also highly associated with the institutional user class (*http*). In the feature list for Mesa, locality-indicative words were ranked highly and associated with the institutional actor class, such as, *arizona, phoenix, valley, azcentral* (regional newspaper), *gilbert* (name of a town), and *kfyi* (local radio station). The plural first-person pronouns, such as *we* and *our*, were associated with the institutional user class, whereas singular pronouns *my* and *me* were associated with the general public user class. Some lifestyle related words such as *life, fan, music, love, student, artist,* or *american* showed stronger associations with the general public user class. Overall, the institutional user-related features were more prominent and consistent than general public-related features. Meanwhile, the top feature list for the Random dataset included fewer media-related terms than the other four datasets.

Error analysis

Our classification model is not error-free. A systematic analysis of the errors committed during testing should offer insight for future advancement on this model. For error analysis, we investigated two types of classification errors in each dataset, specifically False Positive classifications and False Negative classifications. Overall, the model performed more poorly in capturing negative classifications than positive classifications, missing true negative samples more frequently. The inability of the model in identifying true negative samples resulted in higher proportion of False Positive classification (Table 3).

Since the number of negative samples in our dataset is smaller than positive samples, our model sees less examples of organizational/institutional accounts in training. This leads to a small set of features that are representative of negative classifications. Since human coders can pick up on context clues and background semantic knowledge of features to derive classifications, this may not be a problem for humans. However, the model used in this research is unable to do this. To

Figure 6. Top 50 features with highest coefficients.

MESA			BOSTON			BRUSSELS			QUEBEC			RANDOM		
Feature	RF-Coeff	LR-Coeff	Feature	RF-Coeff	LR-Coeff	Feature	RF-Coeff	LR-Coeff	Feature	RF	LR	Feature	RF	LR
news	0.0928	-2.351	news	0.1095	-2.472	news	0.0836	-2.024	journalist	0.0625	-3.3469	personally	0.0332	-1.0777
reporter	0.0432	-1.576	reporter	0.0319	-2.767	reporter	0.0273	-2.595	news	0.0440	-2.2394	kind	0.0238	-1.2549
anchor	0.0276	-1.441	editor	0.0243	-1.726	journalist	0.0263	-2.729	reporter	0.0298	-2.3259	selectively	0.0135	-1.5338
phoenix	0.0265	-1.442	journalist	0.0198	-2.563	editor	0.0185	-1.661	editor	0.0295	-1.8878	culture	0.0134	-1.3466
producer	0.0257	-1.441	co	0.0117	-0.473	co	0.0171	-0.581	co	0.0288	-0.9164	photog	0.0122	-1.1693
journalist	0.0240	-1.835	host	0.0107	-1.794	breaking	0.0162	-0.596	http	0.0203	-0.3014	married	0.0112	-1.2773
arizona	0.0239	-1.429	pm	0.0098	-1.899	http	0.0146	-0.617	com	0.0195	-1.4846	amazing	0.0107	-0.7359
co	0.0174	-0.758	official	0.0096	-1.602	host	0.0116	-1.453	the	0.0136	-0.2927	no1	0.0102	1.3372
fox	0.0168	-1.091	breaking	0.0095	-0.268	radio	0.0113	-1.109	radio	0.0109	-1.2323	cat	0.0102	-1.2122
kfyi	0.0140	-1.129	producer	0.0091	-1.232	my	0.0100	1.011	events	0.0108	-1.0646	pichona	0.0099	-0.8185
editor	0.0134	-1.100	my	0.0091	0.953	your	0.0100	-0.864	writer	0.0099	-0.0774	news	0.0098	-1.4058
http	0.0124	-0.253	anchor	0.0086	-1.609	com	0.0096	-1.512	my	0.0091	0.7435	page	0.0088	-1.0033
valley	0.0118	-1.267	discuss	0.0085	-0.451	community	0.0091	-1.659	media	0.0086	-0.7891	mad	0.0087	-1.0258
com	0.0117	-0.510	election	0.0079	-1.435	public	0.0083	-1.063	politics	0.0086	0.5008	football	0.0086	-1.2879
nbc	0.0113	-0.725	video	0.0075	-1.781	podcast	0.0082	-1.414	shesourpresident	0.0085	-0.7041	cowboys	0.0085	-1.4590
official	0.0109	-0.905	our	0.0072	-1.061	love	0.0082	1.605	member	0.0085	-1.1687	weakness	0.0083	-0.6781
manager	0.0103	-1.301	http	0.0070	-1.141	official	0.0081	-1.114	host	0.0085	-0.8750	perfect	0.0081	-0.7441
endorsements	0.0096	-0.776	https	0.0070	-0.229	daily	0.0077	-0.950	author	0.0076	-0.2908	gay	0.0078	-0.6285
gilbert	0.0087	-0.872	nycstartup	0.0068	-0.451	journalism	0.0077	-1.334	shopping	0.0075	-0.7425	student	0.0074	-1.1376
breaking	0.0081	-0.646	love	0.0063	0.428	provides	0.0071	-1.195	producer	0.0075	-0.4248	va	0.0070	-1.0441
community	0.0081	-1.099	subjects	0.0063	-0.451	we	0.0069	-0.788	sun	0.0070	-1.0028	friend	0.0067	-0.8256
college	0.0080	-0.892	breakingnews	0.0061	-1.392	https	0.0069	0.073	journalism	0.0068	-1.3141	osu	0.0065	-0.3626
azcentral	0.0079	-0.471	providing	0.0060	-1.282	local	0.0069	-0.849	covering	0.0065	-0.6608	bringing	0.0064	-1.0523
crime	0.0077	-0.600	we	0.0060	-0.630	tv	0.0063	-1.365	historian	0.0060	-0.5329	line	0.0063	-0.5225
retweets	0.0071	-0.512	writer	0.0057	0.010	you	0.0058	0.107	blacklivesmatter	0.0059	-0.6494	project	0.0062	-1.1946
sports	0.0068	-0.523	vonvo	0.0056	-0.451	anchor	0.0056	-1.013	all	0.0058	-0.5009	stories	0.0062	-1.1565
tv	0.0067	-0.870	coverage	0.0055	-1.305	updates	0.0054	-0.700	imstillwithher	0.0058	-0.9763	personality	0.0059	-0.5563
writer	0.0064	-1.165	service	0.0054	-1.277	conservative	0.0054	0.851	tv	0.0058	-0.4538	getting	0.0059	-0.8250
crisis	0.0063	-0.305	latest	0.0054	-0.729	today	0.0052	-1.049	you	0.0057	0.9582	police	0.0058	-1.1148
stories	0.0060	-0.785	radio	0.0053	-0.818	new	0.0052	-0.486	things	0.0056	0.7312	professional	0.0057	-1.0006
network	0.0059	-0.515	new	0.0053	-0.880	based	0.0051	-1.093	freelance	0.0054	-0.2760	happiness	0.0055	-0.9911
weather	0.0059	-0.392	station	0.0051	-0.958	info	0.0050	-1.183	community	0.0054	-1.0805	family	0.0054	-0.4283
guy	0.0056	-0.746	home	0.0050	-1.036	show	0.0050	-0.895	theresistance	0.0053	0.1875	dude	0.0053	-1.3578
truck	0.0056	-1.080	no	0.0049	-1.241	top	0.0050	-0.650	california	0.0052	-0.5120	videogames	0.0053	-0.9686
republic	0.0055	-0.375	channel	0.0049	-1.044	trump	0.0048	0.710	social	0.0052	-0.7697	gonna	0.0053	0.3982
legislative	0.0053	-0.767	organizations	0.0047	-0.684	covering	0.0048	-0.999	former	0.0051	-0.1061	profile	0.0051	-0.7583
mesa	0.0053	-1.066	chief	0.0047	-1.524	writer	0.0048	-0.433	political	0.0050	-0.0833	day	0.0051	-0.7272
asu	0.0052	-0.411	you	0.0046	0.505	usa	0.0047	-1.666	life	0.0049	0.3085	land	0.0051	-0.9104
nd	0.0052	-0.646	lates	0.0046	-0.963	life	0.0046	0.616	public	0.0049	-0.1460	member	0.0049	1.2525
new	0.0051	-0.651	england	0.0046	-0.894	music	0.0045	0.631	me	0.0049	0.3022	resist	0.0049	-0.2272
digital	0.0051	-0.270	covering	0.0046	-1.230	text	0.0045	-0.584	music	0.0048	0.8500	noamnesty	0.0049	-0.0338
twitter	0.0050	-0.229	management	0.0046	-1.168	our	0.0045	-0.519	cool	0.0048	-0.5610	geopolitical	0.0048	-0.8030
my	0.0050	0.566	broadcast	0.0043	-0.830	us	0.0044	-0.549	new	0.0047	-0.5569	looking	0.0047	-1.0887
kgun	0.0048	-0.563	online	0.0043	-0.724	producer	0.0042	-1.063	books	0.0046	-0.4110	today	0.0047	-1.0956
president	0.0048	-0.873	director	0.0042	-0.480	associate	0.0040	-0.997	people	0.0046	0.0127	idk	0.0046	-0.1621
safety	0.0047	-0.355	matter	0.0042	-0.351	digital	0.0039	-0.893	gov	0.0045	-0.5778	company	0.0046	-1.0218
emergency	0.0047	-1.037	talk	0.0042	-0.857	me	0.0039	1.140	love	0.0045	0.6705	manone	0.0046	0.5623
phx	0.0045	-0.556	events	0.0041	-0.346	social	0.0038	-0.467	artist	0.0044	0.6004	pro	0.0046	-0.8893
rts	0.0045	-0.172	former	0.0041	-1.076	tweets	0.0038	-0.841	owner	0.0044	-0.6282	lot	0.0045	-0.4400
call	0.0044	-1.228	tv	0.0040	-0.331	talk	0.0038	-0.926	student	0.0044	1.1484	theresistance	0.0045	-0.5106

know if a feature is indicative of a positive or negative classification, the model must see the feature at least once—ideally multiple times—in the training set. A way to overcome this problem would be to include more negative valued descriptions in the model-training stage and allow it to develop a more expansive negative feature set.

A closer look at the data suggests three causes for misclassification. First, as mentioned above, the restrictive negative feature set results in frequent instances of errors. For example, a profile of an

Table 3. Comparison of predicted truth classification in testing set.

Dataset	True Positive (TP) Prediction	True Negative (TN) Prediction	No. of Positive Samples Model Missed (False Negative)	No. of Negative Samples Model Missed (False Positive)
Mesa	140	19	9	5
Boston	229	152	39	32
Brussels	252	79	35	36
Quebec	311	29	39	18
Random	301	14	46	63

institutional user, who has a true negative value, from the Mesa dataset reads: *"3rd Battalion Fire Radio for Monroe County New York. All information posted is heard from the SCANNER. Nothing is confirmed nor 100% accurate..... #kcco"*. To a human coder, this description is obviously used for an organization. The text mentions that the Twitter feed will post fire information "heard from the scanner" and is likely for the residents of Monroe County, New York. Since our model does not reason in such a manner, rather it searches for features that indicate a certain classification, it incorrectly assumes that this is a personal account rather than a Twitter account for an organization. The model was unable to locate features for the negative class because the organizational/institutional users in our dataset predominantly centered around the news media.

Second, there were ambiguous features that could imply a positive classification in one context and a negative classification in another. Since an RF model lacks the ability to reason about features in semantic contexts, ambiguous features are bound to be a source of misclassification. For example, take the personal user from the Boston dataset: *"I love Fox News & Rock 'n Roll and volunteer at animal shelter - rescue is hard but so rewarding too"*. The model falsely made a negative classification with this user. This error is because the terms "Fox" and "News" generally imply a negative classification (or institutional user type). We see in this context, however, that "Fox News" as a feature implies a personal preference. Human coders, unlike machines, could easily pick up on such semantic cues and derive the correct classification.

Third, samples with insufficient information caused misclassification. If a sample lacked enough information to derive a classification with certainty, human coders and machine alike were more prone to misclassify it. For example, the user description with two terms, *"Digital marketing"*, from the Boston dataset received a false, negative classification: This is an example of a Twitter account with insufficient information because there is no context for this text. Only a manual checking of the actual profile page could validate the true classification. Such text was problematic because the present features seemed to weakly correlate with a non-personal user type. At first glance, it may seem to a human coder that this is a personal account because it lacks any reference to a specific organization. However, as observed in many examples in our training sets, the features "digital" and "marketing" were generally tied to organizations. For example, a user may say they do "marketing for company X". Hence, to the machine, this could be a good evidence for a negative class since it has, in training, seen these features associated with negative samples. Thus, lack of context was a major source of errors.

Comparisons between two sample groups

Despite some errors, the models overall performed reliably and thus, were used to classify the rest of the unlabeled samples. To address whether the classified two sample groups show systematic differences according to the proposed hypotheses, we ran descriptive post-hoc tests (Chi-square and Kruskal-Wallis H Test) that compared tweet activities between the two sample groups. Figure 7 provides visual summaries of the differences between the two user groups in the four news-related datasets and the Random dataset.

First, an examination of the human-coded data showed mean differences in terms of retweeting across all four news-related datasets. Specifically, the general public user samples were characterized with *more* retweeting than institutional user samples (H1). Also, Boston, Brussels, and Quebec datasets showed that general users tweeted URLs *less frequently* when referring external information than institutional users (H2). Although the Mesa dataset was not statistically significant for H2, the pattern found in the tweets was consistent with the other three datasets. In terms of language use, general public users showed significantly *less* analytic tones than institutional users across Mesa, Boston, and Brussels datasets (H4). Although the Quebec dataset was not statistically significant regarding analytic languages, the pattern found in the tweets related to the event was consistent with the other three datasets. The use of affective language was significantly *higher* in the general user tweets than institutional user tweets only in the Boston dataset (H5). While the use of affective language was not significant for other datasets, the pattern was, again, consistent across the datasets.

Second, an examination of the machine-labeled samples reaffirmed the differences found from the hand-coded samples in terms of H1, H2, H4, and H5. That is, the variables that were not significant with the hand-coded dataset showed significant differences between the two samples in the machine-labeled datasets. For example, use of affective language became significant in Mesa, Boston, and Quebec datasets when analyzed in the machine-labeled samples, with consistent mean difference patterns. The statistical differences in language styles for general users—lower in analytic tones and higher in affective tones than institutional users—were resonant with previous anecdotal discussions that general users showed more affect in their own content on Twitter than media users

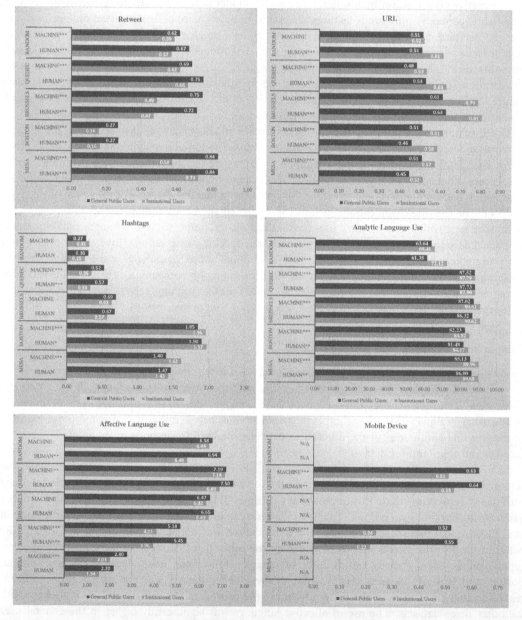

Figure 7. Summary of mean differences between general public users and institutional users. *** $p < .001$; ** $p < .01$; * $p < .05$; Retweet, URL, Mobile Device were tested by Pearson $X^2(1)$. The rest were tested by Kruskal-Wallis rank $X^2(1)$ (with ties considered).

(Papacharissi, 2015). Our findings not only reiterate these previous discussions but also emphasize the importance of separating samples into general users and institutional users to truly understand who is tweeting what and how.

Meanwhile, hash-tagging—as hypothesized as H3—became significantly different in the machine-classified samples. However, the directionality of the mean differences were *inconsistent* across different datasets, thus preventing us from reporting systematic differences between general public and institutional users regarding the use of hashtags. Prior scholarship may explain such inconclusive findings regarding hasthtags: they have shown that news media were not "skillful" in using hashtags and keywords for their tweets even if some news outlets tweeted rather frequently (Engesser & Humprecht, 2015, p. 514). Their discussion implies that institutional users—notably media professionals—are not distinctive from general public users due to the lack of strategic use of hashtags.

Next, we tested H6—difference in tweeting patterns of general public users and institutional users based on the device used to tweet—for the Boston and Quebec events. The results suggested that general public users used a mobile device *twice as often* as institutional users to tweet their posts (H6). This result implies the possibility that "the type of people who tweet from mobile devices are qualitatively *different* from those who tweet from web-based platforms" (Murthy et al., 2015, p. 834, *italics* added). The difference in device usage was also significant in the Quebec dataset, reiterating the results from the Boston dataset, although the gap between the two groups was reduced to 10%.

Finally, we replicated the post-hoc tests on the Random dataset to address the generalizability of these findings. The results from Random dataset remained largely the same as the findings from the four violent-event based datasets. That is, general users *retweeted more; used URLs less; and used less analytic language yet more affective language* than institutional users. While some of the variables were significant only for either the machine-labeled dataset or the human-coded dataset, the patterns of mean differences were persistent. There was no difference in hashtagging between general users and institutional users in the Random dataset, that also reaffirmed the inconsistent results for this variable as found in the other four datasets.

In summary, the overall tweeting patterns revealed systematic differences between the general public user samples and institutional user samples in terms of retweets, use of URLs, and language use, but not in terms of hashtag use.

Discussion and conclusion

This article intends to address sampling issues faced by communication scholars engaged in social media research. Data gathered from Twitter—or any other social media platform—usually involves an examination of complex sets of information. As highlighted in the literature section, the heterogeneous nature of data could induce various sampling biases, specifically predefined sampling frames, engineered noises and proxy misspecifications. Whereas many issues related to these biases are unfortunately beyond the researchers' control, this study suggests that some shortcomings may be improved upon with a computational approach. Particularly, this study highlighted the "proxy-population mismatch" issue, and demonstrated the use of the Random Forest classifier to improve the proxy-population match by disentangling general public users from institutional users in a general Twitter sample.

We manually prepared the training and testing sets comprising 7,000 human-coded Twitter profiles, and then used them to train the machine-learning model to computationally distinguish between general and institutional users. The preparation of coded data followed a rule-based approach, that was later validated by an additional review of the actual user profile page where available. We applied the trained models to four different violence-news related Twitter datasets that centered around a local event (Mesa), a national event (Boston) and two international events (Brussels and Quebec). To address the generalizability of these results beyond specific news contexts, we added a Random dataset and replicated the whole modeling and analysis processes with randomly selected tweets on uneventful days.

The results are evidence that RF modeling may be a useful approach to distinguish between the two types of Twitter account holders within a given news event data, and possibly across news events of a similar nature. The model performed well across all four news datasets: within the Mesa shooting dataset, the performance was above 90% for accuracy, precision, recall, and F1 scores; the results for the other three were also solid, with a performance of higher than 80% for accuracy, precision, recall, and F1. Moreover, cross-validation of the model across the four datasets also showed satisfactory results, suggesting the possibility of using the machine-learning model trained with these datasets for future research on Twitter datasets that pertain to other violence-related news events. The Boston dataset, however, showed results with lower accuracy than others when tested for cross-validation. This result could be due to a particularly large portion of the negative class (i.e., institutional users) contained in the Boston dataset—almost 40%—compared to the other three datasets.

The high performance of our model could be good news especially for social media researcher who would like to implement computational process for a better large-scale sampling. We intended to develop a machine learning model that would be useful in the sampling stage of their research. Thus, one of our practical goals was to reduce the modeling cost by minimizing data-related preprocessing steps and using simple algorithms to do so. While more advanced feature engineering and complex algorithms could have resulted in higher performances, the simplicity of the TF-based feature sets and use of the RF classifier reduced the time and effort necessary to classify the sample in different categories.

Nonetheless, it is important to discuss the limitations of our model. First, this study primarily focused on the proxy-population mismatch issue, using "front-end" data composed of publicly available tweets and user profile data. It could not address problems inherent in a predefined sampling frame or engineered noise issues. Specifically, the most accurate information about Twitter user demographics could reside in proprietary "back-end" data. Restricted access to this back-end data is one intractable limitations that social media researchers often encounter when they estimate the population of interest on a platform like Twitter. Additionally, StreamAPI-based data collection, as opposed to purchasing the data via Firehose, compromises transparency regarding the algorithms Twitter uses to predefine the sample frame available via StreamAPI. Such limitations are a result of how Twitter shares its data with academics and due to their proprietary nature, beyond the scope of this study.

Another limitation pertains with the labeling approach we took when preparing train and test datasets. That is, the profile text-based classification could miss subtle, contextual cues that differentiate between institutional and personal users. For example, the textual description in a user's profile may be insufficient to conclude whether the user belongs to the general public or institutional category. To overcome this stumbling block, future studies may want to adopt the manual checkup of the actual Twitter profiles—which we did for validation purposes—as the ground truth label, and add some additional non-textual features (e.g., profile photo, etc.) when building feature sets. Also, researchers interested in this research might consider a higher n-gram embedding of the data. This procedure could, however, lead to substantially greater computational complexity and possibly a model that over fits the data. A more suitable approach would be to build a new model that considers features within their context more naturally. An example of such a model would be a word2Vec neural network, one that learns vector representations of phrases rather than each term (Mikolov, Sutskever, Chen, Corrado, & Dean, 2013). The current study did not try this model, which is worth further investigation.

Our error analysis suggests that a small size of the negative training set (=institutional users) resulted in a narrow range of features from which the model could learn only partially about institutional users. This led to a high chance of False Positive classification cases. Although our feature set was a relatively solid representation of media/journalism-related users, it could have missed other non-media institutional users. This could be a reason why institutional users were consistently underrepresented across all machine-labeled datasets: Institutional users were less prevalent in all machine-labeled datasets than their counterpart hand-coded datasets. One practical solution to this issue would be to use a training set that has a more diverse representation of institutional users. One might incorporate negative labels from Random datasets into the training set for more accuracy in this regard.

Overall, our study suggests the possibility of a nontrivial portion of institutional user tweets included in a sampling frame if they are not carefully filtered out. Even in the Random data, we observed over 17% of messages were identified as institutional tweets. Filtered sampling could be particularly advantageous in some research contexts where general public user behaviors are of particular interest. Specifically, general public users are likely to (i) retweet others' messages more, (ii) hyperlink external information less, (iii) use lesser analytic and more affective language, and (iv) tweet more from mobile devices than institutional users. These findings imply that researchers' failure to filter out non-general users from a Twitter sample would have confounding effects on a study's results, especially when the purpose is to understand general users' behaviors.

Our finding of general users using the singular pronoun "my/me" more than institutional users adds nuance to Murthy et al. (2015) finding of tweets from mobile devices incorporating more egocentric language than tweets from web devices. A more critical question, though, will be whether the use of egocentric language is a result of the affordance of mobile devices or the nature of the population that primarily tweets from mobile devices. On a related note, only about 20% of non-general/institutional users had tweeted from mobile devices in 2013, as seen in the Boston dataset. The number of cases related to mobile use when tweeting, however, increased more than twice, up to about 50%, during the Quebec mosque attack in 2017. This drastic change within the institutional user samples is interesting, and worthy of further investigation. Researchers could examine whether such change influences the ways in which institutional users frame their messages.

In summary, our study shows that RF modeling offers an effective way of "slicing" a large social media dataset. The RF classifier is useful when separating binary classes under the linearly non-separable data condition. With great promise, however, comes great expectation and the method shown in this article has its limitations. We tested RF modeling for a binary classification using only the Twitter profile texts. Future studies may extend this line of research by (i) investigating multi-label classification problems, and (ii) by addressing more complex features such as network structures or other information available in user accounts, as mentioned earlier. Another problem that the social media research community should ponder is identifying and excluding bot activities when studying human behaviors. Bots are an entrenched problem that not only creates engineered noises but also aggravates the proxy-population mismatch. While it is beyond the scope of our project to disambiguate the human-like bot profiles, there is an urgent need for future research to develop advanced and sophisticated methods in this regard. With recommended future research alternatives, scholars could further enhance the utility of advanced computational techniques in communication research.

Notes

1. Recall, Precision, and Accuracy are the standard metrics to validate ML results. There are four possible classification outcomes: (1) True Positive (TP); (2) False Negative (FN); (3) False Positive (FP); and (4) True Negative (TN). Recall is the rate of correctly labeling general publics out of all the instances supposed to belong to general publics, computed as TP/(TP + FN). Precision is the rate of including correctly labeled general public users from all instances labeled as general publics, computed as TP/(TP + FP). Accuracy is the rate of correct labels of both, the general public and institutional users from all labels, computed as (TP+TN)/(TP + FN + FP + TN). F1 score is the harmonic mean of precision and recall, computed as 2 * (Precision * Recall)/(Precision + Recall).
2. More formally, the GI for a classifier with J labels can be computed via the following:

$$\sum_{i=0}^{J} P_i(1-P_i) = \sum_{i=0}^{J} P_i - P_i^2 ,$$

where $P_i :=$ probability a randomly chosen object is classified with label i.

For the source codes and label data, please see the project repository at https://github.com/jpriniski/TwitterClassification

Funding

This work was supported by the 2017 Emerging Scholars Award from Association for Education in Journalism and Mass Communication.

ORCID

K. Hazel Kwon http://orcid.org/0000-0001-7414-6959

References

Abokhodair, N., Yoo, D., & McDonald, D. W. (2015). *Dissecting a social botnet: Growth, content and influence in Twitter*. In Proceedings of the 18th ACM Conference on Computer Supported Cooperative Work & Social Computing (pp. 839–851). New York, NY: ACM. doi:https://doi.org/10.1145/2675133.2675208

Boyd, D., & Crawford, K. (2012). Critical questions for big data. *Information, Communication & Society, 15*(5), 662–679.

Breiman, L. (1984). *Classification and Regression Trees*. Boca Raton, FL: Chapman & Hall/CRC.

Breiman, L. (2001). *Random Forests*. Retrieved April 10, 2017, from https://www.stat.berkeley.edu/~breiman/randomforest2001.pdf.

Brooks, B., Hogan, B., Ellison, N., Lampe, C., & Vitak, J. (2014). Assessing structural correlates to social capital in Facebook ego networks. *Social Networks, 38*, 1–15.

Burrows, R., & Savage, M. (2014). After the crisis? Big data and the methodological challenges of empirical sociology. *Big Data & Society, 1*(1). doi:10.1177/2053951714540280

Chu, Z., Gianvecchio, S., Wang, H., & Jajodia, S. (2012). Detecting automation of Twitter accounts: Are you a human, bot, or cyborg?. *IEEE Transactions on Dependable and Secure Computing, 9*(6), 811–824.

Cohen, R., & Ruth, D. (2013). Classifying political orientation on Twitter: It's not easy! In Seventh International AAAI Conference on Weblogs and Social Media (pp. 91–99). Cambridge, MA: AAAI Press.

Colleoni, E., Rozza, A., & Arvidsson, A. (2014). Echo chamber or public sphere? Predicting political orientation and measuring political homophily in Twitter using big data. *Journal of Communication, 64*(2), 317–332.

Dredze, M., Paul, M. J., Bergsma, S., & Tran, H. (2013, June). Carmen: A twitter geolocation system with applications to public health. *Papers from the AAAI workshop on expanding the boundaries of health informatics using* (pp. 20–24). Bellevue, WA, USA. Association for the Advancement of Artificial (AAA).

Driscoll, K., & Walker, S. (2014). Big data, big questions, working within a black box: Transparency in the collection and production of big Twitter data. *International Journal of Communication, 8*, 1745–1764.

Emery, S. L., Szczypka, G., Abril, E. P., Kim, Y., & Vera, L. (2014). Are you scared yet? Evaluating fear appeal messages in Tweets about the Tips campaign. *Journal of Communication, 64*(2), 278–295.

Engesser, S., & Humprecht, E. (2015). Frequency or skillfulness. *Journalism Studies, 16*(4), 513–529.

González-Bailón, S., Wang, N., Rivero, A., Borge-Holthoefer, J., & Moreno, Y. (2014). Assessing the bias in samples of large online networks. *Social Networks, 38*, 16–27.

Hargittai, E. (2015). Is bigger always better? potential biases of Big data derived from Social Network Sites. *The Annals of the American Academy of Political and Social Science, 659*(1), 63–76.

Hargittai, E., & Litt, E. (2011). The tweet smell of celebrity success: Explaining variation in Twitter adoption among a diverse group of young adults. *New Media & Society, 13*(5), 824–842.

Hermida, A. (2010). Twittering the news. *Journalism Practice, 4*(3), 297–308.

Himelboim, I., McCreery, S., & Smith, M. (2013). Birds of a feather wweet together: Integrating network and content analyses to examine cross-ideology exposure on Twitter. *Journal of Computer-Mediated Communication, 18*(2), 40–60.

Jackson, S. J., & Foucault Welles, B. (2015). Hijacking #myNYPD: Social media dissent and networked counterpublics. *Journal of Communication, 65*(6), 932–952.

Kwon, K. H., Chadha, M., & Pellizzaro, K. (2017). Proximity and terrorism news in social media: A construal-level theoretical approach to networked framing of terrorism in Twitter. *Mass Communication and Society, 20*(6), 869–894.

Kwon, K. H., Stefanone, M. A., & Barnett, G. A. (2014). Social network influence on online behavioral choices: Exploring group formation on Social Network Sites. *American Behavioral Scientist, 58*(10), 1345–1360.

Lee, K., Eoff, B., & Caverlee, J. (2011). Seven months with the devils: A long-term study of content polluters on Twitter. In Fifth International AAAI Conference on Weblogs and Social Media. Barcelona, Spain.

Loh, W. (2011). *Classification and Regression Trees*. Retrieved from http://www.stat.wisc.edu/~loh/treeprogs/guide/wires11.pdf 10.1002/widm.8

Mikolov, T., Sutskever, I., Chen, K., Corrado, G. S., & Dean, J. (2013). Distributed representations of words and phrases and their compositionality. *Advances in Neural Information Processing Systems, 26*, 3111–3119.

Morstatter, F., Pfeffer, J., Liu, H., & Carley, K. M. (2013). Is the sample good enough? Comparing data from Twitter's Streaming API with Twitter's Firehose. arXiv:1306.5204 [Physics]. Retrieved from http://arxiv.org/abs/1306.5204

Murthy, D., Bowman, S., Gross, A. J., & McGarry, M. (2015). Do we tweet differently from our mobile devices? A study of language differences on mobile and web-based Twitter platforms. *Journal of Communication, 65*(5), 816–837.

Papacharissi, Z. (2015). *Affective Publics: Sentiment, Technology, and Politics*. New York, NY: Oxford University Press.

Pennebaker, J. W., Booth, R. J., Boyd, R. L., & Francis, M. E. (2015). *Linguistic Inquiry and Word Count: LIWC2015*. Austin, TX: Pennebaker Conglomerates. www.LIWC.net

Ratkiewicz, J., Conover, M., Miess, M., Goncalves, B., Patil, S., Flammini, A., & Menczer, F. (2011). Truthy: Mapping the spread of astroturf in microblog streams. In *WWW 2011 Proceedings of the 20th International Conference Companion on World Wide Web* (pp. 249–252). Hyderabad, India: ACM.

Ruths, D., & Pfeffer, J. (2014). Social media for large studies of behavior. *Science, 346*(6213), 1063–1064.

Salganik, M. (2017). *Bit by Bit: Social Research in the Digital Age*. Princeton, NJ: Princeton University Press.

Schroeder, R. (2014). Big data and the brave new world of social media research. *Big Data & Society, 1*(2), 1–11.

Shin, J., & Thorson, K. (2017). Partisan selective sharing: The biased diffusion of fact-checking messages on social media. *Journal of Communication, 67*, (2), 233–255. doi:10.1111/jcom.12284

Smith, M., Ceni, A., Milic-Frayling, N., Shneiderman, B., Mendes Rodrigues, E., Leskovec, J., & Dunne, C., (2010). NodeXL: A free and open network overview, discovery and exploration add-in for Excel 2007/2010/2013/2016, http://nodexl.codeplex.com/. Social Media Research Foundation

Ugander, J., Karrer, B., Backstrom, L., & Marlow, C. (2011). The anatomy of the Facebook social graph. arXiv:1111.4503 [Physics]. Retrieved from http://arxiv.org/abs/1111.4503

Vaccari, C., Chadwick, A., & O'Loughlin, B. (2015). Dual screening the political: Media events, social media, and citizen engagement. *Journal of Communication, 65*(6), 1041–1061.

Vargo, C. J., Guo, L., McCombs, M., & Shaw, D. L. (2014). Network issue agendas on Twitter during the 2012 U.S. presidential election. *Journal of Communication, 64*(2), 296–316.

Varol, O., Ferrara, E., Davis, C. A., Menczer, F., & Flammini, A. (2017). Online human-bot interactions: Detection, estimation, and characterization. arXiv:1703.03107 [Cs]. Retrieved from http://arxiv.org/abs/1703.03107

Woodford, D., Walker, S., & Paul, A. (2013). Slicing big data - Twitter, gambling and time sensitive information. In *Selected Papers of Internet Research* . 14.0. Denver, CO. Association of Internet Research. Retrieved from http://spir.aoir.org/index.php/spir/article/view/914

Zhou, W.-X., Sornette, D., Hill, R. A., & Dunbar, R. I. M. (2005). Discrete hierarchical organization of social group sizes. *Proceedings of the Royal Society of London B: Biological Sciences, 272*(1561), 439–444.

Index

Note: **Bold** page numbers refer to tables; *italic* page numbers refer to figures and page numbers followed by "n" denote endnotes.

accuracy 61, 63, 155n1; average 66; measurement of 66–68, **67,** *67*; prediction 65; of web archives 128–129
adaptability, scaling up content analysis 84–85
Aday, S. 126
Agarwal, S. D. 123
agent-based modeling 4
aggregation 18; sentiment analysis 66
"algorithmic confounding" 138
Amsterdam Content Analysis Toolkit (AmCAT) 5, 79, 83
anonymized data 7
Apache Tika 20
application data, sentiment analysis 62
application programing interfaces (API) 138, 139
archived web data 123
ARChive file format (ARC) 123
ArchiveSpark 124
Archives Unleashed Toolkit 124
Aroyo, L. 48
Austrian parliamentary speeches, sentiment analysis 68–70, *70, 71*
automated content analysis (ACA) 78–80, 85, 86, 90, 91
automatic classification, Twitter 145–146
automatic text analysis 8

background topics 27
Bagging/Bootstrap Aggregating 144
bag-of-words approach 15, 16, 21, 60, 64, 66, 67
bag-of-words model 145
Balmas, M. 6
Bayesian framework 15
Bennett, W. L. 123
Berge, C. 98
bibliometric approaches 96
Biel, J.-I. 19
big data 2, 4, 5–6, 8, 78, 79, 82, 90, 136
"Big Data in Communication Research" (Parks) 79
bimodal network approach 98
Blei, D. M. 14–17, 19, 22, 23

Bode, L. 120, 123
Bodrunova, S. 23
boilerplate content 20, 21, 28
Boomgaarden, H. G. 86
Booth, R. J. 142
Boston data 142, 148, 151, 154
Boumans, J. W. 82, 86
Boyd, D. 130
Boyd-Graber, J. 22
Boyd, R. L. 142
Brown, G. 15
Brunelle, J. F. 128
Brussels data 142
Bulmer, M. G. 106

Cappella, J. N. 78
"Carmen" library 142
ceteris paribus 45
Chang, J. 22
classification learning 145, *146*
cleaning text data 18
Climate Science web archive 125
Clinical and Translational Science Award (CTSA) 103
cloud-computing 81
coder pair 47
coders 43–44, **44,** 50; moral and political views 43–44, **44**
coder training 40–43, 45, 48, 51
coding procedure 45, 46, 49
Cohen, J. 46
Cohen, R. 139
coherence model 128
coherence, topic model 27
coherent ecosystem structure 100–101
collaboration ecosystems 114, 115
color-coding scheme 51
Columbia University 121
communication research 136; data cleaning and preprocessing 18; interpretation and validity 19–20; reliability 19; topics and prior

parameters 18–19; web archives in 125–128, *126*, **128**
communication researchers 5
communication scientists 7–8, 85, 87, 90
computational algorithms, ease-of-use of 5
Computational Communication Science 78
computational methods 9; challenges and pitfalls in 4–5; in communication science 1–2; lab experiments to social environment 3; measurement 6–7; responsible and ethical conduct in 7; self report to real behavior 2–3; skills and infrastructure 7–8; small-N to large-N 3–4; solitary to collaborative research 4
computational social science 120
Computational Social Science (Cioffi-Revilla) 78
computational techniques 136, 138, 155
computing power, lack of 81
contemporary content analyses 48
content analyses: coders 43–44, **44**; limitations 56–57; measures 44; procedures 45–46, **46**; reliabilities **46**, 46–48, **47**; text difficulty 45; text materials 44; *see also* crowd content analyses
content analytical studies 43
content extraction procedures 43
Contractor, N. S. 96
conventional social research 137
Cornell University 125
corpus 14
corpus cleaning 21
Correlated Topic Model (CTM) 16, 22
Crawford, K. 130
Cristianini, N. 87
crowd content analyses 49–50; coders 50; inter-coder agreement 53–55; procedures 51–53; text material and measures 50–51
CrowdFlower 63
crowdsourcing platforms 3
crowd truth approach 50, 56
CTM *see* Correlated Topic Model (CTM)
custom-written program 82

data analysis 88–89
data cleaning 88; of unstructured text data 18
data-driven research 136, 139
data preprocessing, Twitter user samples 145
"data revolution" (Kitchin) 80
data structuring and storing 87–88
data, web archives: completeness **129**, 129–130; determination 125; filteration 127; political communication 123; to research 126–127
decentralized ecosystem 105, 112–114, **113**
degradation, web archives 128; accuracy 128–129; dataset completeness **129**, 129–130
Delli Carpini, M. X. 44
Denny, M. J. 21
descriptive statistics, team interlock ecosystems 106, **107**, *107–108*
"Digital marketing" 151

Digital Methods Initiative 80
digital research 9
digital trace 1–3, 5, 7, 79
DiMaggio, P. 17
Ding, W. 87
Dirichlet distribution 16, 31n1
distributed computing 87, 124
distributed word embeddings 60, *62*, 63–64, 72
distributional hypothesis 61
document 14
document-topic assignment matrix 15
Domahidi, E. 15
Dunning 24

EBSCO Communication Source 17–18, 31n2
ecosystem coherence 105, 110, **111,** 115
ecosystem decentralization 105, 112–114, **113**
ecosystems effects 114–115
ecosystem simulation 96, 105–106
embedding-based sentiment analysis 60, 61; accuracy measures 66–68, **67,** *67*; aggregation 66; application data 62; classification 65–66; evaluation 66; parliamentary debates 68–70, *70*; preprocessing 65; sentence and word tokenization 64–65; sentence embedding 65; training data 62–63; transformation data 63–64, *64*
error analysis 149–151
Evans, M. S. 19
EyeWire project 49–50

feasibility, scaling up content analysis 89
feature extraction 145
Filippov, V. 23
filtered sampling 155
Foot, K. 122, 123
Francis, M. E. 142
Freelon, D. 79, 126
free open source software (FOSS) 89
"friend-of-a-friend" mechanism 97

Gatica-Perez, D. 19
GDELT *see* Global Database of Events, Language, and Tone (GDELT)
general public users 137, 139
gensim 26
Geocities platform 124
Gerbner, G. 78
German language texts, preprocessing of 72
Gerrish, S. 22
Ghosh, D. D. 19
Gibbs sampler 23
Gilliat, Bruce 121
Gini impurity (GI) 144, 155n2
Global Database of Events, Language, and Tone (GDELT) 50
global ecosystem decentralization 115
González-Bailón, S. 6, 138

INDEX

Graham, J. 40, 44
Grčar, M. 61
Griffiths, T. L. 23
Grün, B. 19
Guha, R. 19
Günther, E. 15, 83
Guo, L. 87

hand-coded dataset 148, 152, 155
Hanna, A. 120
Hargittai, E. 6
Harris, Z. S. 61
Heiberger, R. H. 84
Hierarchical Dirichlet Process (HDP) 19
Hindman, M. 4, 79
Hirschman-Herfindahl Index (HHI) 27
Hornik, K. 19
human annotators 86, 89, 91
human coding 44, 48–49, 55, 82
hyperedge clustering coefficient 100–102, 105, 110, **111,** 112, 115
hyperedges 98–100
hypergraph 8, 96; centralization 100, 105, **113**; density 100; hyperedge metrics 99–100; index 105; key components of 99; metrics 100, 106, 109; node metrics 99; to team interlock ecosystems 98–100, 115
hyperparameters 15
hyperparameter tuning 66
hyperties 99
hypotheses linking scientific ecosystems 100; coherent ecosystem structure 100–101; ecosystem decentralization 102–103; local brokerage 101–102
hypothetical statistical generative process 15

inference mechanism 17
inferential statistics, team interlock ecosystems 109
initialization strategy 23, 24
Institutional Review Boards (IRBs) 130
institutional users 137, 142
inter-coder agreement 51–55
International Communication Association (ICA) 136
International Internet Preservation Consortium 123, 124
International Organization for Standardization (ISO) 123
Internet Archive 121, 123–126
interpretability, of topic model 23, 30, **38,** *39*
inter-topic semantic validity 28, 31
intra-topic semantic validity 19, 28, 31
intrinsic coherence 23, 30, 32n5
Ishwar, P. 87
ISO *see* International Organization for Standardization (ISO)
Issue Crawler 20

Jaccard index 20
Jacobi, C. 86
Johnson, C. N. 123
joint-probability distribution 16
Jonkman, J. G. F. 8
Jordan, M. I. 14
JSON-based approach 87

Kahle, Brewster 121
Keeter, S. 44
Keras Python library 65
key metadata 124
Kitchin, R. 79
Kleinnijenhuis, J. 87
Knowledge Discovery in Databases (KDD) 61
knowledge interlock ecosystem 98, 101, 106, 109, 110, 112–116
Kolmogorov-Smirnov test 106
Koltcov, S. 20, 23
Koltsova, O. 20, 23
Krippendorff, K. 46
Kroon, A. C. 86
Kwon, K. H. 6, 8

Lafferty, J. D. 16
Lancichinetti, A. 23–25, 31
language-dependent word embeddings 64, 73n4
language-detection algorithm 20
language pre-processing 18
Lansdall-Welfare, T. 87
large-scale data analysis 90
large-scale network analysis 126
latent Dirichlet allocation (LDA) 8, 88
latent Dirichlet allocation (LDA) topic modeling 13, 19, **35–36**; advantages of 16; building and preprocessing 20–22; challenges of 17; data-generating process 15–16; limitations of 16; model selection 22–26, *24, 25*; presentation and interpretation **29,** 29–30; statistical background of *14,* 14–17; validity and labeling 27–28
LDAvis 26
Leipzig Corpus Miner 83
lemmatization 18, 21
Lewis, J. 87
Lewis, S. C. 79
Lexicoder 86
lexicon-based sentiment analysis 142
LGA *see* Longitudinal Graph Analysis (LGA)
Library of Congress 121, 122
linguistic analysis 122
Lin, J. 129
local brokerage 101–102, 111–112
local ecosystem 102, 111, 115
local neighborhood, hypergraph 99, 100
Log-Likelihood Ratio Test 24
Longitudinal Graph Analysis (LGA) 123–124
Lungeanu, A. 8
Lynch, M. 126

INDEX

machine-assisted sampling 139
machine learning (ML) 9, 60, 61, 65, 79, 87, 143, 144, 148, 154
Maier, D. 8
MALLET 19
manual content analysis 6, 78, 79, 85
MapReduce-frameworks 83
Marshall, E. A. 23
memory, lack of 81
Mesa data 142, 145, 148, 149, 151, 154
metadata 123–124
methodological approach, LDA 20; building and preprocessing 20–22; model selection 22–26, *24, 25*; validity and labeling 27–28
methodological framework, web archives 128
MFD *see* Moral Foundations Dictionary (MFD)
MFQ *see* Moral Foundations Questionnaire (MFQ)
MFT *see* Moral Foundations Theory (MFT)
Milligan, I. 129
MIME *see* Model of Intuitive Morality and Exemplars (MIME)
Mimno, D. 27, 32n5
misspecified/insufficient search parameters 138
mixed membership approach 16
ML *see* machine learning (ML)
Model of Intuitive Morality and Exemplars (MIME) 40–43, **41–42,** 45, 56
model selection 22–26, *24, 25,* 30–31
MoNA *see* Moral Narrative Analyzer (MoNA)
Moraes, R. 65
moral foundations 39, 40, 42–49, 51–53, 57n1
Moral Foundations Dictionary (MFD) 40, 44, 50, 57
Moral Foundations Questionnaire (MFQ) 44
Moral Foundations Theory (MFT) 39–43, **41–42,** 48, 56, 57n1
moral intuitions 39, 40, 42, 43, 55, 57n1
moral intuition salience 40, 44, 48, 56
Moral Narrative Analyzer (MoNA) 45, 50, 51, **52,** 56, 57
Mozetič, I. 61, 65
multi-foundation coders 51, 55, 57n2
multilevel ecosystems 96, 99
multinomial Naive Bayes classifier 66
multiple interfaces, scaling up content analysis 85
"multiple team membership" 97, *97*
Murray, F. 101, 102
Murthy, D. 141, 142, 155
mutual information 19
Myths of Human Annotations (Aroyo and Welty) 55

Nag, M. 17
named entity recognition (NER) 46, 88
National Institutes of Health (NIH) 103
national libraries 121
natural language processing (NLP) 25, 84
Natural Language Toolkit (NLTK) 64, 84
NER *see* named entity recognition (NER)
Neto, W. P. G. 65
network analysis 8

network modeling techniques 3
Neuendorf, K. A. 27
Neuman, W. R. 78
neural network 66
Newman, M. E. J. 97
Ng, A. Y. 14
Niekler, A. 31
Nikolenko, S. I. 23
NLP *see* natural language processing (NLP)
NLTK *see* Natural Language Toolkit (NLTK)
nodes 99
node's degree 99
node's hyperdegree 99
non-organic activities 138
non-random initialization 17
NoSQL database 85, 90
null model simulation 106

Occupy Wall Street Movement 123, 129
O'Mahony, S. 101, 102
online coding platform 45, 51
openNLP 20
open source, scaling up content analysis 83–84
outlined method 127

Paltoglou, G. 6
Pantel, P. 61
Pan, Z. 87
Parks, M. R. 79
part-of-speech tagging (POS) 88, 145
Pennebaker, J. W. 142
perplexity metric 19
person-to-person approach 96, 98, 100, 102
person-to-person framework 8
Pfeffer, J. 139
pointwise mutual information (PMI) 57
political communication 20, 68, 73n3; web archives 123
"political issues" 15, 20, 26, 30
Polyglot 63–65, 68, 73n4
Poole, M. S. 96
Porter, M. F. 52
power law distribution 109
precision 155n1
preprocessing: of German language text 72; LDA 20–22, 30; sentiment analysis 72; of unstructured text data 18
prior distributions 15
probability distribution 15, 16
Prolific Academic platform 50
proprietary restrictions 138
proxy-population mismatch 9, 137, 139, 154; general public users in Twitter 139–141, **140;** random forest classification *143,* 143–144, *144;* tweets on violence news 142; Twitter user samples 144–146, *146*
Python 50, 63, 79, 83, 85–90, 145
Python Natural Language Toolkit 44

Quandt, T. 83
quantitative diagnostic metrics 19
Quebec data 142, 151, 153
Quinn, K. M. 28

Random Forest (RF) classification 137, 143–145, 153–155; algorithms 144, *144*; for supervised machine learning *143*, 143–144, *144*
random initialization 17, 24
random sampling 26, 129
Rank-1 metric 27
Rasberry Pi computers 124
recall 155n1
regular expressions 20
regularization 22, 23, 31
Řehůřek, R. 83
relative pruning 21
relevance, topic model 27
reliability: with regularization technique 23–26, *24*; of topic model 22–23; of topic solution 19
research datasets 5
research-ready tools 127
Reuters, Thomson 103
RF *see* Random Forest (RF)
Riebling, J. R. 84
Roberts, M. E. 23
"robocoder" 53
Rudkovsky, Elena 8
Ruest, N. 129
rule-based annotation 144–146, 153
Ruth, D. 139
Ruths, D. 139

sample datasets 127–128, **128**
sampling, of social media 137
scalability, scaling up content analysis 82–83, 91
scaling up content analysis 78, 80–82, 85–87, *86*, 91; adaptability 84–85; data analyzing 88–89; data cleaning 88; data structuring and storing 87–88; dimensions of *86*; feasibility 89; multiple interfaces 85; open source 83–84; scalability 82–83
Schneider, S. M. 122, 123
scientific ecosystems 96–98; structural characteristics of 100
scientific teams 112, 114
sci-kit learn package 145
Scrapy spider 44
SearchAPI 138
searching 125
semantic network initialization 24, 31, 88
sentence and word tokenization 64–65
sentence embedding, sentiment analysis 65, 72
sentiment analysis 60, 61; accuracy measures 66–68, **67**, *67*; aggregation 66; application data 62; Austrian parliamentary speeches 68–70, *70*; classification 65–66; evaluation 66; preprocessing 65; sentence and word tokenization 64–65; sentence embedding 65; training data 62–63;

transformation data 63–64, *64*; with word embeddings 61–62, *62*
Shah, D. V. 2, 7, 78, 120
Shaw, J. D. 125
Sheafer, T. 86
Shin, J. 140
Shirley, K. E. 26, 27
Sievert, C. 26, 27
single-foundation coders 51, 53, 55
Smailović, J. 61
Smith, John 103
snowball procedure 32n4
Socher, R. 68
social actors 137
"social brain hypothesis" 138
social interaction, in web archives 122–123
social media 3, 5, 7, 136; users 139
social media data-driven research 136; engineered noises 138; predefined sampling frame 137–138; proxy misspecification 138–139
social network analysis 126
Society Works Best Index (SWB) 44, 45, 47, 51
Sojka, P. 83
Soroka, S. 6
sources and concentration, topic model 27
Spaniol, M. 128
Spirling, A. 21
Stanford Named Entity Recognition engine 44
Stanford Natural Language Processing tools 84
Stanford NER algorithm 46
stemming 18
Stewart, B. M. 23
Steyvers, M. 23
stochastic random processes 17
storage capacity, lack of 81
StreamAPI 138–139, 142, 154
Strycharz, J. 87, 91
subsequent multivariate analysis 6
substantive search 19–20
Sudhahar, S. 87
supervised machine learning 62, 137; random forest classification for *143*, 143–144, *144*
SWB *see* Society Works Best Index (SWB)
"system drift" 138

Tamborini, R. 42
target population 40, 130, 137–139
team assembly mechanisms 116
team descriptive statistics, team interlock ecosystems 108–109
team interlock ecosystems 96–98; descriptive statistics 106, **107**, *107–108*; ecosystem coherence 110, **111**; ecosystem decentralization 112–114, **113**; hypergraph approach 98–100 (*see also* hypergraph); inferential statistics 109; limitations 116; local brokerage 111–112; methods 103–105, *104–105*; null model simulation 106; power

law distribution 109; team descriptive statistics 108–109
term frequency (TF) 145
term frequency-inverse document frequency weighting (TF-IDF) 52, 66, 145
terms 14
testing set 143
text difficulty 45
TF *see* term frequency (TF)
Thompson, J. 87
Thorson, K. 140
Tingley, D. 23
tokenization 21
topic coherence 19
topic labeling 27
topic modeling 14, 31, **37,** 83; coherence 27; interpretability 23; presentation and interpretation **29,** 29–30; relevance 27; reliability 22–23; sources and concentration 27; *see also* latent Dirichlet allocation (LDA) topic modeling
topics 14, 15
topic validity 27, 28
traditional content analyses 82
traditional quantitative content analysis 48, 55
trained human codings myths 48–49
trained manual coders 6
training data, sentiment analysis 62–63
training set 143
transformation data, sentiment analysis 63–64, *64*
Trilling, D. 8
TTR *see* type-token ratio (TTR)
Turney, P. D. 61
tweets on violence news 142
Twitter 9, 137, 138; communication activities on 141; data 121, 123, 126, 131, 132n1, 154; general public users in 139–141, **140**; political orientations on 139, 140; in public communication 138; sampling 137
Twitter geo-tagging tool 142
Twitter user samples: classification learning 145, *146*; data preprocessing 145; feature extraction 145; rule-based annotation 144, 145; validation and automatic classification 145–146
two step approach 17, 30
type-token ratio (TTR) 45

unbounded research space 131
unification 21
Uniform Resource Locators (URLs) 50, 124–127, 129, 130, 142
units of analysis 45, 46
unsupervised methods 6
Urgent Question Debate 68, 70, 72

Valiati, J. F. 65
validation: of human annotation outputs 146, *147*; of model performance 147–149, **148,** *149*; Twitter user samples 145–146
validation procedure 19–20, 27–28, 31
Van Atteveldt, W. 83
Vargo, C. J. 87
Virginia Tech 125, 126
visualization, sentiment analysis 66, 72
Vliegenthart, R. 86

Walgrave, S. 86
Walker, S. 123
Wallach, H. 3
Wang, C. 22
Warnick, B. 122
the Web 43, 120–122, 129–131; as communication platform 122, 125
Web ARChive file format (WARC) 123, 124
web archives 8, 121–122; accuracy of 128–129; collecting or accessing data 125–126, *126*; communication platform 122, 125; data and political communication 123; data determination 125; data filteration 127; dataset completeness **129,** 129–130; data to research 126–127; ethical boundaries 130; limitations of 128, 131; metadata 123–124; sample datasets 127–128, **128**; social interaction in 122–123; tools and methods 123, 124; unbounded research space 131
Web Archive Transformation (WAT) 123–124
web-based platform 43
web-crawling procedure 20
Weber, M. 5, 8
Weber, R. 6, 8
web interface 72
Web of Science (WoS) 17–18, 31–32n2, 103
Welty, C. 48
word embeddings 60–61, 63–64, *64,* 71; supervised sentiment analysis with 61–68; *see also* sentiment analysis
word-frequency analysis 44
word-topic assignment matrix 15
word2Vec 63, 154
World Wide Web 120
WOS *see* Web of Science (WoS)

xtas (eXtensible Text Analysis Suite) 80, 83

Yang, J. 120
Young, L. 6
Yule, G. 15

Zamith, R. 79
Zoizner, A. 86